WHAT AM I DOING HERE?

Ken Walker

Published in 2015
© Copyright Ken Walker Publications
23 Village Farm
Bilton, Harrogate
HG1 4DH
ken@kenwalker.org

ISBN: 978-0-95699839-1-6

Cover and Book interior Design by Russell Holden
www.pixeltweakspublications.com

Pixel✳tweaks
PUBLICATIONS

AKNOWLEDGEMENTS

I am greatly indebted to my editor Nigel Perry who spent many hours working on my story. Without his help and guidance the book could not have been completed.

My thanks also go to my friend Beryl who again turned my initial long hand notes into computer text.

A big thank you to Russell Holden. I finally found someone to help me publish who was not just in it for the money, he enjoys what he does and was helpful and enthusiastic from day one. His encouragement helped get the book finished and into print.

I would like to thank all those who contacted me after reading my first book *Nothing Easy*, it was a pleasant surprise and encouraged me to press on with the second part of my life story.

Last of all I would like to mention all those who figure in my story, Good or bad, Thank you, you gave me something to write about!

This book is dedicated to my Mother. She was proud of her Border Country Heritage. Many of her ancestors – Robsons, Hedleys and Grahams were Border Reavers. She loved to visit the areas where they once roamed and the Great Hall at Netherby, once proud seat of the Graham clan. I regret not taking her there more often.

CONTENTS

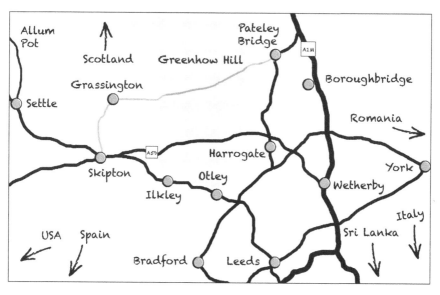

.

PROLOGUE
1977

What happens now? There I was in November 1977, 42-years of age and out of work for the first time in my life. I had been earning some form of wage virtually since I was a boy of ten in Masham. One moment I was sitting in the office of the transport company that I had once owned, my lovely car parked outside, and the next, I was trudging the half mile from East Parade, Ilkley, to my rented apartment in nearby Cowpasture Road. I had no job, no office, no prospects and no car.

The spring had gone out of my step as I made my way along those damp, autumn streets of West Yorkshire's prettiest town I looked around to see the sights of my years of success ... the Rose and Crown, in which I had convivially mixed with my employees most evenings after work, the clothes emporium my wife had owned, the 'Chippy Walker' fish shop and other scenes of enterprise. I glanced at the moors above Ilkley – the Cow and Calf rocks barely visible through the mist. I had often boasted that the view of the moors from my office window was better than from many of the expensive houses in Ilkley ... But that was all in the past.

CHAPTER ONE

PICKING UP THE PIECES

So now in the long afternoon I sat in my flat thinking, "what next?" Everything I had worked for over many years, so hard and at such long hours had gone. I sat pondering my future, trying to look forwards rather than back. But I had to ask myself what was there to look forward to? I had no idea what to do with the rest of my life. There was one thing that made me feel better: though I had little money, for the first time in many years I didn't owe anything. I had a clean slate!

The phone was silent. I lifted the receiver to hear the dialling tone and to check that it was still working. In recent months, I had dreaded the ring as it usually meant trouble. It was often the bank manager calling about his loans and my overdraft. Or it might be someone asking for payment. But it had gone quiet now. I was out of Ken Walker Transport and there was no more Ken Walker Contracting. In fact that name had disappeared with the takeover by the Morgans. To many people who I encountered later it was as if I had disappeared as well. The phone didn't ring and I felt more isolated than ever before in my life.

So I decided to call my friend and solicitor Jack Mewies to tell him what had happened and confess my mistake in handing over the lease. He didn't say, "I told you so". Instead, he invited me to visit him. "Come up to Skipton tomorrow. We will have a meal together and talk things over." I said sorry Jack I don't have any wheels at the moment. "Don't worry; I'll come to Ilkley." We arranged to meet the next day. Fortunately I had not lost my appetite and cooked my favourite fish meal of halibut. This took me briefly back to my wet fish hawking days at Masham. Julia called on her way home from work in Leeds for a while then left to give me some space for thinking. I went to bed early with a book. My sleep was disturbed by muddled dreams but eventually morning, and with it my new life, arrived.

I met Jack and over the meal in a restaurant we chatted for a while. He asked how much it would cost to set me up again in business. He was offering his help. I wish I could have responded positively but at that moment I felt defeated and confused after the turmoil of the past few months. I said I would like to try something different, but only when I was able to get my strength back. I have often thought what a friend he was.

For years I had been used to going to work, often in the early hours. Our working lives are ruled by the clock but now for me time did not matter as I had nowhere to go and nothing to do. I thought, "Maybe I should go to the Labour Exchange, after all I am out of work." While I was deciding the door bell rang. I jumped up a little surprised, then gathered myself together. One thing I felt fairly certain of was that it was not likely to be someone asking for money. Instead, it was Malcolm Booth who had something to sell. "I've brought you some rabbits Ken. How many do you want? I had a good catch yesterday." Malcolm subscribed to my grandfather's adage and had 'a hobby that pays'. He caught rabbits to earn extra cash, though most of what he earned went on beer at the Rose and Crown. But he was good at catching rabbits. Local farmers welcomed him as rabbits are a pest, eating a lot of grass that should feed farm animals. Though it was only a hobby, Malcolm went about it in a very professional manner. I had been hunting with him and saw how it was done. After locating the main entrance to a burrow he would carefully survey the surrounding area for the bolt holes. Some of the smaller of these he would block off before placing nets over the others. He then took his 'professional assistant' out of his pocket, and pushed it down the main entrance. This of course was a ferret. The ferret disappeared from sight but soon there would be fireworks from underground as rabbits do not like ferrets, and sure enough they started to bolt straight into the nets. It was then an easy job to collect and kill them. The day I was with him he caught more than 20 and had no trouble selling them to butchers and friends. On this occasion I told Malcolm I would take two, paid him and he left smiling. I put one in the freezer and kept the other out to make into a stew.

I sign on

I was no longer wealthy. I had managed to salvage a little money but trying to keep the business going for so long had used up most of my cash in paying wages. I would have to sign on for unemployment benefit at what was known in those days as the Labour Exchange. You signed on each week if you were unemployed, registered yourself as looking for work and received the government's unemployment handout. This was not a lot of money but would pay for food. But to get this I had to visit the Labour Exchange and I had no car to get me there.

I was now without a means of transport of my own for the first time in years. Morgans had acquired my company and now took away my firm's car, leaving me with nothing. Driving vehicles of all kinds had been an important part of my life from the time I had steered the cars being towed by my father at age nine. I had ridden motor bikes which I had assembled myself, drove dad's fish and chip van before I left school and was piloting three-wheelers at sixteen. In the RAF I had been a dispatch rider riding the wonderful Triumph motor bikes used by the forces. On these I toured West Germany. I had driven delivery trucks dropping off animal carcasses, the Ledgard array of old and cronky buses, wagons of all kinds, JCB earth movers and more than once had taken a Drott digger on the roads between building sites around Ilkley. Sports cars and racing cars had been as much a part of my life as food and drink. Now I didn't have a vehicle of any sort, not even a push-bike. Alan Morgan Limited had seen to that.

There was only one thing for it – I had to catch the bus to get to the Otley Labour Exchange. The last time I had been on a bus I had been driving. I sat upstairs near the front and looked out at the road I had driven those old blue buses on twenty years before. It certainly was a time for reflection.

As I walked in through the door of the Labour Exchange, facing me was a long counter, Walking up to one of the bays felt strange. Not long before I had employed fifty people; now here I was looking for an employer to give me a chance. I had not shirked from sacking a man if I felt it was called for. I had a system. If a driver had caused trouble, or repeatedly damaged his vehicle, or upset a customer I would confront him and ask for an explanation. Once I had heard this I would go upstairs to my office have a discussion with myself – "How long had he worked for me? How reliable was he? How did he look after his vehicle? Was he married? Did he have a family that relied on him?" When I had asked myself these questions I would make my decision, then go back to him and say, "This is your last chance, do your job right or next time you and me part company". Or it would be, "You've had your last chance and must now join the ranks of the unemployed!"

Well here I was joining them. I looked at the floor. There were no footprints but I felt sure that someone must have stood where I was standing now, sent by me and probably cursing the name Ken Walker. I had never sacked anyone on the spur of the moment or in anger. I always tried to be fair. I am certain that people had liked working for me. For years I had a waiting list and was always being asked in the pub if there were any jobs going. We paid higher than the competitive rates and treated staff well. But it could end in a walk up to one of these bays.

Mobile again

I gave my details to the clerk, signed on the dotted line and made my exit, tail between my legs, trying to think of what to do next. As I walked to the bus station my old friend Barry Normington drove past in a little van. I waved and he stopped. "What are you doing on foot?" he said with a smile. "It's the only way I can get about at the moment," I replied, then told him why. Without hesitation he said, "Do you want to buy a cheap van? You can have this one. Come home with me, I have a car." I went with him and we did the deal. I don't recall the price but it was very cheap. He was a friend doing me a favour. When he gave me the documents and keys he looked at the petrol gauge. "You're lucky. I wouldn't have filled it this morning if I'd known I was going to sell it!" "Well right now Barry I need a bit of luck and you are a friend. Thank you," I said. Had my luck started to turn the corner, I wondered.

Months before as the business went into its last downward spiral I had sold my BMW to pay wages. This had the personalised number plate 5KW. Not wanting to lose this I transferred the plates onto a works pick-up which was now in the possession of Alan Morgan Limited. I pointed out to Morgans that as it was a personal number it was not an asset of the company. I was told that when the vehicle was due for replacement I would be given the opportunity to buy it complete with plate. Months later this did come to pass, by which time the pick-up was knackered and had run out of MOT. Yet they still asked an inflated price as a last kick up my arse. Rather than lose the plate that was quite valuable and also had sentimental value, I reluctantly accepted this as the price I would have to pay. I didn't put it on the van I bought from Barry, which was old and battered, but kept it until such time as my fortunes might have improved. In the event, it was some years before I had a nice car to put them on.

Still on my mind was the fresh young rabbit I had waiting for me at home. I bought some vegetables for the stew. Rabbits from Malcolm Booth were always skinned ready for the pot. I cleaned off a few loose hairs, chopped the rabbit in half so that it would fit into my casserole dish. I added the vegetables and put it in the oven to cook.

After an hour it was cooked and tender, so I served it up with plenty of gravy. I had forgotten to buy potatoes so I mopped up the gravy with bread. But something was not quite right. The meat was tender as the animal was definitely young but the gravy made with vegetable Oxo was darker than normal. It didn't taste bad but was stronger than usual with a powerful smell. I felt uneasy but not put off enough to stop eating until I stuck my fork into the rear portion and out popped a dark brown currant. Well, it was about the same size and texture, but it was not a real currant, if you get my drift! Suddenly I felt sick as I realised why it was strong and dark. When Malcolm had gutted and skinned the rabbit he had missed the pipe that runs from its gut to the back passage. When I investigated further I found more stewed currants. I gulped down water and threw out the remainder of the feast. It was a long time before I ate rabbit again and when I did I carefully checked to make sure there was nothing left between the back legs!

The next day I spoke to my accountant friend David Crowther who told me, "Don't worry Ken. You'll bounce back." It was good to hear but at that moment I felt all the bounce had gone from me. There was still some way to go, I decided, before that corner was to be reached let alone turned.

A Trip to France

Picking myself back up was helped by another conversation with Jack Mewies. He rang the following week and said he was going to France for a short holiday with his partner Jill, and asked whether Julia and I would like to go with them. We would make a foursome and tour northern France for a few days. I liked the idea. Naturally, I was free after my recent business problems and the chance to get away was probably just what I needed. But immediately a problem arose. What would I do for money? I had little available cash.

"You will only need spending money! We can go in my car," Jack said. "Okay. We'd love to go. When?" was my reply. "I'll arrange it," he said. "You just get your spending money together."

I knew that finding enough spending money would be a problem. But an idea occurred. I'd heard that worsted cloth sold at a premium in France where they loved the material made in Huddersfield. Perhaps I could take some to sell. As it happened I knew a man in Bingley who bought suit lengths from a mill in Huddersfield as a side line. I had bought mohair material from him in the past that I had made into lovely suits, so I went to see him and bought a selection of twelve lengths at £4.50 each. Surely I could double my money this way and pay for Julia and me on the trip. I packed the material with care in a case separate to my clothes and put it in the bottom of the boot when we loaded our belongings into Jack's car.

Off we went to France. We toured for a couple of days. Jack liked good food at the best restaurants followed by a night at the casino. I watched him spread his chips on the roulette table and then place piles of them on different numbers. Then I carefully placed just two or three chips on what I hoped would be a single lucky number. He won while I lost, as I couldn't afford to spread a big stake over the table as he did.

On the ferry to France with Julia. 1977

Finally, we arrived in Brittany in the lovely port town of Saint-Malo. The four of us had just finished a large midday meal and walked back to our hotel. "We are going to lay down for a rest, Ken," said Jack. "See you later."

"Right Jack," I said. "I think we'll do the same." This was my opportunity. When things had settled down I went back to the car. Fortunately I had the keys as I was doing most of the driving. I took out the bottom case with my worsted material and set off for town. The case was heavy and Saint-Malo is hilly. It was hot despite the time of the year, and I was sweating, which I put down to part-worry, part-weather. I eventually found a tailoring shop. My French didn't go much further than *"s'il vous plait,"* and *"merci,"* so I would have to rely on the cloth selling itself once the case was opened. I looked through the window to see how many people were in there and which one looked like the owner. I plucked up courage and plunged in.

Shopping in France – Jill, Jack Mewies and Julia

I walked to the counter, put my case on top, opened it and spread out a few pieces of cloth. The shop went quiet as the entire staff and one or two customers came to look. There was not a word spoken more than a few "ohs" and "ahs." However their faces were eloquent. They were obviously amazed as they touched and admired the cloth. With a few words and the use of sign language I asked if they would like to buy. The most important looking one shook his head and said, *"Non!"* emphatically. The rest of the staff said nothing and backed away. I felt deflated, thinking there would be no casino for me tonight. I folded the material and put it neatly back in the case, closed it and made my way out to a chorus of *"Au revoir."* I thought, that's a bugger! Still there must be more than one tailor in the town and set off along the street.

I found another and then another, but received exactly the same reception each time. People obviously liked the material and appeared interested, but didn't even ask "How much?" It didn't help that my case was feeling heavier when in fact I had hoped that by now it would have been getting a lot lighter. I was fast becoming disillusioned. The one thing I couldn't do was quit as I needed the money. I took a deep breath and went into another shop, up to the counter, a little bolder this time, opened the case and repeated the routine. Again, there was the same reaction as before. I could see they liked the worsted but stood back with a firm, "Non!" confirmed by a chopping motion with the hands. As I packed the case for the fourth time a woman customer in the shop came up to speak.

"Monsieur," she said. "I can tell you don't speak French. As I speak English maybe I can help you." "I would be grateful if you can," I said. "I saw you trying to sell the cloth," she said. "Well, recently the French government put a ban on all imported worsted in order to protect the home industry. They think the material is excellent quality but are frightened to buy. They also think that it might be stolen." I thanked her for being so helpful and left the shop, by now realising that my money-making idea was in vain and the cloth would be returning to England with me. It was with a heavy heart that I made my way back to the hotel with a case that now felt heavier by the step. I stowed the case in the bottom of the car boot and went inside for a well earned rest. A few days later at another hotel as I was taking cases out of the boot Jack pointed to the one at the bottom with the material saying, "You haven't had that case out yet Ken." "Oh, I always bring too many clothes with me Jack," I replied. I would have liked to have paid my share of the costs, but fortunately Julia had brought more money than I thought she had. And Jack was very generous paying for the hotels and most of the meals. Once back across the Channel in England we joined the queue at customs waiting while every car was checked for contraband. I watched nervously as the car in front of us went through. The passengers had to get out, the driver opened the car boot and a thorough check was made of everything. The customs officers even looked under the seats. On this particular day they were being unusually conscientious. I tried to stay calm.

"Well my conscience is clear," said Jack. "What about you, Ken?" "I have only a few more cigars than I should and that includes the packet already opened. So I, too, am in the clear." But what I was not saying was what I was thinking. I was worried. Though as a solicitor Jack spent much of his life in court sometimes telling fairy stories in order to defend his clients he was understandably law-abiding. In fact, he was quite a stickler for upholding the law. It would not do to be linked with someone who had not just smuggled something into France, but was now taking it back the other way. My mind was racing. I had visions of the headline in the *Craven Herald* newspaper, "Local solicitor caught with illegal goods at customs." He had been a good friend to me, how would he take it? How could I explain? The customs officials finished with the car in front, and beckoned us forward. I was driving and my heart raced. Sitting in the front next to me Jack wound the passenger side window down and reached out with the passports. The officer glanced at them and handed them straight back, waving us through without another word. It seemed like we were the only car that day not to have been searched. I breathed a huge sigh of relief as I pressed the accelerator and moved off thinking it is amazing what you can get away with in a Rolls Royce! The material was eventually sold back in UK.

Months later we were all having a meal together. After a few glasses of wine I decided to tell Jack about the cloth, but when I opened my mouth and mentioned the French trip I received a kick on the shins under the table from Julia, who had been aware of what I was doing. So Jack never did find out.

Moving away from Ilkley

Apart from my closest friends there were not many people I wanted to spend time with in those first few months after the collapse of my business. It was all too embarrassingly painful. Even sympathy was difficult to take and I quickly became frustrated with having to explain over and again what went wrong. Of course, none of it reflected well on me and talking about it reinforced my sense of defeat So it was better to avoid chance meetings.

There was one person I had known for many years, David Booth, who had also suffered more than his fair share of ups and downs and I felt he understood my depression. We had worked together years earlier when he was in the timber business, felling trees, chopping wood and selling logs. David was 'sharp' and he loved dealing. He would buy and sell anything, from a horse to a caravan. But you had to have your wits around you when dealing with him. You could haggle with him and try to get the price down, but this could go on for ages. As I grew to understand him better I spotted the sign that meant you were getting close to a price that was acceptable. David would wet the tips of his fingers on his tongue then try to catch your hand with his. If he caught your hand it would close the deal as far as he was concerned and he would have no further discussion. That was that! You would have to pay and he was not a man to argue with, being as strong as an ox. I saw him one day on a building site carry a huge stone lintel. It had taken two men to lift it onto his shoulders. Not only was he able to carry it on his own but he also climbed a ladder to pass it to the workmen on the scaffolding above. Experience had taught me to always keep my hands in my pockets or behind my back when discussing a deal with David Booth. He could be something of a rogue and people warned you about him.

He had once owned a butcher's shop in Ilkley and occasionally I had bought meat from him. Though he was a friend I did not trust him and always took care to watch him cut my meat from the carcass. I had to know which animal it came from. One day I called in at the shop just as he was shutting up for the day. "I'm in a hurry Ken," he said. "And I'll have to serve you quickly." He went to the freezer and gave me a small bag of already diced meat ready to cook. I thanked him and later prepared my evening meal. It was dark meat and as I popped it in the pan I was not happy with it. I had worked for a butcher in my youth and later as a delivery driver for the Wensleydale Meat Company, so I knew something about meat. Was this cow beef or something else? I stewed it for a long time. It smelled strong and was full of sinew. I'm not eating this, I thought, and threw it out. My suspicion was that it was horse! Some time after David found himself in trouble with the law for selling suspect meat. At the time he had a contract from the council to supply meat for school dinners and, when tested, some was found to be horse. He lost the contract and received a heavy fine, while I received the confirmation about my earlier meal.

By now David had moved to live near Pately Bridge in the beautiful Nidderdale in North Yorkshire. He knew the area well and most of the people living I the vicinity. He also had his ear to the ground and told me of a little cottage in the sparsely populated village of Greenhow Hill that was empty and in need of renovation. Greenhow was on the top of a desolate hill in the Pennines between Nidderdale and Wharfedale. The cottage was not on the market as the owners had not yet decided whether to sell, but it had stood empty since the previous occupant had died. She had left the cottage in her will to her three children but they could not agree what to do after the tragedy of the death of their mother, who had committed suicide in a fit of depression.

I decided it was worth following up. Without much money and no job I would have to find something cheap, then do it up to increase its value. So this seemed to fit the bill, but when I saw the cottage I realised that it needed a lot of work.

Fortunately when times were good and I had spare money I had invested in some property as a joint venture with a good friend of mine Barry Taylor. Well now I needed that money but it was not easy to get it from Barry and instead of the planned profit I had trouble getting from him what I had invested about two years before but now it would enable me to get back on the housing ladder And it would get me away from Ilkley and the scene of all that was painful. I could hide myself away at Greenhow, which was small and at ten miles from Ilkley far enough to give me peace but still close to those whose company I welcomed. For Julia Nadal, who was living with her parents at High Austby which was on the route to Greenhow Hill, this was only a short journey. And for my sons living with Wendy in Ilkley it soon became a quick trip to a very different and exciting part of the world.

In late 1977 I spoke to one of the old lady's sons. He was keen to sell, and it turned out his brother was too. It was their sister who was against it. The cottage and the manner of her mother's death just held so much sadness for her. I offered the brother to whom I spoke first an incentive that if he could get the family to agree to sell the cottage to me, I would make sure he received a little extra. I explained that we could do the deal without the expense of estate agents and cost of publicity. It would also mean that they would not have people trampling around the house which was the site of so much upset. This made sense to him and he persuaded his sister to let it go to me. The eventual sale cost me less than £8,000 for the cottage and 27 acres of rough grassland close to the moor; a very good deal. I scraped together the deposit and signed up with a mortgage company for the remainder. Now I had to make it into a home. Once, this tiny cottage had been the school house when the old village school was next door. Before that it had been two semi-detached cottages built in the early nineteenth century for the lead miners of Greenhow. In those days both cottages had just one room up and one down. Knocked into one it was still small but for me a location for a fresh start, and a chance to rebuild my life, hopes and ambitions.

CHAPTER TWO

A NEW BEGINNING
Greenhow Hill 1977 - 1982

Bleak is the right word to describe Greenhow Hill. When the wind blows, as it seems to almost all the time, it feels like it can cut you in half. The village is one of the highest in the British Isles at 1,380 feet above sea level and there are not many trees. When my friends heard I was moving there they said, "Why ever are you going to that God-forsaken place?" and spoke of it as if it was the end of the world.

What would they have thought if they knew I was moving to a tumble-down wreck of a cottage in which the previous occupant had committed suicide? I decided it was best to keep this to myself for the time being. But I was pleased for a number of reasons. I no longer felt comfortable in Ilkley. When I had been prosperous and owned several properties I felt a fixture of the town and thought I would never leave. But things had changed some-what. I now lived in a rented flat and was unemployed. I wanted to get away. It wasn't so much that I chose Greenhow; things didn't work like that. But when I was presented with the idea by the dodgy butcher David Booth I thought this would be the right place at the right time. I guess there was a touch of my becoming a recluse, but it would be on my terms. Going to Greenhow sounded adventurous and would give me a clean slate for a new challenge.

Before moving 'on t'moor,' I bought a book on Nidderdale to read about the area. There was much to learn. Greenhow, Ilkley and the place of my upbringing Masham are almost in a line running down from Masham – north east to south west. Each is famous in its own way: Masham is the 'Old Peculiar', so named as an independently administered part of the diocese of York Minster because the Archbishop felt it was too far to visit. It is home to two of Britain's finest breweries. Ilkley is the spa town that serves as a prosperous commuting location for Leeds and Bradford. It is the home of Ilkley Moor which, of course, has given rise to Yorkshire's unofficial anthem,

On Ilkla Moor Baht 'at. Masham has a population of about 1,250 souls and Ilkley about 14,000. Now I was moving to something altogether smaller.

Greenhow, as it is formally known – Greenhow Hill is the local description and if you have ever walked up there you'll know why – had barely a hundred inhabitants. By road it is about half-way between Ilkley and Masham. Its name derives from the Old Norse haugr, meaning a hill and a mound. Its parish church, St Mary's, is reputedly the highest in England at 1,300 feet above sea level. The question that suggests itself is why anyone would want to live up there in the first place. It provided a scratchy existence for a few sheep farmers, but what drew the people were lead mines. There is evidence that these were exploited back in Roman days, but through most of the next 1,500 years the mines were worked by farmers employed by the nearby religious establishments of Fountains Abbey and Bolton Abbey, aided by some of the monks as a penance no doubt. Lead mined at Greenhow was supplied in 1365 for the roof of Windsor Castle, carried by pack animals to Boroughbridge and then shipped by boat to Berkshire. In the sixteenth century the mines fell into private hands following the dissolution of the monasteries and their new owner, Sir Stephen Proctor, expanded their earning potential. This meant he needed a larger workforce so in the early 1600s he built a smelt mill and founded Greenhow village as somewhere for the miners to live.

Joseph Kipling, the grandfather of Rudyard, was a later inhabitant when he became the minister at the Methodist Chapel at Greenhow in the late nineteenth century, and Rudyard himself is known to have visited. He wrote a story using the local dialect called *On Greenhow Hill* which appeared as a chapter in his work of 1891, *Life's Handicap*. This features his *'soldiers three'* of privates Mulvaney, Ortheris and the Yorkshireman Learoyd, the last of whom had lived in Greenhow.

Though now on a hillside in the Himalayas hunting a deserter, the location recalls to John Learoyd his native Yorkshire, as Kipling describes:

"It's along o' yon hill there," said Learoyd, watching the bare sub-Himalayan spur that reminded him of his Yorkshire moors. He was speaking more to himself than his fellows. "Ay," said he, "Rumbolds Moor stands

*up ower Skipton town, an' Greenhow Hill stands up ower Pateley Brig.
I reckon you've never heeard tell o' Green-how Hill, but yon bit o' bare
stuff if there was nobbut a white road windin' is like ut; strangely like.
Moors an' moors an' moors, wi' never a tree for shelter, an' gray houses wi'
flagstone rooves, and pewits cryin', an' a windhover goin' to and fro just
like these kites. And cold! A wind that cuts you like a knife. You could
tell Green-how Hill folk by the red-apple colour o' their cheeks an' nose
tips, and their blue eyes, driven into pin-points by the wind. Miners
mostly, burrowin' for lead i' th' hillsides, followin' the trail of th' ore vein
same as a field-rat. It was the roughest minin' I ever seen. Yo'd come on
a bit o' creakin' wood windlass like a well-head, an' you was let down
i' th' bight of a rope, fendin' yoursen off the side wi' one hand, carryin'
a candle stuck in a lump o' clay with t'other, an' clickin' hold of a rope
with t'other hand." "An' that's three of them," said Mulvaney. "Must be
a good climate in those parts."*

Now, here I was about to join those apple-cheeked, three-handed folk!

Keys to the Cottage

I was quite excited when I got the keys to my cottage, named the Old School
House and built in 1824. I had only looked round from the outside and
through the windows. Now I was in for a shock! Inside the house was dark,
damp and miserable. An old stone sink sat under the kitchen window with
no sign of a tap. I searched and found I had just walked past it - outside.
The tiny fireplace looked as if it would warm only your knees even when
well stoked up. What was Julia going to think? Being country lass brought
up on a farm, she was deterred by little and she was keen on me moving to
Greenhow. But until I had the house sorted out this was going to mean more
than roughing it. Would she be put off coming to visit? And what about my
sons? They were also excited by me living in such an unusual and different
place, but how would they take to this?

Looking further around the house, I could hear a whirring noise and when
I moved towards the door that led to the front room I found it was the wind
blowing. I had to push hard against the draught to open it. Here another
sight greeted me. The front room was dark with only one small window. The

ceiling was low with part of it damp and sagging. The front door opened into an old porch in such bad condition I was surprised that the wind hadn't blown it down.

My excitement was fast disappearing as I thought of the challenge that lay ahead of me. Had I bitten off more than I could chew? When I set off up the stairs I came to a length of wire hanging down from the open trap door into the loft. Though an electric cable it was not part of the electrical system of the house, fastened as it was to a beam in the loft. I pondered for a moment and then worked out why it was there. The poor old lady had obviously hung herself from this, and no one had thought to have it removed. The sadness of the lady's three children was such that they couldn't bear to step foot back in the house. It was a tragedy but why hadn't someone else thought to take it down? Out of respect for the poor woman I quickly removed all signs of the tragic event and did not mention it to Julia, my sons or anyone else. On looking outside I saw the handful of other houses, and thought how desolate and lonely it must have been for the lady with her three grown-up children all gone away. The woman had met a sad end close to where I now stood, but for me life must go on. My task was to make this into a happy, cosy home. It wasn't going to be easy but given a little time I would do it.

Good Samaritan

For a period of time as I ripped apart the house at Greenhow I carried on living in Ilkley in my flat on Cowpasture Road. I would drive in my old van to town to pick up supplies and materials and take them up the Hill. It was winter, in early 1978, and we already had snow at Greenhow. As I walked up Brook Street, Ilkley, I looked up and saw a few new flakes blowing in the wind. More were forecast. A few flakes in Brook Street could mean a few inches on Greenhow Hill and I was anxious to get on my way up there. I jumped in the van and was off. As I made my way through the village of Askwith the road was already white. As I drove up the steep hill towards Snowden Moor the snow was deeper still with a strong wind drifting it across the road.

I turned left at the junction and was surprised to see two bedraggled figures at the side of the road waving me down. As I got closer I could see they were not dressed for the climate. In fact, it looked like they'd been recently undressed! I recognised them immediately as they were well known in Ilkley. He was a prominent businessman. They were married ... but not to each other! As I slithered to a halt they looked a little embarrassed. She knew me and did the talking, her face a little flushed. Was it the cold wind or the recent heat in the car? "Can you help us Ken? Our car is stuck in the snow."

They took me to where the car was jammed in a drift just out of sight of the road. It was obvious what had happened. He had driven off the road with other things on his mind, and without realising had dropped the front wheels into a snow covered rut. While they were pre-occupied the car had settled into the rut as the snow piled up around the car which had now stuck fast. One thing I knew, and that was while he was a better auctioneer than me, I was the better driver. By revving the engine slowly and rocking it to and fro I soon had the car back on the road and pointing towards Ilkley. They were delighted. After thanking me they didn't hang around and rushed off down the road.

A few days later I called in at the Miner's Arms, my local pub and the only one in Greenhow. I ordered a pint but was served instead with a bottle of whisky. John Peel, the landlord, put it on the bar in front of me. "This is for you Ken. The man who left it didn't give his name but said you would know who he was and to thank you for your help when he was stuck in the snow. He was tall, slim and wore a tweed suit." John pulled my pint then stood waiting for me to tell him the story. Pub landlords like to hear local gossip, but all I said was that it was a pleasure to help someone in trouble and left it at that!

Almost freezing to death

I could have done with a little help of my own a few weeks later. Again I had gone to Ilkley for supplies and again it had started to snow. This time I was the one to get stuck and there was no one to come to my assistance. What followed nearly ended my time in Greenhow ... and anywhere else for that matter! I spotted those flakes again as we loaded my van. It was only lightly snowing as I left Ilkley but I knew it would worsen as I climbed towards Greenhow Hill. As I passed Stone House the wind was blowing the snow off the moors and onto the road where it was settling in ever deeper drifts. A strip of road would be laid bare by the wind, then further up the snow would be up to a foot deep. I put my foot down as hard as I could and picked up speed to charge through the drifts, but the higher I went the deeper they became and I was losing momentum as the road got steeper I knew it couldn't last and eventually the old van ground to a halt in a two-foot drift that had built up right across the road. I was still about three miles from home and the snow was continuing to fall heavily, with the temperature dropping quickly in the icy wind. There were no other vehicles in sight. I had a shovel in the boot but that would be no help. I might dig a way through this drift but there were other and thicker ones further along. Worst of all I had no coat, only a light anorak. In the few moments it took to decide what to do the snow had completely covered the car and I couldn't even see out. Quarry wagons used this road and with their huge wheels would find the going easier. If one came along while I was sitting in the van I would be in worse trouble if it didn't see me, so I got out. The only thing for it was to walk those final three miles. Luckily, I had two keys and I left the spare in the ignition so that if anyone needed to move the van, like a snow plough driver, he would be able to do so without the steering lock being a problem. I was not properly dressed for hiking in just an anorak with no hat or gloves, and it was then I realised how exposed that couple must have felt on Snowden Moor.

I set off, head down against the icy blasts. As before, I found the wind was so strong it had cleared parts of the road completely, picking up and dumping the snow in deep drifts where it joined snow blown off the moor. At first when I came to these drifts I ran and jumped them. It warmed me up a little. But as I went along, still climbing higher, it became impossible and I had to wade through drifts that were by now up to my waist. It was bitterly cold and soon I was wet through, with snow sticking to my hair and beard. It was going to take me longer than an hour to walk to Greenhow, but I kept my spirits up by thinking about another spirit that would warm me when I got to the Miner's Arms. I also thought of a book that by chance I had just finished, *The Worst Journey in the World* by Apsley Cherry-Garrard.

He was an acclaimed explorer of Antarctica as one of the younger members of Robert Falcon Scott's Terra Nova expedition of 1910–13, which was the subject of his book. In this he detailed the sufferings of himself and two colleagues seeking unhatched Emperor penguin eggs in temperatures of from –40 °C to –60 °C as they hauled sledges 60 miles to the penguin's hatching ground and back. He later laid stores for Scott's expedition and in November 1912 was part of the party that found the bodies of Scott, Wilson and Bowers. *The Worst Journey in the World* is a classic true adventure tale.

Now compared to what he endured in the Antarctic this was a walk in the park. I kept that fact in my mind as my eyelids iced up stopping me seeing clearly. I swung my arms to help boost circulation but this became difficult as my anorak, thick with snow, had now frozen and stiffened. My jeans were wet through, and becoming frozen to my legs. I was a fit man but the cold was sapping my strength. The wind was blowing the snow off the moors and into my face which was now quite numb. I didn't want to compare what I was going through to Cherry-Garrard's experiences but I knew I could find myself in difficulties if I didn't get to that pub before long. The picture of me thawing out beside the large open fire at the Miner's Arms, sipping a glass of rum or brandy, was comforting. Keep going, I told myself, each step is one nearer warmth and comfort.

Eventually I reached Greenhow and turned the corner from Duck Street onto the Pateley Bridge-to-Grassington road. I couldn't see much because of the ice on my eyelids but I knew I was nearing the pub. At last I could make out the dark shape of the building. Dark shape? This wasn't right at all. Where were the welcoming lights and the vehicles in the car park? That was when I remembered it was Monday – closing day! I was devastated and my heart sank.

But I couldn't stand around and freeze so I set off up the road to my cottage. I had started the renovation work so there would be little comfort in the house. There was no hot water but at least it had electricity and offered shelter from the wind and snow. When I arrived I looked in the mirror. My hair was frozen solid and icicles hung down from my beard to my chest. I had trouble turning my head. I had dreamed of a brandy in front of a big open fire but instead had to make do with a cup of tea, and a rub down with a towel in front of a little electric fire. The snow continued falling and my van sat where I left it for over a week. But the next night, and every night until I was mobile again, I could be found in the Miner's Arms enjoying both beer and warmth!

George's labourer

I applied for planning permission to build a small kitchen extension at the back of the cottage. This would cost money that I didn't have so while I waited for approval I sold twelve acres of land to Alan Firth, a local farmer. The Old School House adjoined the school itself, in which an elderly couple lived together. They sent in an objection to my plans, but there were no grounds for the complaint and approval came through fairly speedily. I had first started work in late 1977 working on my own with Julia's help when she could spare the time from work. But I was not a builder and as the cold winter gave way to spring it was clear I would need some specialist help.

One day in Ilkley I bumped into a local builder, Geoffrey Warr. He was retiring and his workmen were being made redundant. He was particularly upset at having to fire one of his best workmen, a man called George. He was close to retiring age and would find it difficult to get another job. George lived at Robin Hood, Ardsley, between Leeds and Wakefield, and travelled to Ilkley each day. But when I mentioned Greenhow he was not interested because of the extra distance. So I offered to pay cash and petrol money, and eventually persuaded him to help me. He was a wonderful man. The deal was that he would be the master builder (which he was in any case) and I would be his labourer. We worked hard together through the rest of 1978 building the extension and renovating the house.

George was a stone mason by trade and the first thing he did was to rebuild the small fireplace in the living room. Although he was working with second-hand stones he was able to delicately shape and lay them down leaving only a quarter-inch gap. "That's the sign of a good workman," he said. "There should be no big gaps filled in with cement." The next job was the fireplace in the front room. What I wanted here was an open fireplace like a miniature Inglenook with a dog-grate in which to burn wood. Once completed, we let it dry out before lighting the fire. Though it was now several months since the snow I was really excited at the thought of sitting round a glowing open fire with all that promised for the next winter. But I was severely disillusioned. It didn't draw and the smoke went everywhere except up the chimney, I went upstairs to find the smoke curling into the bedrooms from around the window frames and the skirting boards. There were draughts everywhere and all seemed to draw the smoke except the chimney. George looked at me and I looked at him waiting for him to say what we should do – "I told you Ken, open fires are a waste of time. The only way to keep warm is to sit on the roof by the chimney pot, as that's where all the heat goes." We dampened down the fire and had a look up the chimney. "There's no throat," he said. "We will have to make one." A throat is a narrow aperture where a big fireplace leads into a wide chimney and causes the chimney to suck up the smoke. Once we finished constructing this It worked perfectly thanks to George but it always worked a bit better if we left the kitchen door open a fraction to increase the draught.

Since the ceilings were damp and sagging I thought it would be a good idea to pull them down to expose the wooden joists as they are in a traditional cottage. It was an awfully dirty job prising off the old larch laths and plaster with a pick axe, but through the dust we could see something very pleasing. The joists were varnished dark brown and were as shiny as they had been when the place was newly built a hundred and fifty years before. This was before it had been so-called modernised and plastered over in more recent times. When we reached the corner of the room we uncovered the hole where an old staircase had gone up to the bedroom when this had been one half of two tiny cottages.

As the laths and plaster fell to the floor I noticed some old newspapers. We stopped work to let the dust settle and had a good look at them. They had been stuffed in to fill a gap, then plastered over. (A few years later I saw a man doing a similar thing with newspapers but he was stuffing them into the bodywork of a car then pasting filler over the top!) I opened one of the papers carefully though it was folded tight, and it was possible to read part. At the top was the publication's title: The Schoolmaster, and the date: October 25th 1879. Lower down I read some of the adverts for blackboards and machine-ruled Welsh slates which the pupils of the day would have had to write on. Other ads were for books and school furniture, and one I found particularly amusing was headed Teeth £1, which presumably was the cost of getting dentures at the time. It went on to explain that a complete upper or lower set of fourteen pure mineral teeth could be fitted and fixed to the mouth, and all without pain! Another newspaper I was able to decipher was the *Yorkshire Post* and *Leeds Intelligencer* dated December 16th 1881. So that was when the house had been last 'modernised'.

Getting back to work I gave the joists a dressing of linseed oil and they looked great, but we found I had created another problem. When someone walked about in the bedroom above dust and dirt lodged over decades in the cracks where the floorboards joined, sprinkled down onto whomever or whatever was below. Once again George came to the rescue and plastered between the joists. When this was later painted white the ceiling looked fantastic and was, we agreed, a big improvement.

Over many years of working on building sites George had learned all the other trades allied to stone masonry such as joinery, plumbing, plastering, drainage and roofing. He could do them all. I watched him put glass in the kitchen windows then run the putty round with the skill of a full-time glazier. The only thing he would not attempt was working with electricity; he wouldn't even change a fuse and would call me if one blew. He was a nice man and loved the dog he would often bring with him, a Kerry Blue terrier, an unusual but very attractive breed. Though he hated driving the 35 miles each way from Robin Hood, he never missed a day until the job was done.

Nearing 65, George's eyesight was not so good and he wore thick bottle glasses that were often covered with cement dust or blobs of plaster. How he could see to do the high quality work always amazed me. I grew to like him and greatly enjoyed that period of labouring and learning from him. It was good for my soul, too, after the dramatic but depressing last years of running my company, ensuring 50

George pointing at Greenhow 1977

employees were paid each week, and running from pillar to post trying to solve problems and balance the books. Apart from the manner of my dismissal by Alan Morgan, there were other things that had caused great heartache. The bank had held insurance policies in the names of my three sons and took these as part payment of my overdrafts. I was given no choice about that or on losing the deeds to my house.

So in one way it came as a sad day when the building work on the house in Greenhow was completed and George and his dog disappeared down the road in his little harvest gold Austin Allegro never to be seen again. He left me with a few of his sayings which I still use today, "If it was easy everyone would do it," and, "A crying baby gets attention".

By the end of the year Julia was helping me decorate and now we had a decent place in which to live. There was a good hot water heating system without having to rely solely on the fire back boiler that was in when we came, and there was a large kitchen thanks to the extension. The electrical supply was good and as the chillier evenings of autumn drew in I often had a comforting wood fire going: on the evidence of the previous winter this was going to be important. Julia moved in permanently. She didn't fancy the long drive to her work in Chapeltown, Leeds, so she took on a shop selling children's clothes in Ilkley. This was actually in the very same premises used by my ex-wife Wendy to run her boutique a few years before.

Julia and I were very comfortable living together in the Old School House but I still didn't tell her about the hanging electrical cable!

Settling in ... and buying a pony

In that first year in Greenhow the Old School House didn't have a telephone and we had to walk down the road to a public call box outside the Miner's Arms. One day as I approached I saw two hikers who had stopped to speak to a local woman at the bus stop next to the phone box. One of them asked her, "What time is the bus to Pateley Bridge?" She replied, "Two-thirty, the day after tomorrow on market day!" Pateley Bridge was just three miles distant but it sometimes felt that it and other centres of civilisation were a lot further away.

Julia bought a black Labrador who we called Bessie. She gave me company on the days I was on my own. Last thing at night I would take her for a short walk in the field behind the house and that was when I would be reminded of how high we were above sea level. When it was a moonlit evening, instead of looking up at the clouds I sometimes looked straight ahead at them floating by, with the lower ones passing below me further down the steep hills. On the occasions we had fog it was actually more often a matter of us standing in clouds.

On Friday afternoons I would drive down to Ilkley to collect from school my two younger sons, Andrew, now sixteen, and Tim, ten years of age. They loved coming up to the rural isolation of Greenhow which they found a complete change from Ilkley. It was great to be together for the weekend.

Neither boy had any problem with roughing it and the chance of mucking around in the open air really appealed to them. When I was young I had felt that country life had given me the sort of learning experience I wasn't getting from school, and I was happy to see both boys enjoy themselves. Their older brother Jonathan, now approaching twenty, had moved out from his mother's house and gone into digs with some wild mates. Not for him, at least at this time, the rural life.

I had bought a little dumper truck used by builders to transport materials around sites and Tim took it over, spending hours riding round the fields on it. He would be up early on a Sunday morning and out on the machine. Often the first thing I would hear before I opened my eyes was the 'put-put-put' of Tim's dumper. It was his 'toy' and though he was only ten he was already mechanically minded and could wind the handle fast enough to start it then drive and fix it when it went wrong.

Andrew had more traditional country pursuits in mind. Since there was still plenty of grassland on my remaining fifteen acres, Andrew suggested we get a horse. He had learned to ride with a friend in Ilkley, so I agreed to buy a pony. As usual, my thinking was to go to an auction. There was a monthly horse sale at Pannal near Harrogate, and we all jumped in the van to go to the next one. We looked around at the various horses on show and quickly fell in love with a little Shetland pony. He was standing in a pen with his head down, looking forlorn and seeming for all the world like he was waiting for someone to take him to a good home. We stroked him. He seemed docile and good natured so it was an easy decision. When it came to the auction I put my hand up when I sensed the bidding was slowing down, bid twice and the hammer fell. "Details please?" I gave my name to the auctioneer, then went round to the office and paid for the pony.

We all felt excited as we rushed down the yard to inspect our new pet. He looked so sweet. I arranged transport to Greenhow, giving the driver my address. Then we rushed back to wait. About two hours later the Land Rover and trailer arrived. Andrew rushed out to guide him as he backed the trailer into my drive. I led the pony out of the trailer and round to the back field. He had a thick coat and would be all right living outside with just a small shelter for when the weather became really rough. After all, though Greenhow winters may be tough the pony was a Shetland and was built for worse. I don't know who made the suggestion but he was christened Horace. Right away Andrew wanted to ride him but we decided to give him a rest after his traumatic rides to and from the auction. Tomorrow would be soon enough. I slipped off the head collar freeing him to roam and he wandered off down the field. I would soon learn that I had made my first mistake with Horace!

The next day we were all up early but Horace was nowhere to be seen. Eventually we spotted him down by the little pine wood on the edge of our land where he had found shelter from the wind. He was as far away as possible and that is where he stayed for several weeks as we couldn't coax him back. When we approached him he trotted off deeper in the wood. The little docile pony of yesterday was now like a wild animal and no one could get near him. It was obvious he had been given 'something' to keep him quiet at the auction; not all villains are in the car trade! As the weather grew colder towards the back end of 1978 and there was less grass, Horace ventured nearer the house where we put out hay for him. We would watch him when the snow fell thick and it would take him a long time to walk up from the wood, slowly picking his way on his short legs around the humps and hollows of the old mine workings and the drifted snow.

Philippa who lived next door (but was not the lady who objected to the extension) knew more about horses than we did and eventually managed to catch him. But he always refused to allow anyone to sit on his back and went wild if we tried. I thought that I could tame him and sat on his back with my legs almost touching the ground on either side, but he even threw me off! So instead of being ridden Horace became a pet. Andrew got over his initial disappointment and loved spending time with him. Over the next few years, we would feed and stroke Horace but that was all he allowed. No rides.

After selling twelve acres when I first moved in, much of the remaining fifteen acres was let-off for grazing to a farmer from Middlesmoor. But there was still plenty of grass for another horse. Should I go to the auction again or talk to my friend David Booth, the one-time butcher? There was a risk either way. David lived about three miles away on a farm belonging to a friend with whom he bought and sold horses. Actually, together they would trade in almost anything that was likely to show a profit and could get involved in some very shady dealings. I called on David. When I arrived there was no one in the yard so I walked towards his caravan through one of the open farm buildings. Suddenly without warning, a huge shaggy Alsatian leapt out and grabbed my wrist. I froze as his teeth sunk in. Fortunately for me at that same moment David appeared round the corner and bellowed at the dog, who immediately let go and returned to his bed under a cart. It was obvious who the 'pack leader' around here was. My wrist suffered little permanent damage as the Alsatian's teeth had met bone, but I carry a scar to this day. David had another dog, a bulldog that was never chained up and followed him everywhere. It was no danger to anyone as most of its bottom jaw was missing and a great piece of skin and lip hung loose over the gap where its lower teeth had been. There were other marks on the poor thing to show it had been fighting. Though I never saw any evidence of organised dog fighting

I felt sure it went on. The farm was isolated and an ideal place to hide from the law. His bulldog was rather a pitiful sight but strangely enough it seemed quite happy. Though I liked David I did not like some of the things he did. He was a good contact and I benefited from our friendship, though I always had to be on guard.

He showed me a horse he said would be suitable for my boys to ride. "It's bomb proof," he said and was also big enough for me. Then the haggling started. I didn't have his knowledge when it came to valuing horses so I worked on the theory that he would at first ask for far too much and all I had to do was work at getting the price down. It was a slow process and he kept wetting his fingers then looking for my hands. But these I kept well clear, hiding them behind my back. Eventually we reached agreement and shook hands on the deal. "Are you going to ride it home?" he asked. Well, I hadn't ridden a horse for many years but found myself saying, "Yes." "Can you ride bareback?" he asked. "I'd prefer not to," I said. "Well you will need a saddle." "I thought that was included in the deal," was my reply, my tongue firmly in my cheek.

He smiled and I thought here we go again. Thankfully, arriving at a deal was much easier this time, though later I thought he must have done so well out of the horse he had eased up on the tack, bridle and saddle. We saddled up the horse, whose name now escapes me. Then David made a point of showing me how not to be fooled by a crafty old horse when fastening the girth, as they breathe in and hold it until you have fastened up. That way they are more comfortable with a looser girth when they breathe out. (I used to do exactly the same when my mechanic strapped me into my racing car.) It was not a big horse but to help me get on, David gave me a leg-up. A thought crossed my mind as I swung my leg over, "Had he also legged me up on the price," as they say in the motor trade when you have paid too much for something. But the deal was done and we had shaken so there was no going back. To use another motor dealers' phrase, whatever the outcome I was not 'a cocker,' the horse was now mine.

It was about three miles from David's farm back to Greenhow and it was getting dark by the time I got there. We had walked most of the way as I was not confident enough to urge my new horse into a gallop in case I fell off or could not control her. Andrew, Tim and Julia were pleased and would occasionally ride the pony, though this was another that was treated more as a pet.

Jonathan in jail for £27

Since moving out of Wendy's house, my elder son Jonathan had been sharing with friends and living something of a wild existence as far as we could tell. For a while I hadn't seen him, but one day he decided he would like to come and stay with us at Greenhow. Julia, who was always good with my sons, and I were happy and we made him welcome. But whatever we did he did not appear to be happy. He was quiet and moody, staying in his bedroom with little to say. If I wondered what was troubling him I was soon to find out.

We had finished our evening meal and Jonathan had gone to his bedroom when I heard a loud knock on the back door. I opened it and was surprised to see PC Ford, the local police constable. "Is Jonathan staying with you?" "Yes" I replied. "Well, I'd like a word with him." I called Jonathan who appeared at the bottom of the stairs looking sheepish. PC Ford said, "Jonathan I want £27 from you for an unpaid fine. If you do not pay I have a warrant for your arrest." Jonathan didn't say a word but only shook his head. He obviously did not have the £27. The constable then turned to me, "Do you have it Ken? Are you going to pay or do I have to take him with me?" He explained that the fine was for a motoring offence some time before. Jonathan had made no attempt to pay it or any part of it. This annoyed me and I thought he must learn a lesson.

"Sorry, I can't pay his debt," I said. PC Ford looked at Jonathan, "Well get your toothbrush and some clothes. You won't need many. They'll give you a uniform where you're going." Jonathan went back upstairs and returned with a small bag. He then left with PC Ford, who turned to me one last time and asked, "Do you want to pay?" It was now my turn to shake my head as I stood - with almost £100 in my pocket – watching him escort my son to the police car and drive off towards Pateley Bridge.

Jonathan was taken to Armley Jail in Leeds. I went to visit him not knowing if he would want to see me, but relieved that he was taking his medicine like a man and held no grudge. I was nervous walking in and was more shocked than he had been. Armley Jail looked just like an ancient fortress from the outside, a dark grey, miserable Victorian building. It was worse inside as I walked in through a wicket gate in the great wooden doors. It was like stepping back in time. I looked around at the inmates, they had all broken the law most for far more serious things than non payment of a fine and there amongst then was Jonathan. I shuddered at the thought that my actions had helped condemn my son to this. Would he be better or worse for the experience?

I sat down at a little wooden table and Jonathan sat on the other side. I looked across at him in his blue and white striped shirt thinking, "My boy, in such a place!" Worse still, his fellow prisoners included some of the worst criminals in the country such as the notorious criminal Donald Neilson, known as the Black Panther. The warder stood a few paces away keeping an eye on us. There was not much to talk about but I was able to pass him a packet of cigarettes under the table.

I often asked myself if I had made the right decision in letting him go to prison but Jonathan made me feel easier some months later when he said it was a lesson he had learned, and an experience he was determined never to repeat. And he never has! The trivial reason for his jailing came home to him and he understood that there was no escaping the law: you had to face up to the consequences of your actions. If only more first time offenders thought the same. From what I hear many can't wait to get back inside.

Brakes, rocks and rats

I bought a second-hand Land Rover to replace the van that Barry Normington had sold me outside the Labour Exchange. I was sorry to see the old van go, but it struggled in bad weather and the Land Rover would be ideal if we had another hard winter – and we usually did in Greenhow. One day as I drove the Land Rover to Ilkley to collect supplies I sped down the steep hill towards Askwith. I pressed the brake but nothing happened, my foot just went to the floor boards. I was picking up speed and pumped the pedal but still nothing happened. I grabbed the hand brake and all that did was to turn off the engine as it was a transmission brake. I was now freewheeling faster than ever with no brake or engine to slow me. There was no point in changing down a gear, but what could I do? Fortunately, there was no one coming up the other way. As I approached a narrower section with steep banks on either side all I could hear was the drum of the tyres on the road. There was nowhere to pull off but an idea occurred to me. If I could steer into the bank while running alongside it, by holding tightly onto the steering wheel I might scrub off some of the speed. I turned the wheel to the side and hung on as the front road wheel grabbed at the banking trying to ride up it. Thankfully, it worked and I slowed down coming to a halt just before the very narrowest part. When I looked back up the road I saw the cause of the problem. The back wheel, complete with brake drum, had come out of the axle. A furrow along the grass bank had been ploughed making the road altogether a little wider, and I'd had a very close shave!

Julia had settled in at Greenhow and we were living together full time. She was a great help with making the cottage suitable for habitation and loved it when the boys visited. So far, while renovating the cottage, I had lived off my few savings and proceeds from selling some of the land, I didn't want Julia to have to pay more than her share from her earnings at the children's clothes shop, but now we were turning into 1979 it was time for me to again think about earning some money.

The land I owned was a patchwork of grass fields divided by old stone walls that had fallen down in many places over the years. In the summer of 1979 the weather was good and I set about mending the walls. I enjoyed this dry-stone walling though I was by no means an expert. It was a very relaxing way to spend the time after the hectic style of my earlier life. And it gave me an idea. Most of the stone was weathered limestone and the bigger pieces would be good for rockery stone. By making the fields bigger overall I would have a lot left over. Some years before, my horse dealing friend David Booth and I had collected rockery stone from the moors above Threshfield near Grassington, and had sold it to gardening contractors. The stone on my land was similar. All I had to do was to select suitable lumps, start piling them up and find a market to sell them to. I put a few pieces into my Land Rover and drove down to Stephen Smiths Garden Centre in Otley, and was pleasantly surprised to take an order for ten tons. I was back in business.

I could kill two birds with one stone, as it were: mend my walls and earn some money. It would take some time to get ten tons together but the sun was shining. So I put on my shorts and took off my shirt, and went to work feeling good out in the fresh air and a long way from the telephone. When I had the stone ready I phoned an old friend, Derek Symonds, who agreed to deliver it to Otley. Derek had been an employee of mine and the foreman in charge of a near-catastrophic demolition job years before. As detailed in my first book, *Nothing Easy*, the work was to pull down an old hall next to a church at Cross Hills. Unfortunately for us, in demolishing the hall a huge section of wall had come down in one lump and had brought the church down with it. There had been all hell to pay as I found out that church people could be as exploitive as any when they sought compensation

Derek now had his own tipper lorry and, as I discovered, was only too pleased to help his old boss. He was doing me an extra big favour as his wagon had an aluminium body which could be damaged by rockery stone. But as good as his word, Derek delivered the load and a week later I received a cheque. I was in the money and I had space to think of what to do next.

I fenced off part of the field closest to the house, dug it over to make a vegetable patch for our own vegetables. I also fenced off another strip along the wall and put wire netting down for a hen run. Then I bought ten 'point of lay' pullets that started laying a few weeks later. They laid only small eggs to start with, but as the hens grew so did the eggs until they were full size. I fed them corn twice a day which I scattered on the grass to keep them occupied in scratching for it. To boost egg production I also put a large metal feeder in the middle of the pen so they would always have a plentiful supply of food. After a few weeks they were in full production and eating a lot of food. I was always filling the feeder thinking what an exceptionally hungry flock they were. It was not until much later in the winter that I found the reason.

There had been a light fall of snow during the night. When I went out in the morning to feed the hens I was amazed to see a different set of tracks in the snow leading from the wall to the feeder. No wonder the food was going down fast. Unwittingly, I had been feeding a pack of rats that lived in the bottom of the dry stone wall. The feeder was removed immediately and I telephoned the Council Pest Control Department. They didn't waste time and arrived the same afternoon. When they investigated they said that there must be dozens of rats living in the bottom of the wall and, thanks to me, all looked well fed. I had to move my hens to a different field while the pest control people took over feeding the rats on a new special diet. This soon reduced both their appetite and their numbers!

Our own milk

Now we had our own eggs, Julia thought it would be a good idea to have our own milk. So off I went again to the solver of all problems, dodgy David Booth. He sold me a nanny-goat that was in-kid and due soon. There was an old shed behind the house which we patched up and added straw to make her comfortable, naming her Florence. There was not a long wait before she gave birth to two kids. The white one was very strong and soon stood on its own feet and was feeding. The little brown one though, was very weak and lay huddled in the straw. We made frequent visits to check on its progress, but it could not stand to drink. The mother was not interested in it and licked and fed just the stronger one.

It was a cold night so we decided to take the kid into the house and warmed it by the fire. It started to revive and eventually stood up. We took it back to get a drink of milk from Florence but she was having none of it and would not allow him near. I took hold of Florence by the horns while Julia propped the young kid up at the rear where the milk came from. But as soon as we let Florence free she turned round and butted the kid so hard he flew right across the shed. She wanted nothing to do with him. We would have to do something or he would not survive.

I had an idea that I remembered from my pig-keeping days. I fixed a 'creep' in one corner, fenced off with rails to make a little refuge for the kid where mother could not reach him. That's where he spent most of the time when we were not in to feed him. Occasionally he would be brave and venture out, but as soon as Florence saw him he would duck under the bottom rail back to safety. We had to go in three or four times a day. I would hold Florence while he had a drink. She did not like it but she had no choice. He was quite nimble and kept out of her way in his creep. When he heard us at the door he would dash out to meet us for his feed time. This went on for weeks until he no longer needed mother's milk and they all learned to live together, though Florence never really accepted him.

When it was time for Florence to mate I borrowed a billy-goat from a friend. While our neighbour Philippa, the one who helped us with our horses, couldn't have been nicer, our other neighbour had been most difficult from the first day. We worked out that she had wanted to buy the Old School House before me and was awkward whenever she had an opportunity, such as objecting to our small kitchen extension. Well as it happened, our large front garden ran right up to her front door and the grass needed eating off, so I tethered the borrowed billy-goat on a short rope as close as I could to her door. You may or may not know that billy-goats stink. The smell is vile even when you're not close and I made sure he was as near as possible to my nasty neighbour. When he had eaten all the grass I fed him hay and left him there for almost a week. Neither the neighbour nor her husband said a word about it but I'm sure they got the message. As their front door led directly into their front room she and her husband would be sitting watching television only a few feet from the excruciating aroma of our billy. We never became friends but for the rest of the time I lived in Greenhow I never had another problem.

Scaffolding

Making money was constantly on my mind. I bought an old Bedford wagon and one day I took some scrap into Bradford for a friend. I liked looking round scrap yards and on this occasion I noticed among a huge pile of scrap steel a lot of scaffolding tubes. I spoke to the manager and agreed to buy seven tons of scaffolding at little more than the price of scrap. Most of the long poles had slight bends in them but I had an answer. A friend in Burley-in-Wharfedale, Charlie Ridley, had a machine for straightening steel. He was a bit eccentric but a clever engineer. "Sorry," he said. "You can't use my machine but I'll make you a smaller portable one that will do the same job and you can take it away with you." Good enough, I thought, and I hauled the scaffolding from Bradford to Greenhow then picked up the straightener from Charlie and set it up on a bench outside my house.

All it consisted of was a steel framework with a hole at each end to thread the scaffold pole through and a hydraulic jack in the middle. The pole was pushed through till the bend was over the jack, then you pumped to apply pressure and straighten it. To check it was now straight you used 'rack of eye,' as they called it, looking along the length. The hard part was pushing a buckled length of steel through the machine. Though it was a slow job I managed to straighten them all out. I put an advertisement in the local paper and sold the lot to local builders, making myself a tidy profit.

My next money-making venture was to buy a second-hand JCB earth mover. I took it home, painted and serviced it, then placed an ad in the Yorkshire Post newspaper. I waited for the interest to flood in, but I waited and waited. Greenhow was a bit out of the way for buyers from Leeds and South Yorkshire who could not even find it on the map. I had to remain patient but eventually a local firm did show interest and it was sold at a smaller than hoped for profit.

Car dealing

I drifted into the motor trade. I had never liked car dealers who in my experience were mostly a shady bunch of characters. But here was I now becoming one, although not a particularly successful example! A top car dealer once said to me, "Ken, look them in the eye and then screw them." Well, I could never bring myself to do this. I tried to give a fair deal but as far as my experience goes that is not the recipe for success in the car business.

I became friends with Geoff Buller, owner of Nidderdale Motors in Pately Bridge. I bought some of his older part-exchange vehicles, cleaned and sold them. He was very helpful and, aware that I did not have much money, he would often say," Take the car and pay me when you sell it." He became a great friend and I always made sure I paid him promptly. One day he offered me a nice Rover 2000. All it needed was a good clean. I took it home to Greenhow, put an advert in the *Yorkshire Post* and made it ready to sell. I had to work outside but it was a dry day, though the wind was sneaking around as usual. I made a thorough job of cleaning the car, inside and out, and when I'd finished it looked like new. I felt confident that it would return a profit. Two days later when the ad appeared in the paper the telephone rang and a foreign-sounding gentleman asked me questions about the car. He said he lived in Leeds but would like to see the vehicle and asked where I lived. When I told him he was none-the-wiser, never having heard of Greenhow. I tried to explain, but after several goes between us and a third party who I assumed was helping him with the language, he asked if we could meet at Otley bus station. I wanted to sell the car and so agreed.

I was there early and parked in an obvious place where I could be seen. Eventually two men appeared, recognised the car and came over. They told me they were from the Sudan and were staying with friends in Leeds. They wanted a car to take back with them to Sudan, and had been advised to buy a Hillman or a Rover. They looked round the car and liked it, but said they didn't understand much about cars and asked if a friend inspect it. "He works in Bradford."

This knocked me back a bit but I wanted to sell the car so, in for a penny in for a pound, I agreed. One of them climbed in the front with me while the other opened the rear door. A look of horror appeared on his face as he saw Bessie, my Labrador. "Don't worry. She won't bite," I reassured him. He eased into the seat and sat as far away from her as possible, almost trapping his arm in the door as he closed it, while Bessie, sensing his unease, also backed away into her corner.

We drove to Bradford where their friend was a tutor at the University. One of my passengers went inside and returned with the news that we should wait for 30 minutes for the lecturer to finish the tutorial he was conducting. Eventually he appeared, smartly dressed. He was obviously a clever academic, which made me wonder how much he really knew about cars. I was soon to find out as he strolled round pausing to kick a tyre or run his hand over the paintwork. He looked in the boot and scrutinised the spare wheel and tool kit. After a good look inside, including sitting behind the wheel, he looked at the engine. I raised the bonnet and he peered inside, instantly looking a little bewildered. With hindsight I would say this was first time he had ever looked at a Rover engine. He did not reach for the dip stick to check the oil or look in the radiator, but he did notice that the water was low in the windscreen washer bottle. He did not ask many questions only looked and kept his thoughts to himself.

By now a number of their other friends had gathered round. The two buyers, the lecturer and the others gathered in a huddle for all of fifteen minutes. There was plenty of heads nodding, arms waving and pointing at the car, and they spoke in Arabic while I stood like a spare part. Eventually one came over and said his friends like the car and they would buy it. I expected the next question to be, "What's your last price?" But instead I was asked if I could take the buyers to Leeds to get the money from another friend. I'd gone this far, so agreed. We said goodbye to the dozen or so friends and the two buyers climbed into the car, one in the front with me, the other in the back with Bessie, as before sitting as far apart as possible. By the time we were close to Leeds the petrol light started flashing. We had covered some miles and I thought, "Bugger it. Take the chance," and I didn't look again at the gauge.

Eventually we arrived at their friend's house In Chapeltown, then as today a run-down area. We turned off the main road into a housing estate where there were purple, graffiti-covered wheelie bins on the pavements, derelict cars with flat tyres and smashed windows. I was directed to a house in a corner and as I pulled up the man in the back was out before I had applied the hand brake, dusting himself down to remove any dog hairs. They told me to wait and disappeared into a house. The thought crossed my mind that perhaps I had been used just as a free taxi ride home. I waited nervously but not for long. When they returned one said, "We don't have English money." My heart sank. I thought, "Please don't ask me to accept a cheque on a Sudanese bank."

"But we can pay in US dollars. How much do you want?" I just happened to know the current exchange rate: $2.40 for £1. I soon had it converted and told them the amount. They went back inside. I prepared a receipt and filled in the transfer of ownership on the registration document and waited. I couldn't quite believe what was happening. They were soon back with yet more friends. But I was delighted to see they also had a bundle of greenbacks which they handed over for me to count. Once done, I stuffed the cash into my pocket and handed over the documents and the receipt. Other friends arrived and now I was standing in the middle of seven people none of whom I had ever seen before this day. I was quite worried, they had the car, the keys, and a receipt for proof of ownership, all they had to do now was take the money back off me and I would not be in a very good position to do anything about it.

They looked at the car and at me, "How will you get back home?" "Don't worry about me," I said. "I'll catch a bus to Otley and someone will pick me up." There was no other car there and I doubt if they had insurance for this one, or a license. I was a bit worried and just wanted to get away from where I was badly outnumbered in a strange part of Leeds. I did not have a lead for Bessie so I took off my belt slipped it through her collar. Fortunately my trousers were a good fit and did not slip down. I bid them farewell and set off towards the main road feeling a little easier as I put some distance between us. I was greatly relieved to get on the first bus that came by and felt much more relaxed when I sat down and felt the wad of dollars in my back pocket pressing against the seat.

The Miner's Arms

Mention has been made before of the Miner's Arms in Greenhow, where it was of course the only public house, just a short walk down the road from my cottage. The first time I had visited the pub was long before I moved to the village back in the 1960s. I was working with a tractor driver called Barry Bramley and we had been

The Miners Arms

spreading lime at a farm near Pateley Bridge. It was a warm summer's evening when we drove past the pub on our way home and Barry said, "Do you fancy a pint Ken?" The brakes had been applied before the words had left his lips. We ordered two pints of bitter, looked around and felt ourselves step back in time. The walls were whitewashed, the floor just bare flagstones, the tables were scrubbed but no longer white, and had long benches on either side. There were two old chairs either side of the big black fireplace. An old lady appeared behind the bar and told us to sit down and she would bring the beer to us. Barry sat by the window and as I turned to follow, I noticed that there were no beer pumps. The old lady reached up and took a large jug from a row of different sizes hung from a ceiling joist above the bar, bent down to a large wooden barrel on a rack tilted slightly backwards, turned the brass tap and the beer flowed into the jug. She moved the jug up and down to create a froth. I sat by Barry and she was not far behind with two glasses in one hand and the jug in the other. She put the glasses on the table then poured beer into them, repeating the movement to create more froth, before handing the jug over to us. It was the first time I had drunk beer straight from the barrel and it was so good we had another jug.

Fifteen years passed and now I was living in the village and calling in at the pub most evenings, except Mondays of course. The old lady was long gone and the pub was now run by the popular John Peel, a landlord who always made you welcome especially in winter when the few of us would gather around the huge fire. I told John about how different things were all those years before. He told me that things had changed very little when he first took over the pub. He'd opened one of the cupboards to find a stack of old brass spittoons. "Where are they John?"? I asked, sensing a little earner in what could be interesting collectors' items. "Oh, I threw them down the tip at the back of the pub. But that was years ago and they're now buried under tons of builders' waste." I went around in daylight and with his agreement conducted a search. But he was right. They couldn't be found – or someone else had been there before me.

During the long winter evenings when the snow was deep, I would walk to the Miner's Arms listening to the wind whistling through the telephone wires strung on poles along the side of the road. As the wind increased it would build from a hum to a shriek, the slack on the cables thrusting out sideways almost torn from the posts. Then it would suddenly drop and the wires would briefly sag waiting for the next onslaught, and they didn't have long to wait. I often stood for a few moments underneath listening to the music as the noise went up and down. It was exciting and wild, and the comforting thought was that John's cosy fire was little more than a hundred yards away. Such is the pleasure of country life.

Sometimes there would only be eight or ten locals in the pub to have braved the snow. John would say, "You're all welcome to stay as long as you like. There is no closing time as the roads are closed and we're cut off, so there will be no law man coming tonight." It wouldn't

John Peel in good spirit

have made much difference, as our local constable was often there with us also having a pint long after closing time.

They were all characters. One regular, Les Myers, appeared in winter often looking like a snow man. He would scrape off the snow then remove the sack tied with string around his shoulders for extra protection. He would shuffle into the bar and order a pint while having great difficulty getting the money out of his pocket with cold numb hands. Les lived in a little farm over a mile away, but he was a good shepherd and whatever the weather he would tend his flock, checking that they had found shelter. Sheep can survive for a while buried in the snow but need to be found and dug out before too long. Les always wanted to know exactly where they were. He would check some of them on his way to the pub, have a pint and a warm, then walk back to look at the remainder on his way home. Though many sheep were buried in snow for days and lost during the hardest winters, I don't think Les ever lost any.

We few regulars had some enjoyable late-night drinking sessions during those winters. Often, I was the last to leave about midnight with John bolting the outer door behind me. The snow would be swirling round in the wind and I would button my coat, dig my hands deep in my pockets and set off up the road to my home. One night I hadn't gone far when I heard a meow. Huddled behind the telephone box sheltering from the snow was the pub's small kitten. I thought, "Poor thing, it will never survive on a night like this. John must have forgotten about it." The kitten was pleased when I picked it up and tucked it into the front of my coat. What had been a cry for help turned into a purr of satisfaction. I thought that John would worry if he

41

couldn't find her in the morning, so I retraced my footsteps to the pub, which was now in darkness. John lived at the back of the pub so I had to hammer loudly on the front door, which eventually opened a few inches and the end of a double barrelled shotgun pointed out.

"Who is it," he called. "Me John, Ken. I've rescued your kitten." The gun disappeared and the door opened wider. What confronted me was an angry pub landlord in his sleeping attire. "She's out because I put her out," he spluttered. "I put her out every night and no harm has come to her yet. Now f**k off home and go to bed. Good night!" With that the door slammed and the bolts were rattled into place. I gently put the kitten on the ground and turned for home. I think that was the only time I saw him angry. He was a good landlord and was almost always jolly. He was not very tall but light on his feet as he flitted from one end of the bar to the other, occasionally stopping by the whisky optic to top up his glass. He knew his customers, knew their tipples and would often have the glass half-full by the time they had put in their order.

The Miners Arms was very popular, not only with the locals but with people driving from far and wide. I guess that the remoteness of Greenhow meant there was little chance of being breathalysed. John enjoyed an unusual domestic situation. He was helped in the pub by both his ex-wife and his new spouse. John and his new wife lived in one part of the house and the ex lived in another. His ex-wife, Joyce, was the cook while her replacement in John's affections helped out behind the bar.

Imagine my surprise when one day my son Jonathan told me that he and Joyce were getting married. Jonathan was half her age but that didn't stop the two of them getting married, at the time Jonathan was at a loose end and I think Joyce felt she could, mother him though marital bliss did not last the test of time and it wasn't long before they parted and divorced. Joyce was very understanding and for Jonathan it was part of his growing up I guess.

Sadly, in 1980 John Peel died suddenly. He was not old and it was a shock to the whole Greenhow community. The Miner's Arms never again reached the level of popularity it enjoyed during his time. His funeral service was held in the parish church, a mere hundred yards up the road from the pub, and he filled the Church just as he had filled the Miner's Arms. He was well known and liked and the congregation was so large it spilled out of the church with people listening from outside. I was one among them.

During the winter of early 1980 Greenhow was cut off from the outside world for a few days with snow drifts up to eight feet high. Finally, a snow blower made it through from Pateley Bridge, cutting a single track not much wider than a car with the snow steeply banked on the sides. I had great fun driving as fast as I dared through this corridor. If I clipped the side it didn't damage the car as you just bounced off the packed snow. I nearly came unstuck one day driving through and spotting a Land Rover coming the other way. It was far off and I tried to change gear to cut my speed, rather than just skid over the packed ice if I used the brakes. Nothing happened! As we approached each other I was still going too fast and braced for a head-on

Greenhow, where the snow comes thick and stays long!

collision. I threw the car sideways which wedged it across the corridor but at least stopped any forward momentum. And just inches away the Land Rover stopped too. The driver climbed out laughing and helped me dig my vehicle out. There was then a half mile drive in reverse for me to get to a spot to let him pass.

Park Rash in the snow

I am sure that many of us must have a few key moments in our lives which looking back we find hard to believe really happened. I think about these and wonder, "Did I really do that?" One of these occurred during the Greenhow days. Luckily, I have a witness to prove I didn't dream the whole thing.

Again it was winter, this time it was New Year's Eve 1981, and once more there was a heavy blanket of snow all around. Julia Nadal had attended Liverpool Art College some years before, and friends from those days decided to come up to the Dales for the New Year from their homes in London. They rented the Shepherds House in Woodale, located in Coverdale on the road from Leyburn to Kettlewell, about 25 miles from Greenhow. Julia suggested we join them for the New Year as there was plenty of room in the house and we could stay overnight. I agreed and took out the map to plot the best way to get there. It had been snowing hard but in the previous few days had eased a bit and the main roads were thought to be passable. There were two options: Greenhow-Ripon- Masham-Middleham and then from Leyburn to Woodale. The alternative was the Greenhow-Grassington-Kettlewell-Park Rash-Woodale route, which was half the distance but was over much higher roads. *(Part of the route can be seen on the front cover of my book Nothing Easy)* Yes, you probably guessed right! The shorter but more difficult way was the one for me. In those snowy conditions it would be an adventure, though I had no idea just how much of a challenge it would turn out to be. I reasoned that the Kettlewell to Woodale part of the route was less high than the road outside our front door at Greenhow and you could drive along that – just about! What I overlooked was that the Kettlewell road was little used. To add to the problem we left it late to depart, setting off just after four o'clock as dusk was approaching. The snow had almost stopped but there was a cold wind blowing. I had sold the Land Rover so we would have to go in Julia's little Fiat 128. The one good bit of sense I had left reminded me to put a big shovel in the boot.

The first part of the journey was quite easy the roads had been cleared earlier in the day and we reached Kettlewell without a problem except that it was now pitch black. We wound our way through the tiny village and out on the back road past the signpost that would have read Leyburn had I been able to read it, marking the road to Woodale. This road was rarely used and was covered in snow, with just a few tyre tracks to show where drivers had gone before. Not far from the village we turned a corner where the road suddenly became much steeper and the tracks petered out ... or should I say they stopped in skid marks, followed by squiggles where drivers had turned back. Well, to paraphrase Margaret Thatcher, "I was not for turning." The thought of going all the way back home and taking the long way was out of the question.

Julia said nothing. She obviously trusted my judgment. But was I so sure? I stopped the car and walked up the hill. The snow had blown across the road near the bend and formed deep drifts in places. Further up it had blown off the road altogether, leaving almost clear patches of tarmac between smaller drifts. There was no sign that anyone else had attempted the climb, so we were going to be the first.

I told Julia that it was not so bad further up. I took out the shovel and dug a track through the drifts for the wheels, backed the vehicle down the hill, then charged up with as much speed as possible. The Fiat ground to a halt about five yards further on from the highest wheel marks. I repeated this a few times and eventually burst through one drift, then another and turned a bend before once more coming to a halt. I got out and surveyed the road again. It was patchy with occasional heavy drifts but fortunately it had stopped snowing. The headlights lit up the road ahead. I cleared channels through the deepest drifts for a short distance then charged them until I once again ground to a halt. The process was repeated and eventually we made it the level ground at the top of the hill. It was easier now as more stretches of the road had the snow blown off by the wind but progress was still slow. Several times more I had to dig a route. Then we came to a down hill section.

At first I was delighted until I found that the snow had blown into hollows where it lay deeper.

By now the moon was up in a cloudless sky with stars twinkling brightly overhead. It looked beautiful with pure snow in every direction. Romantic! But there was no time to dwell. With all the shovelling I was sweating. As soon as I stopped the freezing wind chilled on my back.

We escaped from the hollow and were now climbing up the steepest section towards the notorious hairpin bend at a place called Park Rash also passing the point of no return. Where the wind had blown the snow into drifts these were deep. The car had front wheel drive, good for traction in normal conditions but these were far from normal. As the Fiat pointed up the steep hill at Park Rash the weight became transferred to the back where there was no traction. So I decided to turn round and reverse up the steepest parts. It would not be easy negotiating the hairpin bend on a 1-in-3 gradient going backwards but what else could I do? At least, we were slowly getting nearer to Woodale. I did some more digging to clear a track and started to reverse. When I felt the tyres biting on the cleared road surface I pressed the accelerator harder to get some momentum but suddenly the front end span round and came to rest firmly embedded in a huge drift. Snow was piled against the driver's door and I couldn't open it. And the car was now leaning at a bad angle. I clambered across Julia and out of the passenger side, It did not look good. Now that we were higher up there was an icy wind blowing. We would never survive a night out here and there was not a sign of a farm house or even a barn that we could shelter in. The only lights were from the car, the moon and the stars. Julia was quiet and was not showing stress or asking, "What will we do now?" She climbed out and together we cleared the snow from around the front wheels. Under one I came to grass so we had slid off the road on that side. Again I was sweating from the exertion but had to keep going or I knew I would freeze. I started looking along the roadside for a miss-shape, a hump that didn't look like a natural drift. I knew there had to be one close. Eventually I stabbed my shovel into what I had been searching for, "A gravel heap," I cried. These were put out in winter on steep hills, often with salt mixed in. I cleared more snow from the front then applied a good few shovels of grit on a line up towards the top of the hill. I had to make my next attempt count as there would be no second chance. If the wheels skidded and didn't get us moving forward the car could slide sideways further into the drift. Then we would be there for the night!

I stood up straight to ease my back and take a good look round. The moon was high, reflecting from the snow so brightly it was almost daylight. Except for the car and a few skid marks the whole area was white, blanketed in snow for miles around. The stars were out and twinkling. Then I noticed a large patch in the sky where there were none. This was strange until I realised we were looking at the silhouette of Great Whernside thrusting 2,310 feet up into the night sky. For a second we were spellbound: it was a sight that only the eye can appreciate, as no photographer or artist could ever capture what we were seeing. The shutter in my mind clicked and I remember that image as clearly to this day. Suddenly, I was brought back into the real world as a cold blast cut through my clothes to the sweat on my back. This was no time to be standing around. Before getting into the car I took another look at the curve and tried to remember the line of the road. It was not going to be easy to negotiate going backwards. More air was let out of the tyres and Julia stood ready to push. "Every little helps," as the old lady said when she peed into the sea. I eased up on the clutch, gently using low revs to get traction to avoid spinning the wheels. It worked! The car moved slowly out of the gutter onto the road and backwards up the hill. I stopped on the patch I had gritted, got out to breathe a sigh of relief and survey the next stretch while Julia climbed back into whatever warmth there was in the vehicle. We were by no means home and dry, but the fear of spending the night there had receded a little. One more gritting session and we were over the steepest section. I turned the car round to go forward: it would be much easier looking the same way as we were going!

Now here is a coincidence that takes some believing. When we were stuck in the drift on the steepest part we were less than twenty five yards from where I had crashed my motor bike almost thirty years before, as told in *Nothing Easy*. On that occasion I was in a bad way for a while but managed to get home to safety. Now I would do so again. I also felt some relief because there was nothing as steep in front as what we had just left behind. So one way or another we would dig a way through. We had to as it was out of the question to even think of going back the way we came. It had been extremely difficult coming up hill but going down would be impossible, I would never be able to control the car going round the hairpin down the steepest part it would just slither down and most likely end up stuck in a drift.

Over the next mile or so the gradient was less steep. The road that led up towards the moor was sheltered by walls and trees on either side that had deflected much of the snow apart from the occasional open gateway where the snow had funnelled through and left a huge drift across the road that had to be cleared. Eventually we came to a gate leading onto the open moors which was almost hidden by drifted snow. I soon had it cleared and Julia held it open for me to drive through as the wind tried to slam it shut. The road was straight as we drove along the side of Little Whernside, and almost level with the moor making it hard to see where moor began and road ended. I knew from the past there would be drainage channels by the sides of the road, now completely hidden by snow, and it was vital that I didn't let my wheels drop into them. Thanks to the gale-force wind blowing up here the snow coverage was only a few inches deep and there were few drifts so we made good progress through this part of the journey. My headlights shone bright across the moor with nothing but whiteness as far as we could see. I had blanked off most of the front of the radiator with a piece of cardboard and we now felt the benefit inside the car. Julia said her feet were thawing. She had felt the cold more than me as I was keeping active. Adding to my concerns was that we were using so much power from the battery with the engine running so slowly and us making frequent stops. If the battery ran down it would not be easy to get a jump start! We slithered over a frozen pool of water as we went down a slight hill. The back end of the car slithered sideways but I managed to keep it going frontwards. I reached over and squeezed Julia's hand. There was now a little warmth through her woolly glove.

Suddenly things came into focus and what looked like a snow drift with a few holes in it blocked the road. I quickly realised that we had arrived at the second gate that led off the moor. The wind had driven the snow hard against the gate and the walls on either side had been joined almost completely into what looked just like one long drift. I climbed out of the car took the shovel and hacked away at the snow. When I had scraped most of it off I grabbed hold of the top part of the gate and gave it a tug, but all it did was lean towards me a few inches then spring back. To my dismay I discovered that the bottom part was frozen solid to the ground. The gateway was in a hollow and ice had built up round the bottom part. I was exasperated, a few minutes earlier I felt as if we were nearly there and getting off the moor, but now we were faced with this new obstacle. In my frustration I heaved at the top of the gate and almost caused a catastrophe. It was an old gate and almost fell apart. I had to calm down, take my shovel and patiently chip away at the ice surrounding the bottom rail until it was free. It was painfully slow work but eventually it was done and I managed to push the gate back far enough for the car to get through. I thought about leaving it open as there were no sheep around to wander through but my countryman habits stayed strong and I pushed it shut. I even found an old post laying under the wall and propped up the bottom of the gate so that it stood out of the hollow and would not freeze to the ground again.

Driving down from the moor was a little easier. Eventually Woodale, our destination, came in view. It is just a scattering of less than a dozen houses on either side of the road and we were not sure which was the Shepherds House. By now it was late and predictably there was no one walking along the road. I stopped at a house where the lights were on. The back door faced up the village the way we had come. I climbed the steps knocked on the door and eventually a man appeared. He looked a bit surprised to have a shivering caller at that time of night. "Can you direct me to the Shepherds House," I asked. "Carry on up this road," he said. I interrupted, "We've just come down that way." "You haven't," he said. "It's been blocked for three days. No one has been through." "Well, I'm telling you I've just come from Greenhow via Kettlewell. and I have a witness in the car. Mind you it wasn't easy."

Hearing that he reached out and grabbed my hand. "If you've come over from Kettlewell I will shake your hand. What vehicle are you in?" "A Fiat 128," I told him. "I don't believe it." He slipped on his wellies and followed me down the steps to see the car and my witness, standing there scratching his head. He took my hand again and wished me and Julia, "Happy New Year." We had to turn round and drive back a few hundred yards to the Shepherds House, which stood back a little way from the road. Our friends were as pleased to see us as we were to see them. They had already started celebrating the turn of the year, but we soon caught up with them.

Later, settled into a comfortable chair with a glass of wine I began to relax as I felt the warmth from the log fire. I started to think how close we had come to disaster. As Julia's college friends listened we told them how we'd struggled through the snow. And the thought crossed my mind, "Do they think we're mad?" Once again I had taken a big risk and could thank my lucky stars, many of them twinkling in that dark cold night, for a happy ending.

Time to move

There is no doubt that the best stories and my clearest memories of Greenhow are set in winter. But there was much that occupied me for the rest of the year. Once the snow had finally disappeared I would dig over the vegetable patch. The soil was rich and dark but at an attitude of 1,300 feet the growing season was short no matter how early I planted. At that height, Dales farmers would say you are above the cut-off point for anything other than grass. Certainly, the few trees up there never grow tall. There was a sycamore in my front garden that was no more than thirty feet high. I saw an old photograph taken in the 1930s and it was just about the same then. Whatever the weather the green shoots would not appear until two weeks after the ones lower down in Pateley Bridge or Harrogate. Another problem was the constant wind. The tops of the potatoes and vegetables took a beating until I built a wind break of tin sheets around the garden but with hard work and a bit of luck I could get a reasonable crop each growing season.

During the course of 1979 I found a garage in Harrogate where I could display my cars for sale. But this meant a round trip of forty-odd miles and after several hard winters, Julia and I decided it was time to move. Greenhow Hill had been good for me. It was isolated enough for me to put all my troubles behind but still close enough to those I loved. Renovating the cottage had taught me much. And it had been an enjoyable place to live in where my sons could lose themselves in a rural life, and Julia and I could make ourselves a home. At times I had felt guilty about locking myself away up there but I felt I'd failed those who had helped me in the past, and I didn't want to see them again until I could do so again with a measure of success. I didn't realise how long this would take. By the time the tide turned for me I had lost contact with many to my regret, so I take this opportunity in this book to make my peace.

Julia started looking around for a house and found one in Boroughbridge. Quite quickly after I had put the Old School House on the market there was interest and I came under pressure from a man anxious to buy the house. He and his wife kept horses and were keen to get a place with 15 acres of land. Philippa next door had by now adopted Horace as a pet and that was where he remained. The other horse was sold back to David Booth at a small loss. Thanks to buying cheap and making the improvements with George, I could reap a useful profit on the sale of the house. We had enjoyed the experience of living at Greenhow but it is a wild place. Up there even in summer the clouds can hang around for days leaving the village shrouded in mist. I have often driven down to Pateley Bridge to find the sun shining in the valley, then later in the day driven back up the longest hill in Yorkshire to find it still swathed in clouds.

Starting the vegetable patch

CHAPTER THREE

ORNHAMS GRANGE, BOROUGHBRIDGE
1982 - 1992

After Greenhow Hill a move down to Boroughbridge in 1982 was like returning to civilization. It marked the restitution of my confidence and the ending of a period of virtual exile. Boroughbridge is a quiet, spacious and typically leafy Yorkshire town. It sits on the River Ure a few miles downstream from my boyhood home in Masham. It was founded on a ford close to Aldborough, the site of the Roman town Isurium Brigantum, which was also the headquarters of the Celtic Brigantes tribe. Aldborough became called the 'old town', while the new town became first the 'New Borough on t'Brigg', and later 'Borough on t'Brigg', before finally Boroughbridge. It's funny how these names work out.

We found a house, Ornhams Grange, that we liked on the southern outskirts of Boroughbridge. Or I should say, "Julia found it." The owner was anxious to move and we agreed a good price. As I had made a tidy sum from the sale of the Old School House and between us we now had reasonable incomes, there was a need only for a small mortgage. After my disasters in Ilkley I no

Julia with Bessie at Ornhams Grange

longer felt like a loser. I had made some good decisions and was on my way back. The Grange was a wonderfully large, detached house, which seemed enormous after the cottage at Greenhow, having five bedrooms, two bathrooms and a large lounge with an open fireplace. It stood in its own grounds surrounded by a large garden made even bigger by the addition of a chunk of the adjoining field the size of a small arena, acquired by the previous owners as exercise ground for their horses. The garden was well manured and part of it made an excellent vegetable patch. There was a sycamore tree in the corner of the front garden just like we had at Greenhow, only this one was three-times the size. The house was Victorian with large bay windows and walls in rustic brick covered in ivy.

Why did we plump for such a spacious house when there were just the two of us? Well, there were a number of good reasons, not least that it was within easy reach of work in Harrogate. We bought at a reasonable price and a big house would show more appreciation in value as the years went by. Also, we were not strapped in to a big mortgage that usually goes with a large house. The downside was that we were right next to the A1. We had moved from one Roman road – the Pateley Bridge-Grassington Road in Greenhow followed a Roman trackway, and here we were living by the main north-south Roman route, built in the first century AD. We were told the A1 was scheduled to be realigned and would be moved further from the house, further boosting the value of our investment. We thought then it could be worthwhile to apply for permission to build a second house on the ample vegetable patch.

After living on top of a hill for four years with the wild wind howling around us, Ornhams Grange seemed strangely calm. In altitude we had dropped 1,000 feet. In short order we settled in and in the space of a few months it seemed as if we had been there for years. Now the focus for me was to concentrate on business and to make some money. The Dragon Service Station on Skipton Road in Harrogate, from which I was operating my used car business, was too cramped to offer much hope for expansion. The forecourt had room for only four cars. Eventually I found a bigger garage, half a mile further up Skipton Road in Regent Parade where I could display up to ten vehicles. The place was a bit run down and the owner was close to retirement, but its position was good, close to the main road. At first, I didn't have enough capital to fill the site and other car dealers would loan me cars on a sale-or-return basis, though invariably they were old cars with high mileage and difficult to sell.

The tyre business

It was agreed that the forecourt and a small office would be for my use. Another part of the garage was rented (though he never seemed to pay any rent) by a man called Jimmy Overton, who used it to sell tyres. He would arrive each morning full of enthusiasm, sell a few tyres and then when it quietened down he would disappear to the Cabana café on Knaresborough Road. While he stoked his caffeine count, he would feed the profits from his morning sales into a one-armed bandit gambling machine. I would next see him in the late afternoon when he was often skint and miserable. In the meantime he would have missed out on business while he was feeding his gambling addiction. Jimmy also had a band. When, as was inevitable, the tyre business folded he concentrated his energies full time on music. This looked a good opportunity for me so I bought his tyre equipment, tools and machinery and set about reviving the business. I had some cards printed and went around the streets wherever cars were parked looking for any with bald tyres. I then left a card on the windshield with a quote and my garage address. This meant a lot of leg-work but it eventually paid dividends and trade increased. I also started selling second-hand tyres. I made contact with a man in Bradford called B. who brought container loads of them from Germany where tyre regulations were much stricter. Many taken off cars there were still legal in Britain, and they were inexpensive. I had to pay cash for them but they could be sold for cash at a profit and I made a good income.

This tyre trader from Bradford, though, was a bit of a mystery. B. operated from a huge warehouse that had been once an old woollen mill. He filled it with thousands of tyres of every size and make imaginable. Our business together grew and I began to sell him old casings for remoulding that I had taken off vehicles. All went well for a while, but one day the police arrived at my garage asking questions. Apparently, a wagon load of old scrap tyres had been dumped during the night on a track by the side of a wood near Allerton Park. One of the officers held up a tyre bearing my name written in white letters. "Can you explain this and where were you last night?" I gazed at the tyre in genuine bewilderment, but it didn't take me long to figure out what had occurred. When I went to collect tyres from B. I always took some old ones with me. They would be put in a stack with my name chalked on ready for inspection by his grader. Any that were good enough would be sent for remoulding and B. would pay me a few pounds for my trouble. Any that didn't make the grade he would keep and they would be disposed of later. The tyres would be marked in special chalk and B. used white chalk for this purpose. And this tyre in the hands of the policeman certainly bore B.'s markings. I winced. Once I had been told by one of B.'s drivers that they would load a wagon with all the scrap tyres that couldn't be remoulded and a driver would be paid cash to go out after dark and dump them somewhere quiet. B. neither knew nor cared where they went as scrap tyres were difficult and costly to dispose of. Now one his drivers had been careless and I was implicated. I had to think fast.

A possible solution suggested itself. While I bought second-hand tyres from B. all my new tyres came from National Tyres, a well reputed company on Ripon Road in Harrogate. Maurice, the manager, was very helpful and occasionally let me throw in some of my old tyres for disposal with theirs. I explained this to the policeman and said I guessed that was what had happened. I was sure Maurice would verify this. There was no mention of B.. As soon as the police departed, I telephoned Maurice to make sure he confirmed my story. In any case I could prove where I had been on the night in question and there was no suggestion that I had been involved in the dumping. Maurice was happy to help and the police went away satisfied.

"Do you want a caravan?"

I always got on well with B. He was a bit scruffy, dressed in old, dirty, pale blue overalls usually smoking a slim roll-up that looked more like a 'fold-up'. But he always had a grin on his face, and seemed a truly happy and contented soul. I learned later that he was heavily into drugs. In fact, the tyre business was just a cover to launder the money he made on selling illegal narcotics. When I look back on this time I wonder if his permanent grin didn't owe itself to something more than just tobacco. He often had two or three caravans in a corner of his warehouse. One day while I was waiting to be loaded I went to have a look at them. He came over and said, "If ever you want a tourer Ken, I can sell you one cheap. Just tell me what you want: size, make and how much you want to pay. I'll fix it up. If I don't have one that's suitable I will find one." And find one he did!

About two weeks later he rang me up. "Do you still want a caravan Ken?" "What have you found?" I asked. He went on to describe a four-berth Fleetwood Garland top-of-the-range model, and added that it was in very good condition. It was fully equipped complete with an awning, but warned, "You must make your mind up quickly as I have another man waiting to buy." He gave me all the assurances I needed as to the quality and I knew he felt he owed me a favour for keeping his name out of the recent discussions with the police. So we agreed a price subject to sight of the caravan. "Have the cash ready this afternoon and we will deliver it to Harrogate," he said. "Just give me an address where you want it." There was no room for a caravan at the garage so I made arrangements to park it on a caravan site at Bilton, where my older sister Freda lived. I gave him the address and said I would be there at 3pm. I called at the bank, and then went to wait for the delivery. At twenty past three a big black Ford Granada appeared, towing what I could see was a beautiful, nearly new caravan. I pointed to where it was to be parked and the driver skilfully reversed it in. There were three of them and all looked shady characters. Still, I thought, the folk who work for B. don't turn up in suits and ties. The driver took the money, jumped back in the Granada and with his two mates disappeared down the road. Now I felt uneasy. It had all happened so quickly and when I looked round the caravan I found there were no keys. It was certainly fully equipped with water carriers, cups and saucers, pans, a small black and white TV, children's toys and some clothes. When I looked in the drawers I found papers bearing an address near Bradford. It looked as if it could have been used yesterday. My worries grew!

It was a good van for the price I had paid but where did it come from, or worse still had it been stolen? The more I thought about it the more suspicious I became. Over the years in my line of work I have rubbed shoulders with villains. I have had to accept it and some of them were also entertaining company. But I didn't want any of their stolen gear. When most people sell a caravan, one thing on which you can rely is that they will clear out their personal possessions – even if they let odds and ends of equipment go with the sale. On the other hand, sometimes caravans are repossessed by finance companies that can be quite ruthless. They will employ people like B. As they have the right resources and men for this kind of work. In such circumstances it is unlikely that the finance companies care who snatches it from the defaulter or who ends up owning it; they only want to recover the outstanding dues owed to them. It was possible this was one such example and that would also explain why the price was so cheap and the keys absent.

I had to find out and called B. Before I could utter a word he said, "How do you like the caravan Ken? I told you it was a bargain." "I like it well enough, but there are no keys." "Don't worry. They forgot to leave them. You can get them when you next come for tyres. Go on, get it coupled up to your car and enjoy caravanning." Well, I certainly had a bargain but what could I do to feel easier? Contact the person whose address I'd found? Call the police and involve B. and others in an investigation, or sit tight and use it? My conscience was clear. I had bought the caravan in good faith – though I had no receipt. Could I be accused of receiving stolen goods or worse still, actually stealing it myself? I wanted to enjoy my new possession but I didn't like the thought of someone looking out of their window at an empty space where a caravan had once stood. B told me it was a repossession and assured me there was nothing fishy about the deal. I went back to work for the rest of the afternoon and decided to sleep on it. The keys never did turn up but neither did the police. So I used the caravan for a short time before selling it on.

I was beginning to enjoy the tyre business which always put money in my pocket to pay the mortgage. Meanwhile the small profits on the car deals met our living expenses. I wasn't ruthless enough to make a fortune out of second-hand car deals, but I had a happy time in those years as it was a good way of meeting people who often had an interesting story to tell.

Home at the Grange

With such a large garden one of our first priorities was to dig over a patch to grow flowers and vegetables. Julia took charge of the flower growing, in which I had little interest though I do like to see them, while my focus was on raising vegetables. When I pick peas, beans, cabbages and carrots, or dig up a few potatoes and have them on the table ready to eat a few hours later I feel rewarded for my efforts. Probably this goes back to my childhood and my mother, and my grandfather's instructions that everything had to pay. In addition to gardening, I also trimmed the hedges and removed much of the ivy from the external walls of the house. Nothing had been done to tidy these up for years and both hedges and ivy were full of old bird's nests. I took care to do the trimming when there were no new nests.

Julia started a new business venture. Prior to leaving Greenhow she had been running the children's clothing shop in Ilkley, which had been a step on from designing children's wear as she had done in Chapeltown when she left College. Now the Ilkley shop was given up and she combined her designing and selling talents with that of manufacturing. She turned one of our spare rooms into a machine shop. Here she would design apparel, then have the fabric prepared before it was shipped to outworkers in the area who would machine it up to her designs to make the finished children's wear. We would make a weekly tour of the outworkers, one in Ripon, one Harrogate, one in Leeds dropping off panels of fabric and patterns, and picking up finished garments. When Julia had cut out the panels of fabric they had to be over-locked together before going to the outworkers for final machining. One of my jobs was to work the overlocker – an electric stitching machine that is pedal-operated as you needed both hands to feed the material through it. It took three threads of cotton and stitched around the edges of the fabric to prevent fraying and held the panels together ready for the final machining. It was a wild thing and very difficult to control. I thought my foot trained on an accelerator would find it easy, but far from it, just a little too much pres-sure and it went crazy and I could not feed the fabric through fast enough … and to make matters worse it had a cutter to trim off the edges. If I couldn't keep up the pace it would slice off the corners and ruin the cloth. To operate this machine you needed a great deal of skill and plenty of practice … well I got plenty of practice but never acquired a great deal of skill – just enough to keep the job! Though years later I impressed some garment makers in Romania when I sat down and worked their overlocker!

Julia would sell the clothes to other shops, at craft fairs and markets all around the country and I would often accompany her at the weekend. She gained a good reputation with large numbers of parents, and many children grew up wearing her clothes.

When you move to a different area, you soon make new friends. I remember one American couple who lived near us in Boroughbridge, Jim and Lulu. He was a US Army sergeant based at the top-secret Menwith Hill, nominally a RAF base but actually an American military communications site located high in the Pennines between Harrogate and Skipton. In the evenings, we would often have a drink together in one of Boroughbridge's excellent hostelries, our favourite being The Black Bull. Jim was an interesting chap and had served in several different countries during his long army career. One night we were discussing the horrors of the war in Vietnam and I told him that I had read suggestions that most of the US troops had taken drugs. "Is it true?" I asked. I was a little surprised at his frank answer, "Sure, we all did. In that war you could be blown away at any moment you may as well go high."

Our house was on a North-South tourist route. There seems to be a well-trodden route for foreign visitors starting from London, going north to take in Wales, the Lake District and then across to Edinburgh, before returning down the eastern side to Newcastle and down the A1 to London. Being almost exactly half-way between the Scottish and English capitals on the A1 meant that Boroughbridge was convenient as a stopover. We had the spare rooms and decided to open up a Bed and Breakfast accommodation service for weary travellers. I erected a sign a hundred yards up the road from the house but no one called in. In a moment of inspiration I took this down and moved it a further three hundred yards, and almost immediately the doorbell started to ring. Our guest house business took off and we often used three of our spare rooms at any one time to house visitors.

When foreign guests arrived I always made a point of finding out what country they came from. If they were not from the English-speaking world I'd take out my phrase book and greeted them in their native tongue as they came down for breakfast in the morning. In a short while I could say, "Good morning. Did you sleep well?" in many different languages. Most of the time people were impressed but there was the occasional observation about my accent. I enjoyed cooking and serving the breakfast and chatting to our guests, many of who had very interesting tales of their own. Americans especially loved it when I told them that the road outside the house they had just driven along followed the course of the old Roman road built some nineteen hundred years before.

Masham revisited

Things were going well for Julia and me in the mid-1980s. I had recently purchased a BMW and fitted onto it my personalised registration plates, 5KW. I had acquired these in the early 1970s and had used them on one after another of the luxury cars I drove in those days all the way up to 1977 when I was sacked by Alan Morgan Limited. After the struggle with the Morgans to get the plates back I hid them away in a drawer while I was driving my old van and the Land Rover. But now as my life picked up again and I could afford a late model BMW I thought it was time to take the plates out of the drawer, dust them down and put them to good use. It was a symbolic moment. Now I felt right back on my feet.

Chris Cope, a friend of ours, had recently moved to Masham to manage the Kings Head Hotel for Theakston's Brewery. He was a very good chef and instantly made a success with the restaurant. He asked Julia if she would help on Sundays when they were particularly busy. For me it meant I could take her to work on Sunday mornings, and then roam around revisiting the scenes of my upbringing I had not seen since I was a boy. I could also look up some of my old school friends. It turned out to be a wonderful experience. I always took my camera and our Labrador Bessie.

If the weather was fine I would sometimes watch cricket being played on the recreation ground by the River Ure, known to us as 'the rec'. I had played cricket for the junior team there in the late 1940s. Bessie and I would walk upstream or downstream along the river along two superb pathways. I remembered every bend in the river and every stile. We used a little foot-bridge that was no more than a plank over a stream flowing in to join the Ure from the direction of Marfield. Near this spot I once caught a grayling using a bent pin and a length of cotton. The paths were just as I had left them.

My favourite walk was one that followed my footsteps almost every inch of the way from Park Square up Red Lane, past the tiny old cottage where I had lived for the first few years of my life. Now there was a bathroom inside the house, whereas when we lived there it was a case of a visit to an outside lavatory and a tin bath on the rug before the fire. Though change is often slower in the country I noticed other new features in Masham. At the top of Red Lane, the Fleethams farm buildings were gone and had been replaced by houses. I walked around the corner past Theakston's Brewery, which looked just the same as it did in an old photograph I have of my father and mother around 1930. At the time they had been courting and mother worked as a maid for the Hendon family at the big house across the road.

Around the next corner there was nothing familiar. The single storey Nissan-style huts that had been there housing the NAAFI canteen for the large contingent of troops stationed in Masham in the war had gone. After the war they had been bought by a Mr Harrison who rented one of the smaller ones to my father. He had fitted out one end as a workshop; the middle part was for storing potatoes, and the rest became a preparation area for dad's fish and chip business. As a lad I had peeled more than half a ton of spuds there every week. The workshop was where I kept my first motor bike, a 250cc hand-change BSA and the little Rudge that I had rebuilt from a frame, second-hand engine and spare parts. This had been an exciting land-mark in my young life giving me a measure of the independence I craved. Now the huts had gone and were replaced by new houses.

I continued up Swinney Lane along the side of the beck. When I was a boy there was a wide grass verge and parking area on the right hand side. Here, when not in use, the wooden horse-drawn snow plough was parked. It was also where the road menders left their big green caravan, their tar sprayer, steam roller and water bowser when they came to repair the Masham roads. Further up the lane I turned left and walked over the bridge where Eddie Jameson used to sit on the wall watching the traffic while I flew over on my BSA as fast as I dare, always to his great amusement. The bridge had been widened in recent years to allow Jameson's wagons to pass over. I continued up Foxholme Lane making for what the farming Fleetham's family always referred to as 'the top fields' or 'far fields'.

Foxholme Lane was now just a track running up a gentle slope between the fields. In the distance I could see a cluster of farm buildings, including the dark silhouette of the old barn towering above the cow house and other sheds. I never heard any of the Fleethams use the words, "Mistle" or "Cow byre". It was always cow shed or cow house. The huge barn looked black, no doubt from the many coats of creosote it had soaked up over the years. At this point I was close to what we as boys called the 'Secret Garden'. There really wasn't anything particularly secret about it and you could hardly call it a garden. But to us as youngsters it was a place full of intrigue and excitement. Even in the 1930s and 1940s it was overgrown, but as we clambered through the briars and nettles to get to the gooseberry and blackcurrant bushes we wondered when it had been properly cared-for. Now looking at it decades later it was clear that it was just a small area on a slope between the fields, separated by a hawthorn hedge on one side and a wall on the other. There was a little gate at one end that long before had been painted white. To the left were the remains of the lilac tree, now looking dead with neither leaves nor blooms. Yet I am sure I caught a whiff of the scent from the deep purple blossom of my youth. Inside, was some low stonework, all that remained of a small building tumbled down into a pile of stones. But these stones were different, they were not from the fields. They consisted of big blocks and some were white as if they had been on the inside of a building. If there had once been a dwelling in this secret garden, it could only have been very small. I wished I had asked Muriel or Wallace Fleetham, the two older children in the Fleetham family, about the place.

When I was a little boy I used to pick daffodils on the slope, snowdrops near the gate and tiny violets growing under the hedgerows and take them home for my mother. Violets were not easy to pick as the stalks were so short. Now forty years later the garden was so overgrown and wild there was little sign of anything that might have been planted there. What had survived were the gooseberry bushes. There were many different kinds but my favourite gooseberries were the small hairy red ones, sweet and juicy with thin skins. When I was young I could hardly pick them fast enough and was a regular visitor when they were ripe. In the lower part of the garden there must have once been an orchard of apple trees, but these were now outgrown and what remained of the branches straggled into each other. Such fruit as they presented was not much bigger than crab apples. As I left the garden

I carefully closed the gate, though why I don't know as there was nothing inside to escape and no animals in sight that might venture in. Perhaps I was closing off one of my childhood memories.

Farther on the track levelled out as it ran along a hedge to a gate opening into a farmyard. It felt as if I was expected as the gate was opened half-way. Frankly, it didn't look like it had been touched for decades and was ready to fall apart. The farmyard wasn't as I remembered either, and was really just a cobbled strip between the buildings. None of these were any longer in use and all had been neglected. The great hay barn looked forlorn, now just a tall empty shell, the wind blowing straight through tin sheets flapping. I stood by the gate making sure I didn't lean on it, and looked at the yard and buildings. Memories came back. Though I could not have been more than five or six, I remember the barn being built. This had been what was called around there a, "Do it thysen" job, using second-hand telegraph poles for the uprights.

At hay time I would help tread down the hay in this barn as it was forked from the carts. As the barn was filled Muriel or Wallace Fleetham would first fill a large sack with hay, then stand it in the middle of the bay and fork the hay all round. As the hay became piled higher and higher one of them would pull up the sack just a little at a time. I would continue to run around ... or should I say stagger – trampling down the hay. Eventually when the barn was full to the top, the sack would be pulled out leaving a ventilation shaft down the centre so that the hay could breathe as it settled. I was always sent down a ladder to be safely on the ground before this was done. I climbed down from what seemed such a great height, holding on tightly with my hands while feeling with my foot for the next rung. Simpler times!

Though the barn had lost some of the woodwork and sheeting the second-hand telegraph poles were still doing sterling work, standing up as straight as when Wallace put them in more than forty years before. At the end of the barn there were the remains of the implement shed. Here as I watched they would clean and oil the grass cutter and other machines after hay time. These would be stowed away, locked into each other like parts of a jigsaw puzzle to get them all into a small space. To make hay the Fleethams used five different implements, all horse-drawn. The mower needed two horses to pull it, but the others could be managed by just one. I strolled through the yard to the far end and gazed across to the big field that ran along the boundary of what had been Fleethams Farm. Believe it or not, this field was called Jonathan. My eldest son is called Jonathan but I can assure you there was no connection.

When I was a boy, hanging on a wall next to a clock in the farm house was a framed map of the farm showing the house buildings and every field with its name and acreage. Every field had a name but only a few were used regularly. The grandfather clock was what you might call a one-off. The living room that it had stood in had a low ceiling and the clock had been made to fit. Fancy pieces of woodwork had been removed from the top and the broad part of the body butted up to the ceiling. I think a bit had been also docked off the bottom though it was not as obvious. The tick-tock was so slow I often expected it to stop. I would watch it being wound up with the big weights on chains. Old Mrs Fleetham's rocking chair was by the fireside. I often saw her asleep and thought that slow tick-tock was responsible by lulling her to rest.

Another location where there had been much change was on the moors outside Masham. Here as a teenager I had practiced riding up the steepest parts on my motor bike. During the war it had been used by the military and there were tank tracks scouring the area. These had now all disappeared. In the past the moor had been largely tree-free, covered just with bracken and heather. Now there was still bracken around the edges, but the moors themselves were covered by tall firs. Fortunately visitors were still able to walk around and there were plenty of tracks through the trees.

These Sundays with Bessie in tow, waiting for Julia to finish work, were always very special moments. After a day wandering through my memories it was good to finish off with a pint in the Kings Head. Here I would sometimes meet one of my dad's old football pals, George Bramley, who he played with in the Masham team. No doubt they had themselves often sat in this pub, drinking together after a game. But half-a-century later there was just George here, still fit and healthy in his seventies and long outliving my father.

We lose two dogs

Eventually our old dog Bessie died. Julia and I felt sad because, as dog lovers will understand, they can become a real part of the family. We buried Bessie in the garden and planted a little tree close by in commemoration. We did not want to be without a dog so Julia and I set off quickly to find a puppy. Bessie, a black Labrador, had been so special that we decided another Labrador was the breed for us. The one we bought was a golden Labrador puppy and we were assured that she was pure bred by the man who sold her to us. But as she began to grow I had my suspicions. For one thing her legs were much longer than a normal Labrador's. Even when she was still young she stood tall. She was always lively and a fast runner to boot. I sensed a bit of greyhound in her, but thankfully she had the calmness of a Labrador.

We called her Maudie. Her favourite toy was an old Wellington boot which we threw for her to retrieve. One Sunday morning I left her playing with it on the lawn and went inside for a cup of coffee, but when I came back she was laid on the lawn with her head stuck fast in the Wellington. I pulled it off but I was too late, she had suffocated. I tried to revive her but could not bring her back. Her body was limp and lifeless, and her long legs looked even longer as I laid her gently on the grass, her little body still warm. It seemed she had been sniffing inside the boot and sucked it onto her head. Ever since we had bought her, except when asleep, she had never been still, bouncing around on those long gangly legs. I was annoyed at myself for leaving her alone with the boot, but who could have foreseen such an accident.

We buried Maudie close to Bessie and now the tree served for them both. This time we didn't feel like rushing out and buying another dog and left it for a few months. But at last our spirits rose again and we found a new puppy, another golden Labrador, who we called Bella. She turned out to be the most special of the lot. Bella grew fast and with all the land and fields surrounding us it was always convenient to get her out for plenty of exercise. By now it was the late 1980s and, as with so many other men entering their fifties, my thoughts turned to golf. I'd often practice my swing in the adjoining grass fields. At first I left Bella indoors but she didn't like that idea one little bit, so I let her come out with me. She liked nothing better than to charge off after the balls I had hit to find them and bring them back. She was now growing past her puppy stage. After a few weeks of finding the balls I noticed that she started to look low. Her tail hung down limply and she started to wander about looking miserable. Julia noticed it too. We could not understand what the matter was as she was always so lively. We would have to consider taking her to the vet If she did not pick up. Then one morning when I came downstairs I noticed by Bella's bed two golf balls in a pool of slimy green sick. I looked around and not far away was another. (You might want to put the book down for a while if you're about to have dinner.) One of the balls was white, one a pale green, but the third was stained dark green and looked as if it had been in her stomach for some time. She looked first at the balls, then up at me as if to say, "That's why I was off colour!" Bella was a natural retriever and liked to carry things in her mouth, but the problem was she did not want to leave anything behind. She would cram as many golf balls as she could find into her mouth and occasionally one had been swallowed. I found she could carry three at a go without a problem so that became the new rule. I would drive three in my practice sessions, but never more until she had brought those three back. And we had no repeat of the upset.

Bella was smart, what I would call 'a thinking dog.' When we'd hike across the fields she always carried a stick in her mouth. But the way back into our garden from the fields was through a narrow gap, just about eighteen inches wide. I could squeeze through but I knew Bella was going to have a problem with the long branch. But as I said she was smart and soon learned a solution. She would poke one end through and follow sideways, straightening out when she was on the other side with her head held high in a cocky manner as if to say, "Did you like that?" I loved that dog.

Julia liked horse riding. She had grown up with horses on her parents' farm. Julia and her sister Gina had been through that phase many girls enjoy of being absolutely horse-struck. She had ridden in show jumping competitions and fairs and fetes all over Yorkshire. She

Bella

continued to ride, and had sat astride our second pony at Greenhow. But she preferred the larger horses her mother kept on the farm and Julia would go there to take one out to hack around the countryside. When we went on holiday her idea was to go off riding on some of the days. Why didn't I learn and we could go riding together

As far as I was concerned I had always preferred things mechanical like motor bikes and cars. But with Julia's expertise and encouragement I agreed to have a go. Being a country boy I was quite used to sitting on a horse but riding properly was another matter. So at Julia's urging I decided to have formal lessons. That way we could go riding together around North Yorkshire and when we went off on holiday, and I would have a chance of keeping up with her.

I enrolled for lessons at one of the best riding schools in the country which, luckily, was not far away from Boroughbridge in the hamlet of Markington between Ripon and Harrogate. In fact, the school continues to prosper as the Yorkshire Riding Centre and today attracts pupils from all over the country. I took to horse riding and began to really look forward to my weekly lesson. It was all very different to driving a motor car or riding a motor bike where you could take charge and, if necessary, thrash the engine. Here, you had to employ a totally different technique and the key was to get the horse to co-operate. If you don't have a gentle, though firm approach you are not going anywhere except to finish off flat on your back but In one respect there is a similarity with motor racing cars in that you need to develop a sixth sense about what is going on through 'the seat of your pants,' as they say. While I didn't become an expert by any means, I did develop a good seat and was able to hack around the countryside with Julia without falling off.

On one occasion on a holiday in Spain we were riding through the mountains when we heard this loud clanking which spooked my horse completely. He took off, leaping, rearing and bucking around the hillside, and doing everything he could to part me from the leather of the saddle. It took a while but I calmed him down, and we found out what had been the matter. Two mules were foraging around the bushes and were hobbled by chains which scraped on the rocks and caused the noise.

The boys grow up

My three sons kept in touch. Jonathan had wedded again. His new wife, Sandra, was closer to his age and they made a very happy couple. They said their vows at Harrogate registry office in a service Julia and I attended, and have remained married to this day. Sandra already had a daughter called Helen and together they had another, Sharleen. After his spell in Armley Jonathan pulled himself together and didn't again fall foul of the law. When he came out he first went to stay with a builder friend in Pateley Bridge to learn his trade. He started off labouring moved on to the excavation work then onto stonework, picking up the other building trades as he went along. By the late 1980s Jonathan was the contracts manager doing well by both his boss and himself. He would later go on to start his own building company which has remained successful.

Andrew was the one to embrace education. I had always hoped that all three would take up the opportunity that had been barred for me by my father's attitude. On many occasions I would be held off school to work for dad in his car renovation or fish businesses. But education is not for everyone. Both Jonathan and Tim were happier getting out of school when they could and getting jobs. They learned to work with their hands and make a success of their lives. But the middle one, Andrew went off to the School of Oriental and African Studies, part of the University of London. He did very well to be accepted and had the laudable aim of using his studies to help those in the Third World after graduation. He also wanted to travel and once he completed his studies he went abroad to Sardinia. He used his time there to teach English and learn Italian. He then moved to Spain teaching English at first before taking a job in music production and distribution. Although not very musical himself, he had a guitar but I don't recall anything more than a little strumming. Andrew found his niche and remained in the industry after returning to Britain in 1998 when I drove down to Barcelona to pick him up with his possessions.

Timothy joins us

Timothy's story became more problematical just when his elder brothers were starting to find their feet. He was just fourteen when we moved to Ornhams

Grange from Greenhow, and was beginning to have difficulties at home and school like many others of his age. Wendy had taken up with Ian Gledhill when our marriage broke up in the 1970s, and Ian had been a good and positive influence on the boys. But Tim was perhaps the most unsettled by our divorce and was again upset when Wendy and Ian moved from Ilkley to live near Leeds. He was a little lost for a while and it was thought by all of us that it would be better if he moved in with Julia and me in Boroughbridge.

So, at the age of fifteen Timothy became a permanent resident at Ornhams Grange. We had plenty of room for him to enjoy himself inside or out of the house even when we have paying Bed and Breakfast guests. He had a huge garden where he could ride around on the dumper truck we had brought down with us from Greenhow, and which he always enjoyed. Though he wasn't keen on schooling Timothy was bright, so we were able to enrol him in King James' School in Knaresborough, one of the best state schools in the county and just a short car journey away. Julia was wonderfully supportive with Timothy.

The three of us decided it would be nice to have fresh eggs again as we had at Greenhow. So after a quick visit to a farmer friend we were soon hosting six bantam hens and a cockerel. Bantams are small chickens, often just half the size of normal breeds. The cockerel was also smaller than a standard rooster, but was just as aggressive as he strutted about asserting his dominance over his harem. Our hens laid smaller than normal eggs but usually we had plenty of them. When one of the hens became broody we let her sit on some eggs waiting impatiently for them to hatch. Before long there they were: seven lovely tiny chicks. Tim put them in a little pen protected with wire netting close to the fence. He looked after them, fed them and soon they were almost as big as their mother.

One morning I was awakened in the early hours by a loud cackling noise. When I looked out of the landing window what I saw gave me quite a shock. It was just light enough to pick out the features of the mother bantam franticly running up and down along the inside of the pen. While she was doing this her brood has scattered in all directions in a state of panic. Then I saw what was causing the trouble. A fox was sitting outside the pen only a few feet away calmly watching them and no doubt selecting one as his next meal. I was dumbfounded and my first thought was to shoot him. But at that moment I couldn't decide what was best: grab my gun or my camera! While I dithered, the poor mother hen had worked herself into a dreadful state, trying all she knew to protect her family. Like me the cockerel was doing very little to help. But I'd have to say that all that running up and down and cackling was not having much effect on the fox. I gave up wondering what to do and opted to watch. Clearly neither the fox nor I wanted to miss anything, and the cockerel was keeping a low profile. It was slowly getting lighter with the dawn when the fox suddenly stood up, turned round and slowly ambled off towards the wood. After a short distance he paused and picked up first one thing then a second, before carrying on his calm deliberate way, gliding across the field and disappearing into the wood.

At last, the mother hen started to settle down, though she remained uneasy and kept walking up and down the pen. The cockerel came out to take charge now the fox had disappeared. Likewise, I decided the time had come to act, and got dressed, went out and made a count of the chickens. Two of them were missing. I checked the wire but to my surprise could find no hole in the wire or tunnel underneath. The lost chickens must have been taken by our visiting Reynard but how the fox had managed to swipe them was a mystery, as it has remained to this day. He had reached them somehow and had taken them out into the field before returning to taunt their mother. It gave me a new understanding of the phrase, "As crafty as a fox." When I spotted him he was perhaps looking for a third but as dawn broke decided to settle on two as being a good night's work. We carried on keeping bantams and raising chicks, but neither the fox, nor his kin ever returned - which was doubly strange in its way.

Tim was philosophical about the chickens but became increasingly unhappy at school. He was nearing his sixteenth birthday when he would be able to leave, but the progress towards this deadline seemed very slow to us all. He hated it and could not wait to get a job, and the crowd he was hanging around with were not much help. Many of his school mates had tattoos on their arms and this was in the eighties when they were yet to acquire the trendiness - with both sexes - that they gained later. Tim wanted to be like his pals but I did not like the idea being old-school, and I associated tattoos with something undesirable. I have never had any done myself and stopped Timothy at that time. I knew I couldn't prevent him for ever, but I put the restriction that he had to wait until he had left school. By then he might have grown out of the idea I thought, or at least he would be near enough to becoming an adult when no further ban from me would be effectual.

One day a letter arrived from school saying that Tim had been in some serious trouble and invited me to call in on the school as the headmaster would like a word. I drove in and sat with him, and Timothy was invited to join us. The headmaster told me that Tim had hit a girl. This was completely out of character and I was shocked. He then went to great lengths (as teachers sometimes do) to tell me what happened. Apparently, Tim had sat in the girl's seat and she grabbed hold of him to pull him out. He jumped up in a bit of a temper and pushed her so hard she fell on the floor grazing her knee and hurting her elbow. "We take a very dim view of this, Mr Walker, and if anything like it happens again your son will not be accepted back into this school. This is his last warning." Tim looked sheepish but said nothing other than to apologise. However, when we got home the truth came out. A few days before Tim had been to Leeds and, against instructions, had his arm tattooed. When the girl grabbed hold of his arm she had caught the very same spot which was still very tender. I felt more disappointed with him more for going against my wishes than in pushing a girl, who probably fell a little too easily – just as modern footballers sometimes do. Still, his sixteenth birthday became an even more important date in all our diaries. True to form, he left school as soon as he could and before long found himself operating dumper trucks and earth movers. He showed competence from day one – not a surprise to anyone who knew him ... and has gone on to earn himself a good living and an enviable reputation.

CHAPTER FOUR

ITALIAN HOLIDAYS
1982 - 1991

Towards the end of the time we lived at Greenhow I started to regain my work-play life balance. As mentioned, in 1982 it was time for a return to the 'real world' of Boroughbridge, and I celebrated with a Greek holiday with Julia and her mother Peggy. With the flourishing of my car and tyre businesses, Julia's children's clothing enterprise and our joint B&B undertaking, we develop the taste for other foreign vacations. And where better for us to go than Italy.

This was the obvious holiday destination given Julia's ties with the country. She was half-Italian and though she did not speak a word of the language she encouraged me to learn. Her father, Giulio Nadal, was an Italian who had come to England as a prisoner of war in 1944. He had stayed on after hostilities ended and like so many Italian POWs found it easy to integrate into British society and in 1951 he married Julia's mother, Peggy. Her father set them up on a farm and together they lived first at Blubberhouses and then at High Austby near Ilkley. Peggy liked horses and Giulio had kept a herd of milk cows. Julia and her sister Gina soon followed. When their parents separated in 1974 – there was no question of divorce due to his Catholicism so Giulio returned to Italy to the family home near Treviso, north of Venice. Each year Julia and Gina went to stay with him for a holiday, but in 1982 Gina couldn't make the trip so I was pleased to take her place. It was my first visit to Italy for over a decade. In 1971 I had raced in the European Sports Car Championship at Imola, a very exciting experience as described in my first book *Nothing Easy*.

While I had long known and liked Julia's mother, Peggy, I had never met her father before, though I'd heard plenty of tales of this larger than life character. I will never forget that first time. We travelled by aircraft to Italy and then by train, to Sacile, the nearest railway station just north of Giulio's home in Veneto province. There he was, waiting for us and rushed up to his daughter, flinging his arms around her and kissing her on both cheeks. Then in Italian fashion, I was given the same treatment, his stubble prickling my face. This was another new experience but I did not complain as I had been a bit on edge wondering how he would react to me, an older man with his much younger lovely daughter. He drove us to Orsaga a village not far from where he lived and delivering us to a small hotel by the same name where we could be in comfort. This was better than staying with him in his old rustic farmhouse, he explained, which had few modern facilities.

In what became a series of visits, we timed our trips to coincide with *vendemia*, the Italian harvest and helped to pick the grapes in Giulio's vineyard. I had imagined grape picking as very easy relaxed work snipping a few bunches of grapes stood in the sunshine. It is not quite like that usually very hot with flies, bees and cobwebs in your face the whole time. Some bunches of grapes have rotten ones that crush when you grab them and the sticky juice runs up your arms, it is always more fun drinking the previous years' crops rather than picking the present one! But for Julia and me the lifestyle was one we really enjoyed. It was a whole new experience and a more tranquil pace of life in warm weather. I'm not sure I could have lived that way all year round but for short trips once or twice a year it was *paradiso!* When we stopped for lunch, we would drink a glass of wine sitting in the shade or, "In the shadow," as Giulio called it. There would be fresh bread and cheese, with huge tomatoes picked straight from his garden and often still warm from the sun. Dessert would be a couple of figs again plucked from a tree in the garden.

Apart from our trips each Autumn for the vendemia we started also to visit Italy in Spring whenever we could for sightseeing and I enjoyed every minute.

Don't mention antigelo

This was so different to anything I had previously experienced. I started to learn the language and my skills improved little-by-little with each trip. To help me practice Giulio insisted I place the order whenever we visited a bar or restaurant. This helped though it did cause great embarrassment on one occasion. In April 1986 I read the news of some wine growers in Italy putting antifreeze in their wine which had caused a great international furore. Next time we went to a bar, this one near Cortina in the southern Dolomites, I walked in and asked in Italian for, "Three glasses of a good local wine, but please without antigelo (antifreeze)!" Fortunately, not many of the locals heard but Giulio quickly took me to one side. "Please do not ever say anything like this again," he whispered. "We are most embarrassed by this scandal which was done by a few fools. It has been blown out of all proportion but has given us all a very bad name." I had practiced the antigelo/ antifreeze phrase for several days and can remember it to this day, but I took the warning on board and never, ever used it again when ordering wine.

Giulio would take us to visit his friends and relations for huge meals, often held on Sundays at local homes or restaurants. I specially loved the family gatherings where there would be three generations of the family all wining and dining, and enjoying each others' company. Julia would be spoilt with all the attention and I would be the subject of much ribbing over my attempts to speak the language. The younger children would run around free of any restrictions. Their *madre* and *padre* (parents) would be gabbing away in between the many courses of food and wine. The older *nonni* and *nonne* (grandparents) would sit and smile, occasionally dozing off in the warm weather as these meals went on for hours. At one gathering I decided to try another phrase I had learned. This time I was careful to make sure it couldn't cause offence or be open to the wrong interpretation. We were sitting at a long table and had, as usual, eaten a superb meal. Afterwards, the women cleared away the plates and dishes, and started washing them at a sink in the corner of the kitchen watched by the men. After rehearsing several times under my breath I stood up and blurted out my latest new phrase, *"Posso autarla lavari i piati?"* (Can I help wash the plates?). Though politely refused my offer caused much laughter. I offered on many occasions but was never taken up on it. They were always amused as you never saw an Italian man near the sink.

Giulio became a firm friend. It was wonderful having a personal guide who knew the country so well. He took us to many interesting places, often in an old Fiat that looked like a Lada. Or I should say that when the Lada first appeared it looked like this Fiat as it was the model design which was sold by the Italians to the Russians who used it for their first Ladas. On one occasion when he collected us from the station I was sitting in the back when I noticed over Giulio's shoulder an unusual line across the instrument panel at an angle, darker below than above. It looked like a shadow but wasn't one. Perplexed, I asked what it was. "Oh you see, last winter I ran off the road into a ditch that was flooded. It was a few weeks before we could get the car out. That's the line where the water came up to." Without wanting to be rude, I have to say that Giulio was an awful driver. I soon discovered this was a bit of a national trait, as was the constant honking of the horn. When other drivers honked him he would wave his fist and shout back, *"Va la inferno!"* (Go to hell!). At the same time he would turn around to me in the back and say, "Did you see that Ken?" while swerving across the road and causing more chaos.

Thankfully, when we made our first visit to Venice we caught the train from Treviso, a town about 30km to the north, changed in Mestre then caught another train across the lagoon to Venice. I had read guide books that described Venice and had seen programmes on television, but nothing quite prepared me for the wonder of sights and the unique beauty of its setting. To walk down the steps from the Venezia Santa Lucia Railway Station to the banks of the Grand Canal, and gaze along towards the Rialto and St Mark's was a very special experience. At that moment I wanted nothing more than to stand and stare, but as I did I caught the smell. I have heard people say that Venice stinks. Well, I cannot entirely agree with that but there certainly is a strong smell of the sea– at least I think it is the sea.

Julia and Giulio on the train - Italy 1983

Ken and Giulio -1983

The Grand Canal is like the main street of the city. Every one and everything goes up and down it. As I stood on the station steps watching, a vessel passed by loaded with crates of beer. That was followed by a waterbus crowded with a mixture of locals and tourists. Then a most unusual sight caught my eye, a boat stacked high with shiny black wooden coffins immediately followed by a barge overflowing with a heavy load of building materials and workmen.

A Venetian storm

We took the vaporetto waterbus down to St Mark's Square and spent a few hours looking around the Piazza, the Basilica, the Clock Tower, the Correr Museum, the Rialto, the Doges' Palace and, of course, the Campanile of St Mark's Church. It was glorious and left me in a daze. Then it was time for a cup of coffee, an espresso for Giulio, an Americano for Julia and a cappuccino for me. A little footsore we sat at a table outside a café in the Square. The waiter was soon hovering over us ready to take the order. As usual Giulio kept quiet and let me do the work with my growing command of Italian. I must have spoken correctly as the waiter nodded, turned and walked back into the café. Giulio laughed, "Soon they will think you are a local." The waiter returned and set down three cups on the table, placing *il conto*, the bill, beside one of the cups. Giulio was quick to move and snatched it from under my nose. As always, he was generous and would pay if I didn't out-manoeuvre him. As he glanced at the total, though, his face turned purple and he looked on the edge of going berserk. He jumped up and brought the waiter back, towering over him – Giulio was a big man. "You are a bloody robber," he spluttered. "If this is what you charge tourists no one will come to Italy. But you made a bad mistake when you tried to rob me. I am a Venetian." By now the waiter had turned as white as the tablecloth and was shaking. People at nearby tables turned to watch. Julia flushed crimson and stood up to calm her father down, while Giulio was in full flow. So we had the white-faced waiter, an embarrassed Julia and her father purple with rage. I stood up, too, but remained my natural pink. The café manager appeared and tried to settle things with Giulio. The unfortunate waiter took a few paces back to leave his manager in the firing line. Concessions and apologies were offered and Giulio was persuaded by all parties to accept both. We finished our coffee, paid a much reduced bill and departed without leaving a tip.

It didn't ruin our day in Venice but it was a reminder of the risks for the unwary visitor. We took the train to Treviso and Giulio drove us in his Fiat back to our hotel. We rested for a while and changed before he was called again to pick us up to go for a meal. On the way to the restaurant I noticed the sky was getting dark and it looked as if a storm was brewing, thinking that the colour of the sky actually matched Giulio's face in the afternoon. We were seated in the restaurant and were half-way through our meal when the storm broke. I have never experienced such a violent downpour. The wind grew stronger until it was blowing a gale and shook the whole building. Thunder began to crash all around us and lightning lit up the place. In fact, it wasn't long before we lost the electricity and candles were brought out. Rain lashed down on the roof making a deafening drumming noise and just when we thought it could not get worse a huge window blew in, the glass shattering into thousands of shards as it crashed on the tiled floor. Thankfully, no one was hurt. The curtains flapped crazily in the gale and the rain blew inside causing even more mayhem. Then I realised that it was not rain at all, but hailstones the size of marbles which bounced off the tables and crockery. Diners had left their seats and were now lined up with their backs to the wall at the far side of the room. I won't say there was panic but I have never seen tables empty so fast. Then as suddenly as it started the storm abated and there was a strange calm with only the odd spot of rain. The curtains hung still and limp with drops of water falling from where the window had blown in. The electricity connection was restored and the lights came back on. Those who were farthest away from the damage returned to their tables and resumed their meals, as men appeared with brushes to sweep up the glass and mop up the puddles. It was fascinating to watch. Two men came in carrying a ladder and a great sheet of hardboard. This was hoisted over the broken window and hammered into place. In no time at all things were back to normal and diners were back at their tables, resuming their conversations as if nothing had happened. It seemed that Italians were more used to freak storms than we are.

Once the meal was over, we prepared to leave. The bill was paid (thankfully it was reasonable) and we set off. It truly was calm after the storm but all around the restaurant there was plenty of evidence of how violent it had been.

Vines were ruined, grapes lay on the ground and the ones that had hung on had been shredded. It was a disaster but just a few kilometres away the scene changed completely. Unpicked grapes were untouched by the hailstones and were ripe for harvesting. It had been a very localised storm. Luckily, Giulio was one of those that it had missed. I suppose it is called a micro-climate where one farm catches the full force of a storm and his neighbour just down the road escapes it. Clearly, it was not an unusual occurrence and Giulio told us that most growers had insurance. That night I added a new phrase to my Italian vocabulary ... *de tuoni e de lampi*, (thunder and lightning) and had other occasions in Italy on which to use it.

More sightseeing

The next time we visited Italy Giulio took us to *Pieve di Cadore*, the birthplace around 1488 of the great Venetian painter *Tiziano Vecelli*, better known as Titian. We looked around the town calling in at the *Palazzo della Magnifica Comunità*, then made our way to the church which doubled as a museum where many of his paintings can be seen. Unfortunately it was Monday, closing day in this town just as it had been at the Miner's Arms a few years before. Typically, Giulio was not to be put off. He went to the adjoining monastery and banged on the great door until a monk appeared. By now I could understand quite a bit of the language and heard him say to the monk that his daughter and friend were visiting from England, and had come specially to see Titian's birthplace and some of his famous works. The monk told us to wait, then disappeared. A few minutes later he returned with a huge bunch of keys and led us to the front door of the church. He selected the biggest key, unlocked the door and took us inside. He then closed and relocked the door,

Julia, Giulio and Ken - Venice 1983

giving emphasis to the fact that we were being treated as special guests. He was all smiles as he gave us a private guided tour and seemed not a bit upset at our untimely visit as he explained everything there was to see. It was real VIP treatment for more than an hour and a half we learned much about Titian.

On the way back we stopped where the road crossed the river *Piave* and Giulio showed us where the battlefield ran alongside the river. The river was wide and shallow where the Italians had withstood an Austro-Hungarian offensive in the famous battle of June 1918. Between them, Italian and Austro-Hungarian losses numbered 150,000 men. Giulio would have been only a year old at the time, but he was remarkably well informed and pointed out what was held by different troops and one area where the fighting was so fierce the river was said to have run red with blood. I did not ask him but thought that was where his father had fought. His father had returned from the war so badly injured he died soon afterwards and Giulio could not remember him. Later he showed me a book entitled, *'Battaglia del Montello,'* published in 1968 on the fiftieth anniversary of the battle. Before he died Giulio gave it to me and it is one of my most treasured old books. Though it is in Italian I can understand most of it.

A few days later we visited the magnificent *Duomo di Milano*, the White Cathedral of Milan. We spent some time looking around then went up on the roof to look out across the city. Milan is the second largest city in Italy after Rome and the financial centre of the country, especially well known for its fashion and opera houses. While we were up on the roof it gave us a chance to have a close-up look at the intricately carved stonework of the spires of the Duomo. I didn't count them but the brochure said the Cathedral has a hundred and thirty-five spires. It is a remarkable building with great beauty jostling with odd shapes and different styles. This is hardly surprising when you consider the Duomo took six hundred years to build, work starting in 1386 and not being finished until 1813, and only then because Napoleon had threatened the townsfolk with retribution if they didn't get the job done! Many people have said it mirrors the Italian work ethic in some way. Goodness only knows how many thousands of workmen must have worked on the Cathedral over those six centuries, each adding their own thoughts and, unfortunately, different standards of workmanship. Though built in the

Gothic style, there were so many changes of opinion over the years it isn't really surprising the finished result is something of a hodgepodge. It is a huge construction, the fourth largest cathedral in the world, and the best place to see its many intricacies is on the roof.

We came down to ground level for a last look inside the cathedral. The Duomo houses all sorts of interesting works of art, mausoleums and sarcophagi, all worth seeing. As we neared the main door to leave we came to a standstill with those in front hesitating to go outside. I saw why: another thunderstorm had just started and the heavens had opened. *De tuoni e de lampi,* had returned. We squeezed through to the sheltered area at the entrance and it was then that I heard this loud voice calling out, *"Impermiabiles,"* Though it had only started raining a few moments before, an enterprising young fellow had arrived with a pile of what looked like plastic bags under his arm, and people were rushing to buy what turned out to be cheap plastic macs. I don't recall the price but they were inexpensive and he was doing a good trade earning a few lire from the tourists. I looked back at the Cathedral as we wandered off under our impermiabiles thinking that while it may have embodied something of the Italian character, so did the guy selling the macs.

The hotel and the cantina

On our first few trips to see Giulio we stayed in the Orsaga Hotel run by three sisters and their brother, lovely people who always held out a welcome. One of the sisters did most of the cooking, which consisted mostly of traditional fare and local specialities, which were truly excellent. The brother tended the bar. He had been a champion skier in his younger days and there were trophies everywhere on shelves, in glass cases and hung on the walls of the hotel. He must have been a top competitor as there were dozens of them. Next to the hotel was the town's cantina where grapes from the whole region were brought to be made into wine. During the vendemia as many as 20 tractors and trailers at a time would queue waiting to unload along the main road, snaking past the hotel and around the corner to the cantina. I had never seen such a sight. In Yorkshire I had watched as trucks queued to unload potatoes or sugar beet, but trailers piled high with grapes was something new. Until then I had only thought of grapes as being in a bunch or a few bunches in a small box. To see them in such large quantities was different. As many of the tractors and trailers were quite ancient the growers would lay a plastic sheet in the bottom before loading. This covered the numerous cracks and holes so that the juice from any crushed ones would not seep away. They wanted to lose nothing. One day, a farmer must have forgotten to do this and I noticed a can pushed under the corner at the back of one of the trailers catching the juice dripping into it. Obviously it had sprung a leak. When it was his turn to move forward, he picked up the can and placed it on top of the trailer then It was returned to its place under the corner when he stopped. This went on for the full length of the street until it was his turn to unload.

I was curious to have a look inside the cantina so I told them that I was from England and had never seen anything like it, asking if I could look around. Italian-fashion, they gave me the VIP treatment. There were three huge, stainless steel silos in the middle of the factory that held the thousands of litres of grape juice to be made into wine. In the yard at the back was a large pile of grape skins, seeds, pips and stems continuously being added to from an elevator. These would be made into the Grappa, a rough strong brandy with which Italians like to lace their morning coffee. If you haven't had it, try some but be warned, it is a very strong spirit. I have often seen them in the morning rushing along the pavement on their way to work, then nipping into a bar for a quick one. To a small glass of strong black coffee they add a similar amount of Grappa, which goes straight down the hatch. Then, suitably primed, they go back on the way to work full of strong liquor and a hefty doze of caffeine. It is hardly surprising they drive the way they do!

As an aside, it was around the time I toured the cantina that we had a sad reminder of home. We were watching the TV news in the hotel when news broke of the tragedy of the Bradford City football stadium burning down during a game against Lincoln City on 11th May 1985. Julia and I watched in horror as the flames spread like wildfire through the old woodwork of the stands taking fifty six lives. Nearly three hundred more were injured, many seriously. This was news from home that we could have done without as we knew the area and had lived not far away in Ilkley. Within minutes many of our Italian friends came around to express their condolences. We were far from home but they made sure we did not feel alone.

The sights and sounds of Rome

It was time to see the Eternal City. When he heard that we had plans to visit Rome, Enzo the brother at the hotel offered to ring ahead and book us into accommodation. We were pleased to accept his offer and scribbled down the name and address of the hotel he gave us. We jumped on the Rome train at Treviso and enjoyed the view of the Italian compagna it gave us from the top deck But Rome came as a bit of a shock. We knew to expect crowds, it is one of the most visited places on earth, but it was heaving a little extra as a huge film festival was being staged. We joined a long line to get a taxi and it was an hour or more before it was our turn. We gave the address to the driver who looked down his nose and chuntered. Just as we had waited a long time in our queue so he had too in the line of taxis and he was not pleased that ours was going to be a short trip. Just as Italians came be the most welcoming of people sometimes they can be the most churlish, as he made his displeasure known to us. We cancelled his tip!

We were pleased to have a pre-booking for a hotel with the city so crowded. But when we were dropped off at the hotel our spirits fell as we were told there was no room at the inn. They were full! I had no trouble in telling the receptionist, using my best Italian, that we had a reservation but to no avail. He made the excuse that we were late by a few hours so he had let the room. It was more likely he took a higher price from someone who was desperate. The more we argued the less progress we made, and the receptionist also said he could not recommend another place to stay. So we picked up our cases and set off in search of a bed for the night. We had no idea where to look and just trudged up and down the streets, calling in wherever there was a hotel or Bed and Breakfast sign, but with no luck. The further we walked, the later it became and the closer we moved into poorer streets.

It was now dark as we worked our way along a row of what had once been large five-storey terrace houses, the front doors of which you approached by climbing wide steps from the road. Once grand and impressive, these buildings had grown scruffy and unkempt. We found one with a hotel sign and walked in; it must have been the twentieth we had tried. We made our way to the tiny reception desk while looking round at the untidy and unloved surrounds. Any sign of what we were thinking we struggled to keep off our faces as we spoke to the old lady manning the reception. By now I had practiced my, *"Che un camera libero,"* so many times I could be taken for a native. When she asked how many people and how many nights I almost fainted. She had room. We booked ourselves in for two nights. As she wrote down our details I glanced round, avoiding Julia who was doing the same. We both felt identical thoughts: it was late and any bed is better than no bed. I signed on the dotted line and took the key. The receptionist pointed to the wide stairs and told us our room was on the fourth floor. There was no lift. We climbed up and saw that no matter how rough the reception had been, the décor became worse the higher we went. These walls had not seen a lick of paint for many years. We passed a tall shady-looking character with a huge gold chain around his neck. Next there were two girls all tarted up looking as if they were going to work - on the streets. When we eventually found our room I was shocked to see how many times the door had been patched up, and how many times the lock had been replaced and refitted.

When we stepped inside the room it was even worse. The carpet was filthy, the furniture was broken, a tall window at the opposite side of the room was half open, the long shutters were yellow and the curtains were faded with age. The window looked out into a narrow courtyard. Julia inspected the bed with the same distaste that I felt and would not even sit on it. We stood there in a state of shock. The day had started off so well when we left Sacile but was now ending disastrously in a Roman slum.

I did not want to touch the bed sheets but with two fingers I peeled them back just a little and just a little was enough. I don't know when they were last changed but I would not get in there even with my clothes on. I noticed more than one colour of hair when I turned the pillow over; curly black ones, long greyish blonde ones, and many that were indescribable. Julia was standing quite bewildered. Eventually we had to settle down to rest and make the best of it. I spread my coat and other clothes on the bed and Julia sat on them. That's how she spent the night while I sat in a chair. There was a constant stream of people moving outside in the passage. I locked the door and wedged a chair under the handle. Eventually from sheer exhaustion we dozed off, but I came to life when a severe vibration started to shake the shutters. It felt as if the place was going to fall down but then it stopped as abruptly as it had started. I dozed off again only to be wakened once more by the same vibration. I looked out the window but could not see anything untoward. There was no fire or anything else wrong. I settled down again but the night dragged on and I must have slept again. The next time I awoke it was because of a terrific explosion. The room shook as did the nasty pictures on the wall. Julia was awake and we were terrified, wondering if a bomb had gone off. There was no sign of anything outside the window. A couple of people passed our door going along the passage, and they didn't seem to be in a hurry. Dawn was breaking when I eventually plucked up courage to open the door.

Along the passage was plaster and bits of wood that had fallen off the walls and ceilings. A large hole in the wall next to our room had appeared and in the middle of the passage lay a door that had been blown off its hinges. There was no panic and people just calmly stepped over the debris carrying their cases. We hastily packed ours and went down to the reception area where everything looked normal. What had happened: a bomb, a crashed aircraft, an earthquake? Our friend the old lady receptionist told me with a shrug that the gas boiler in a cupboard next to our room had exploded during the night. That explained the explosion but what about the earlier vibrations? "Oh that was just a tremor from an earthquake several kilometres away. It often happens in Rome. No one takes much notice!"

Well, no one else might but now it was daybreak the first thing Julia and I set about doing was to find somewhere else to stay. Now we could see properly we noticed that the building next door was also a hotel and looked far better and cleaner. We asked about a room and were pleasantly surprised to hear that one had come free due to a cancellation by one of the film festival guests. So we booked for one night and went back for our cases glad to get out of the dirty place. But imagine our surprise when we saw at the reception desk the old lady had been replaced – by the man from next door! The truth dawned on me that they were owned by the same person and as I had said some uncomplimentary things I felt a little embarrassed. Still, we had made our bed, so to speak, and took the key for the hotel next door up to our room. With trepidation in our hearts we opened the door but happily found it was an improvement, not big, but clean enough for one more night in Rome.

Up early as we were, we made a prompt start to our sightseeing. There is so much that Rome has to offer and we were determined to do as much as we could in just one day. Our first stop was the Vatican to see the unbelievable paintings of Michelangelo. *The Last Judgment* on the ceiling of the Sistine Chapel, which had taken him four long years to complete, held us spellbound as it has millions of others. We gazed with awe at those magnificent works of art in the Chapel and in St Peter's. We climbed on the roof and saw across Rome, picking out what we would do next. We wanted to get back to the hotel as late as we could manage to make as short a night of it as possible, so we planned our day carefully. We took in the Trevi Fountain, the Coliseum, Forum, Pantheon, museums and trattorias all around the City. Exhausted, we nevertheless slept fitfully in our room, before departing next day to the north by train to Cornigliano, and then to Sacile. We had each thrown a coin in the Trevi Fountain, a gesture said to signify our wish to return one day. But at that point I don't think either of us really wanted to go back to Rome – or at least we would handle the hotel booking ourselves.

Giulio the Anglophile

In many ways Giulio was more British than the British. It always seemed strange to me when I considered that what had brought him to the country was his capture by British soldiers who imprisoned him as an enemy soldier. Like a lot of Italians he had no appetite for Mussolini's war and was just thankful he faced the British in North Africa rather than the Russians on the Eastern Front. Giulio had lived in Yorkshire for over twenty five years and much of the way of life had rubbed off on him. In his eyes everything about Britain was good, a view that did not always go down well with his Italian friends He made himself unpopular at the time of the Falklands War, not only with friends and acquaintances but with his family too. Three of his brothers had emigrated to Argentina after WWII and their families were still living there. His niece Perina owned a small bar, Bar Alla Bruna, close to the crossroads in Calderano, not far from where he lived. This was where all the locals met to drink and play cards, and most had sympathy for Argentina once the fighting started in 1982. But not Giulio. "Margaret Thatcher will kick them out," he would proclaim in a loud voice to anyone in particular and much to their disapproval. Eventually he was proved right but he made things worse for several years by seldom hesitating to remind his neighbours.

My first visit was after the ending of the Falklands War, but Giulio had an uncanny talent for bringing it up in conversation. I'd go with him to his niece's bar and we would watch the old-timers playing cards. They would argue and shout at one another, wave their arms about and throw the cards on the table in their anger. I quite expected a fight to start any minute. Then Giulio would add spice to the argument with his tales of the British Army in the Falklands and I thought, "Here we go, I'm being dragged in now." But there was never a blow struck, and all would quieten down while the next hand was dealt. Then it would erupt all over again. Over the years I spent quite a long time in Italy but I never understood how Italians can get so agitated one minute, then be serenity itself the next. It was only hot air. At that time a local factory produced kitchen units for export to UK. When the British wagon drivers turned up to collect them they stayed overnight and usually found their way to Bar Alla Bruna where they would enjoy talking English with Giulio.

He loved to do the football pools. I would post copies of the coupons to him from England and he would telephone the numbers for me to fill in on his behalf. He was always convinced that this was going to be his lucky week. One time when he phoned he told me about his new car and was very excited at the prospect of driving it on the roads of northern Italy. "You know Ken, I have searched high and low and at last I've found a British car. You will like it. It is wonderful and much better than the Italian muck. It is a special export model and comes with velour seats and all the extras for hot weather." "What's the make," I asked. "An Allegro," he replied. What could I say? The Allegro was a dreadful model brought out by British Leyland in its last gasps as a major car manufacturer. Faced with a choice of all the Italian makes, who would buy an Allegro – or 'All Agro' as we used to call it. But it was British, which was all that mattered to Giulio. I congratulated him and said I was looking forward to seeing it. As it happened, this car turned out to be the exception to the rule and served him very well. Together, he, Julia and I travelled many miles around Italy in it.

Though we couldn't stay with him, Giulio was the perfect host in every other way. So it was with great pleasure we heard of his decision to pay a return visit to England for a holiday. He agreed to stay with us at Borough-bridge. We could make him welcome and repay a little of the kindness he had shown us. We knew he liked nothing better than horse racing so we took him to the races at York. I had a Rover SDI at the time, which was quite luxurious. Giulio sat in the front with me, leaning back with a smile on his face. He turned to me and said, "Ken, what more could any one want than a car like this British Rover. It is simply the best." I remembered the Ferrari I had driven in the 1970s, and some of the other wonderful Italian and German makes but decided to keep my views to myself. We had a good day at the races. He was always optimistic that the next race would be the one in which he would win big, the same attitude he had with the football pools. He actually didn't do badly at the trackside but I'm sure that the biggest kick he had out of the day was being chauffeured in the Rover.

Illness

Sadly, it wasn't long before things changed dramatically for the worse. After returning to Italy Giulio became ill. He phoned to say he had been to the doctor and was taking medication, though he would not say what the problem was. During our next visit he appeared to be a little better despite having lost weight. He told us he had been given the wrong medicine, but was now on the correct course and felt improved.

As usual, we prepared for the grape harvest. I located the tins, secateurs and other equipment while Giulio went for the tractor and trailer. I watched him as he walked along between the vines. When someone called to him, he turned to see who it was but staggered and grabbed at the branches to avoid falling. For me that was the first real sign of his illness. I was too far away to help but I realised all was not well. He regained his composure and continued his work. He was a big, strong, uncomplaining sort but it was clear there was something seriously wrong with him and I kept close watch.

We brought in the harvest and then, all too soon, the holiday was over and we returned to Boroughbridge. We hadn't been back more than a couple of weeks when Giulio rang and told us he would have to stay in bed for a few days to regain his strength. This was worrying news as he lived on his own and had no one to look after him. His home was an old farm house that was actually the original family home, and had never been modernised or properly maintained. It was owned equally between the brothers and Giulio had been allowed to use it when he returned from England. There had been a trend in northern Italy where everyone, even newlyweds, wanted a newly built house. One of Giulio's friends, a fellow named Evio, worked in his spare time slowly building a new house. When it was eventually completed he got married and moved in. Unlike in England, old houses in Italy just stood empty waiting to fall down; no one wanted them.

Julia and I discussed the situation. We agreed to go back to Italy see what was the matter and if we could help. Julia booked the flights and over we went. Giulio's niece Perina, the bar owner, had been visiting him whenever she could, but she was old and could not give much of her time. Shortly after we arrived, an appointment was made for him to go into hospital for an exploratory operation and a few days later the ambulance came for him. As we didn't know where the hospital was, it was agreed we would follow the ambulance in Giulio's Allegro. And to help us further, or so he thought, the ambulance driver put on the blue flashing lights and drove like he was

on the track at Monza. I had trouble keeping up with him. As we sped through towards Treviso the police stopped other traffic, waving him through with me hanging on behind.

The operation was carried out the following day and we called in

Julia, Peter, Giulio and his sister Perina – Bar Bruna Calderano Italy 1983/4 during the evening to see Giulio propped up in bed looking pale and weary. The doctor asked to see us and we were ushered into his office. His solemn look said it all, and I felt my gut churn as he told us the cause, "Cancer!" He turned to Julia, "Your father has cancer at a very advanced stage. When we look inside he is full of it and does not have long to live. It is too late for an operation. You must take him home and look after him for the remainder of his days, as we can do nothing." When it is a routine part of your job to say such words to people who are desperate for hope, it comes out cold and heartless. We were stunned. He asked again, "When can you take him away." "Take him away? Where can we take him to? We are from England." It was clear he was in no condition to attempt a trip to Britain. His brothers were in Argentina and his niece had the bar and her own family to look after.

"Well I need the bed so he will have to go somewhere," said the doctor. "I will let him stay here for a short time while you find somewhere, but one of you or someone from the family must stay with him in the ward 24 hours a day." We shook hands and left his office. What next? In Italy, the family cares for elderly or sick relatives. We spoke to his niece who could not help or suggest any other member of the family who could. A search started for a nursing home but at that time they really didn't have such places in Italy. The only hospice-type centres were run by the Church but these were few and far between, and it was unfair for us to move him a long way from his friends and family. We started the first of what became a long series of all-night vigils in the hospital ward. Other family members agreed to give us a break during the day so we might look for somewhere for Giulio. This was one of our hardest experiences of our lives, sitting all night on those uncomfortable hospital chairs by Giulio's bed trying to stay alert in case he wanted a drink or a pee.

There were eight beds in the ward and most were occupied by terminally ill old men waiting their turn. It was usually at night that the ends came. I sat listening to the sorrowful sounds of the chronically ill, with snoring from one who had managed to get to sleep, or a quiet sob from another trying to keep his pain to himself, and laboured breathing with moans and gasps from others. I would hear an occasional call for water or a bottle for the other end. Like us, there were relatives of other patients on standby, each sitting on a chair at the end of the bed doing what we were doing. You seldom saw a member of the staff during the nights. I made a count of the beds in that part of the hospital and I think the ratio was about one orderly to 50 patients. There was a long wait if one of them was needed. Julia and I kept a close watch on Giulio but could do little for him other than administer to his basic needs.

One night he was feeling restless and asked me if I would massage his back as it was going numb. I pulled him up, leaning him forward and rubbed gently at the base of his spine to get some circulation. After a while he said it felt better and leaned back onto his pillow. He looked up at me with a faint smile and said, "You are a good man Ken." Another night he suddenly sat bolt upright. I rushed to his side, he looked bewildered as he turned to me and said, "What is happening Ken?" What could I say to that? I am seldom at a loss for words, but not only was I speechless I was gutted and felt close to tears. I stuttered out some sort of answer. Giulio was not my father but in the few years I had known him he treated me like a son. If he thought I was a good man, I certainly knew him to be one.

The hospital was enormous. The wing he was in had a long corridor with fifteen to twenty wards running off one side, with external windows on the other. Julia and I would swap shifts with each other sitting by his bed at night. When not on duty I would try to read by the dim light in the corridor, or I might try to find somewhere to snatch a few hours sleep in a slightly more comfortable chair, or I would find myself just gazing out through the windows into the darkness and what seemed like endless rain. Inevitably, time dragged. The occasional hospital trolley would rattle past or a visitor would shuffle by. Most of these visitors seemed to be old people with glum faces dressed in dark clothes. The hospital was connected by an underground network of passages. Occasionally when Giulio appeared to be settled, Julia and I would walk along these passages to other parts of the hospital, stopping off at a coffee machine. The aim of this was more to stretch our legs than to drink the dreadfully strong coffee, though this did help us keep awake. Often we would hear the rumble of a trolley being pushed along with a large metal coffin on top. We learned to tell the difference between one that was empty and another that had an occupant. If it rattled with a hollow, tinny sound it was empty and on the way to make a collection. If the note was more of a rumble and took more effort to push it was on the way to the morgue. The busiest time was the early hours of the morning.

The weather had been wet and foggy for days. Then early one morning as I was trying to get a little sleep in the corridor and while Julia sat in the ward, dawn started to break. I came awake, stood up and looked out of the window. It was as if a curtain of grey mist had been lifted and now the vista was clear all the way to the snow-capped mountains far off in the distance. As the sun rose the snow became first pink then brilliant white. I must have clicked the shutter of the camera in my head as I can see it now. These were the mountains Giulio always referred to as the Pre-Alps, that led up to the Dolomites, Cortina and Austria beyond.

We were again summoned to the head doctor's office. "When can you move him?" he asked. We told him what we had been doing to locate somewhere for Giulio but added that nowhere had yet been found. "Well, you can't keep him here. You must find a bed for him elsewhere quickly." I had a feeling he was fishing for a hand-out. There was so much corruption in public positions in Italy. But all I said was that we would keep trying. In actual fact, we had come to one dead-end after another.

A funeral

Tragically, it was Giulio himself who provided the answer the following night. He breathed his last! I have seen people waste away over a long period while being tortured by cancer. At least he was spared that and was given a relatively quick end from the time he had been first taken ill. His niece made all the arrangements and we met her and other family members at the undertakers for the funeral. The funeral house was running late with another interment and we had to hang around waiting. To pass the time I walked up and down the road outside what the Americans call 'the parlour'. Then I glanced in at the back of the undertakers' yard. Imagine my surprise when I saw a man sat on a stool with a welding torch sealing the lid on Giulio's metal coffin. I watched for a while and noticed he was taking great care, slowly working all the way around until it was one unit. I had never seen anything like this before and had no idea this was the way things were done in Italy.

Eventually, the coffin came out of the front of the parlour covered in flowers. Julia and I walked directly behind the hand-drawn hearse, first to the church then on to the cemetery. I had experienced both great joy and sorrow in Italy. I once attended a very enjoyable wedding when a lovely lady sang Franz Schubert's musical rendition of the Latin prayer Ave Maria to the happy gathering. That was wonderful. But this funeral was the saddest occasion of all, and here was the hymn being sung again. At the cemetery there was another surprise when the coffin was hoisted up shoulder high and pushed into a square hole in a wall, then cemented in. A photograph of a young Giulio as he would have wanted to be remembered, and a small bunch of flowers were fastened on the wall. That was also how it was done in Italy. Giulio had been born in 1917, the youngest of eleven children. He never remembered his father and his mother also died when he was young. He had been brought up by elder sisters.

There was little more we could do. He had few possessions. His bank and pension books had disappeared. I had heard of pensions being drawn by relatives long after the person had died, but which of his relatives took them we will never know. The house in which he lived returned to his brothers who were anxious to sell it and the vineyard to a building developer.

So our adventures in Italy came to an abrupt and sad end. We had seen so much of interest and learned much about the country and its people, and were fortunate to have such a terrific guide as Giulio. He loved Italy, though as a proud Venetian he preferred the north. On my travels, I have been surprised to find how often in countries there is a north/south divide. There is certainly a big difference in Italy. The northerners often refer to the darker-skinned southerners as 'Arabs,' and they in turn describe the northerners as 'Germans'. Occasionally, if we were served in a café or restaurant by a dark-skinned waiter Giulio would mutter, "Look at him, they come up from the South taking our jobs!" Isn't that the complaint of people the world over. But on balance, there is much to love about Italy and I cherish my memories of the place and of Giulio in particular. Luckily, the habit of photography, started with the old camera that my granny bought me from the sale room when I was still at school means I have much to help me remember.

CHAPTER FIVE

A TRIP TO THE U.S. OF A.
1992

Holidays abroad had now become the norm. With the sad passing of Julia's father, Giulio Nadal, Italy was put to one side and we looked across the Atlantic for our annual vacation in 1992. I had mixed feelings about America and Americans, though I liked most of those I'd met we always heard about how much bigger and better everything was there, I had listened to them now I would take a look and form my own opinion these were my thoughts as we took off for Florida that September day in 1992.

Our idea was to stay in Fort Lauderdale, twenty three miles north of Miami, and use that as a base to visit many other parts, including Cape Canaveral, the Everglades and Miami itself. We had plenty of advice from friends, especially about Miami where we were warned to stay away from the dock area. We rented a car and drove to Key West, past the southern tip of the mainland. We stopped on the way to enjoy the delicious key lime pie, a local Florida speciality. Similar to our lemon meringue pie but made using the tart, aromatic Key Limes that are indigenous to Florida. In Key West we took a quick look around the Hemmingway bars. There is a large number of these but how many he actually visited we will never know. The Overseas Highway, an extension of Route 1, hops over from one of the Florida Keys (a corruption of Cayo, the Spanish word for island) to the next and is one of the most spectacular drives I have ever taken. You can still see remains of the original old causeway built to carry a railroad, and much of the road is low, narrow and close to the water. This causeway and its associated bridges were wrecked by the Labor Day hurricane of 1935 with the loss of over 400 lives, which put paid to the railroad and led to its conversion into a highway. Knowing this certainly added to the excitement of our drive.

The weather in Florida was always warm and it would have been nice to just sit around and soak up the sun with the 'snow birds,' as they call the retired folk who migrate south for the winter. But we wanted to see something of this big country and decided to tour around some of the Deep South. Both Julia and I particularly wanted to see New Orleans, so we flew there from Florida, planning to rent a car and return by road along the Gulf of Mexico coast. Internal flights were and still are relatively cheap and Americans are as used to catching a plane as we are to hopping on a bus or train. It was easy getting to New Orleans, the adventure would be in getting back. We spent two most enjoyable days in New Orleans looking around the old town. I was amazed when I stood on the levee at the corner of Bourbon Street in the French Quarter and saw how much higher the Mississippi river was on one side than the street level was on the other. I felt an uneasy foretaste of the devastation to come years later when Hurricane Katrina struck and the water burst through, drowning most of the City. What New Orleans has in abundance is good food and Traditional Jazz, the main reasons for our visit. And we enjoyed both. It was an incredible experience for Julia and me to wander from one Bourbon Street bar to another. I realised that what we were hearing was mostly 'jazz for the tourist' but it was my kind of music and I loved it.

All too soon we had to plan for our return journey and made for a car rental company. America thrives on the rental market but what we hadn't realised was that we would not be able to hire one vehicle for the whole drive back. A car could be used only in the state in which it had been rented. The only way we could get a car for the whole journey was if we paid a driver to bring it back to Louisiana, which was out of the question. We looked at what it would mean to drive to each border town, leave the car and walk across the border to get another vehicle. But that wasn't practical either. We appeared to be stuck.

The Greyhound Bus

We had seen nothing of the South from the window of the aircraft flying over and did not want to return the same way. There was one choice left: the Greyhound Bus. This is the cheapest form of long distance travel in the USA and we had heard about the type of people who we might meet on the way. But needs must and though we felt uneasy, we proceeded to buy tickets and climb aboard the next bus to leave from New Orleans bound for West Palm Beach, Florida. It was to be an interesting trip.

We settled into our seats about 10am on a Thursday morning, and a few minutes later we were on our way. The bus felt powerful as it had to be to cover almost half the continent. It surged forward when the driver accelerated. Having been a bus driver myself, operating those old Ledgards bangers in late 1950s Leeds, I took a professional interest. My idea of a 'busman's holiday' was to have a close look at bus, engine, gear change and most particularly the skills of the driver. On one occasion in Italy on a coach tour, I was so impressed with the driver I immediately learned a phrase to compliment him, "You are a very good driver," I said in Italian (buon autista). He was pleased and it probably meant as much to him as the small tip I was able to offer. Complimenting someone on their driving is a fairly rare experience in Italy.

Whatever the official road distance, as the journey panned out it quickly emerged that it would be longer. There were many stops to make and as Greyhound buses also carried parcels we had to make detours to Wells Fargo stations, many of them in back streets. We didn't mind this as it did offer a glimpse of what the tourist does not normally see. Whenever new passengers got on, the driver made a short speech outlining the Greyhound Bus Company rules. I wish I had written these down because of the insight they gave into American life. But I can remember the last two: "No spitting and no marijuana". Judging by the sweet smell wafting from the back of the bus for most of the trip the last of these was routinely ignored.

We settled down to see a little of what the Deep South had to show, both rich and poor, good and bad. We passed great colonial style houses surrounded by palm trees with front gardens reaching down over the white sand to the waters of the Gulf of Mexico. At the other extreme were grubby back streets with equally dirty and ragged children and teenagers, black, white and Hispanic, looking bored and resentful, scenes that you don't really expect to see in a prosperous country like America.

Passengers climbed on and off at every stop. It grew dark outside and we turned to our books. I remember at the time I was reading Harold Robins and some of our fellow passengers looked so shady they would not have been out of place in one of the author's thrillers. I became a little more uneasy when I noticed that the overhead light was picking up the sparkle from my diamond ring as I held the book. In fact, I felt as if everyone else had seen it. Discreetly I turned the ring around so the diamond was on the inside of my hand. Julia was asleep, judging by the occasional shake.

As we sped through the night that sweet smell wafted forwards again. I just hoped the dope smokers were sitting as far away from the driver as possible. Most of the passengers merged into the darker recesses of the bus. My main thought was to stay awake and keep reading. Suddenly, I almost jumped out of my skin as a big black hand reached across and tapped my ring hand, "Ya'll got a light man?" I turned to see a large face very close to mine as he leaned over from his seat, his eyes flashing in the dark. "Sure," I answered, trying to appear casual as I fumbled in Julia's bag for a lighter while not waking her. Eventually after turning everything over two or three time I found it at the bottom and handed it to him.

He lit up. The smoke didn't smell like what was coming from the rear so I breathed a little easier on that score. "Thanks mister," he said handing back the lighter. "You guys English?" I used the same language back, "You bet." Well, that was the start of a most enjoyable conversation that lasted much of the night. He was a nice guy, obviously wanting to pass the time in conversation and to be friendly. We discussed many things. I asked him about the USA and he was very interested in anything British. I was curious to know what he did for a living and was tempted to ask but thought it best not to; I did not want to give offence by prying too deeply into personal matters.

I had seen him earlier in the trip when he first boarded the bus. He was a huge man, exceptionally tall and very broad. As he walked along the aisle he had to stoop and ease his great body sideways. He wore a black shirt, dark suit and homburg and you could not tell where he finished and the shirt and suit started. I noticed several gold rings and a heavy chain. I couldn't resist glancing at his jacket to see if there was a bulge from the inside pocket area where he might have a gun. To my English eye he looked like a real gangster, but he was good company with others on the bus. But he really helped pass the time as we droned on into the night until tiredness caught up with me and I fell asleep.

When I awoke it was dawn and soon afterwards we stopped for a short break at a Greyhound pick-up point. It was time, too, to change drivers and we took the opportunity to stretch our legs. Greyhound bus seats are more comfortable than most I have sat on but the upholstery does wear thin on the bits you sit on. Maybe this doesn't matter to some passengers who might carry a bit more upholstery themselves, but my bum had gone numb and I needed to stand for a while. We had a snack as there is always food wherever you are in America. We ate a sandwich that was as much as a full English breakfast, drank some coffee and then were on the road again. I liked the way the driver called out the place names in his southern drawl, "Mobile, Pensacola, Chattahoochee, Tallahassee," lovely long names dragged out even longer by his accent.

Eventually, at 3.30 on the Friday afternoon we reached our destination at West Palm Beach, Florida. We had been travelling for twenty nine and a half hours and had covered 1,500 miles. It was good to walk again. My new friend was off the bus before us and I watched his large, slightly stooped figure taking slow deliberate steps as he set off along the footpath. My imagination got the better of me: was he a 'hit man' or on his way to do some other gangster job. He certainly looked the part, but here I was judging a book by its cover again.

We walked towards the beach. The weather was hot but there was a light, cooling breeze blowing in off the Atlantic Ocean. It felt good to get the circulation going again in my bum and legs. It was amazing to see so many Rolls-Royces parked around the edge of the beach. Some were quite old but I supposed they don't rust here as they do in the UK, and often make their way back across the pond. In fact I heard that many old Jaguar and MG sports cars bought in the USA also eventually find their way back to Britain.

Virgin Islands and Puerto Rico

Sooner than we had expected or planned we found ourselves back at our Fort Lauderdale base and had a few days to spare. The British Virgin Isles were just a relatively short trip away and Julia's sister Gina would be migrating to work there the following month. So we decided to go and have a look at the place where she would live. First, we flew to Puerto Rico, then took a small six-seater plane on an island hop over to Tortola, the main island in the British Virgin Islands group. This was an exciting flying experience going low over the green-blue shallow waters where you could often see the ocean bottom. We called at several islands on the way which felt almost like dropping in at bus stops. I remember one where the airport was only a shed looking like a World War Two hanger. To decorate the inside they had hung great blue sheets with white clouds painted on them.

Tortola is a beautiful island and we enjoyed the view from the taxi as we drove in from the airport. Actually, this taxi was a green Transit van with painted on the side in large letters, 'Frank's Taxi Service'. The driver gave us a guided tour pointing out places of interest on the way to Road Town, the capital, though in reality only a small settlement. It did not take long to look around. We found the solicitors' offices where Gina was to work, and introduced ourselves to the owner. Gina had been interviewed in England and had taken the job sight-unseen. I felt sure she was in for a surprise, but a very pleasant one. The harbour was beautiful with rows of expensive yachts moored along the quay. Once we had seen the place we did not hang around and returned to Puerto Rico where we intended to stay for a couple of days.

While Tortola had a British influence, Puerto Rico was a mixture of the Hispanic and American styles of living. As we walked around we came across a rather unusual-looking circular building. The door was open so we went in and had a look around. I was amazed to find that it was a cock fighting arena. Thankfully, nothing was going on at the time, but I was surprised to find that such places still existed and this one obviously operated in full view. We quickly left and walked along the white sand by the edge of the sea. Looking across at the forested area we saw that many poor people were hanging around and staring at us. Several were collecting empty beer or coke cans which they hammered flat and bagged them up to weigh in for scrap. There were hours of work here but all for just a few cents.

We found a place where they kept horses. It was not a school as such but they agreed to let us ride as we explained we were experienced and, of course, gave them money. After my lessons in Yorkshire I was confident I could cope and, of course, Julia was an expert horsewoman. These horses were different to those we had come across in England. There, I had ridden school horses who knew the routine. These looked different: sleek, fit and excitable, fidgeting to get moving. They were more like the ones I had seen at Wetherby Races and in cowboy films, I felt my confidence drain a little.

There were four other riders in our group and all looked experienced as I watched them mount. I did the same and climbed into the big saddle, taking up the reins while eyeing the others. I realised it was Western-style riding with the reins held in one hand, rather than two as we did in England. I took them in one hand casually as I didn't want anyone to know that this was another first for me. I looked across at Julia who sat nonchalant and comfortable on her horse, no doubt thinking about how the next few minutes might be a real test for me - just what I was thinking. When you go to rent a car they ask for your driving license, but when you hire a horse there is no such requirement, they just take your word and your money.

We set off towards the beach. I was amazed and heartened at the response I had from my horse when the reigns touched its neck. I was used to horses that were usually slow to respond, but this one was lively and aware. I sat there like a cowboy, feeling it was easier than I had expected. The fun would come later. We cantered off through the forest past the make-shift shelters of the aluminium can collectors. Full sacks had been stacked ready for sale and young boys were hammering out cans from a large stockpile. As we neared the sea I noticed my horse was getting eager and wanting to speed up, but I restrained him until we were clear of the trees. The leaders took off and galloped along the sand and I followed. I had never gone as fast on a horse and clung on to the pommel with one hand and tried to keep control with the other. The horses were fit and wanted to get to the front so it became a real race. This was hair-raising stuff - even for me who was going a little thin on top! I was relieved when we came to the end of the open part of the beach. The next section was fenced off for public use and no horses were allowed. So we came to a slow walk.

The woman who ran the show told us what to do next. On the way back we would ride into the sea but first only into the shallows. She advised us to keep tight control as the horses love the water and would want to go deeper.

Their favourite trick was to roll in it and this can be dangerous for riders. "So keep a tight rein, get your feet out of stirrups and be ready to jump off, but if you do, keep hold of the reins," she warned. Well, I was feeling both excited and nervous at the same time. I held back and watched Julia and the other riders go first. Some had obviously done this before. Taking a deep breath, I cautiously followed them in. It was a wonderful experience. First, your feet and legs are cooled, then the water creeps up round the horse's belly and up to his neck. For me, that was my high water-mark, quite literally. Julia and some of the others went in further and I could see how excited the horses became. They obviously loved it and were shaking their heads and splashing around like children, but they needed tight control. When we came out of the surf we galloped on the beach to dry off and called at a little bar, tethered the horses to a rail Western-fashion and drank a cool beer. Later, the woman in charge led her horse into the sea by the reins to show us how they love the water. The horse rolled over and over, and thrashed his legs. Then, in the warm afternoon sun we walked them back to the stables where helpers took over. After another exciting experience we walked slowly back to our hotel to prepare for departure the next day.

Leaving problems

The following morning we walked around the town, returned to the hotel for our mid-day meal then packed our cases. We still had some local currency we wouldn't be able to spend elsewhere, so rather than bother changing it we decided to spend it on two or three Puerto Rico t-shirts. Simple enough you would have thought, but something that would lead to a lot of inconvenience later on. When I left the room Julia was just putting the last few items into her case. Mine was packed but left open ready for the t-shirts. But when I returned the cases were gone. "The porter called for them and I had only to zip up yours and he took them," she told me. The problem was that I had left our passports in my case hidden among the folds of my clothes, and now they were on their way to the airport. As quickly as we could we raced down to the taxi rank and sped off in pursuit, hoping we would get there before they were checked in.

At the airport the bags had gone through, we were told. But we weren't going anywhere without passports. We went to the luggage department and explained what had happened. The woman we spoke to said she was sorry, but there was nothing she could do. "What?" I exclaimed. She did not even look sorry and true to her word did nothing. I asked for the supervisor who eventually appeared, looking very serious. "If you think I'm going to have 200 cases taken off the aircraft so you can look for your passports, think again!" We had no choice but to report to airport security. I won't say we were arrested. We were not handcuffed but the Puerto Rican police took it much more seriously than did the luggage department. They allowed us to fly but we were made to feel like criminals, isolated from the rest of the passengers and escorted by one of the customs officials who stayed with us until we boarded the plane. Once in our seats responsibility for us was handed over to the crew, who then put us back into the charge of customs officials when we arrived in Miami.

At that time foreign visitors needed a visa to enter the USA. Well our visas were in the passports, so we could look forward to a long wait and more explanations. Our new escorts took us first to the immigration department office for another interrogation. We were then put back into isolation until the baggage had been unloaded. Immigration officials then took us to the carousel, by which time our cases had been, like us, isolated as they were the only ones still going around. We collected them and were taken back to the immigration office where I opened my case watched by six officials. None could muster even the merest hint of a smile as I pulled out the passports from inside a neatly folded shirt. In my experience Americans are usually friendly to us Brits, but not on this occasion. They did not see it as a mishap but totally over-reacted and ended up treating us like illegal immigrants or drug smugglers. We were let through to pick up the rest of our baggage and spend the last few days of our holiday in Fort Lauderdale. When our holiday over and we were coming into land at Gatwick Airport I have to say I had a strong sense of relief. It's a lesson really: just because you can push people around doesn't mean you should.

CHAPTER SIX

I HAD BEEN HERE BEFORE
1993

Back in Boroughbridge we were recovering from the ordeal of being taken for criminals on our flight from Puerto Rico to Florida. Julia was back designing children's clothes and selling them at markets around the country and I was in the groove at my car sales and tyre business.

Without ample capital to stock up fully I was continuing to follow the practice that had helped me get established in the first place: taking cars from other dealers and selling them on a commission basis. This was okay but not very profitable and it left me with all the other problems of accepting another car in part-exchange and having to provide a warranty. The cars I sold were at the cheaper end of the market and while most people accept that you get what you pay for, some were never satisfied and would come back time after time to whinge about minor problems. At the outset I had been told that to become successful in this line of business you had to look people in the eye and screw them, but I never could. And I often caught a problem with car buyers who were themselves far and away from being innocent in such circumstances. You often hear about unscrupulous car dealers but I can add a few stories about how unscrupulous Joe Public can be, some finding it fair game to screw the dealer. The one trick pulled by the public most often was when they come to do a deal they tell you the car they are planning to part-exchange is a year newer and therefore worth more than it actually is. You agree a deal based on the information they give you and prepare the vehicle he or she is to buy. You have this serviced, MOT'ed and polished ready for the buyer to collect, but when the time comes for them to bring in their old car for the exchange they tell you they can't find the registration document. You have the choice of cancelling the sale or applying for a new document, so you do the latter. When it arrives it is, as you suspected, for a car a year older than you were told. The buyer has got away with a better deal, but there is one crumb of comfort: they are not likely to come back complaining for warranty work having first cheated you.

Many old cars I accepted in part-exchange were well past their sell-by date and had numerous faults. But the person who traded it in could suddenly become very discerning with the newer vehicle he had bought from me, complaining at any minor fault to get something from the warranty you had provided.

One day an old man walked into the garage holding a bunch of keys in one hand and a handkerchief in the other, wiping his eyes. "I want you to sell my car for me. I have just driven up Knaresborough Road and could hardly see where I was going my eyes are so bad." I could see how bad they were, all red and watery. "If you get it ready to sell I will bring you the documents later. Get me a good price and I will pay you commission." I looked at the old chap and thought how brave he is to draw a line under his driving years. I remembered how excited I had been when I first passed my driving test, and how much I enjoyed the freedom that motoring brings. This old chap had come to the end of the line and must start walking everywhere when his old legs were no longer good. I imagined how I would feel when that day comes and felt sympathy. So I cleaned and polished his old Austin Maxi, prepared it for sale, put an advertisement in the local paper and soon had it sold. He did not live far from the garage so I went around to give him the money as it had been a cash sale. He was living on his own and invited me in. His house smelled of the pipe that was seldom out of his mouth. "Sit down," he said. "I told you that it was a good car and would be easy to sell." I placed the cash, which was in a roll tied up with an elastic band, on the table in front of him and his eyes lit up as he drew on his pipe. He counted the notes carefully. "£950. That's right, Ken," he said. "Thanks for everything you have done. I promised to treat you and here you are," he drew two £10 notes from the bundle. I was speechless but managed to force out, "Thanks Jim," as I left. I could still smell his damned pipe on me as I walked back up Knaresborough Road. I had expected £100 to cover my cleaning and preparing of the car, and the expense of the advertisement that had cost £25 on its own. I was well out of pocket - and I had been feeling sympathy for him!

Mean old Bob

Around the same time there was a break-in at the Yewdale Garage. The garage's owner was a person named Bob Knowles who rented me the display area for my cars, space for my tyre business and an old office. He used the garage for his car maintenance business and had an office of his own which had a desk, a couple of chairs, an old filing cabinet and a safe. Thieves sprayed foam into the alarm box on the wall, though they need not have bothered as it was not connected to anything. Then they forced a window to get in. They used Bob's cutting torch to burn the handle off his safe door, before realising it was not even locked. When they opened the door they must have been disappointed to find the safe had nothing of value in it, only a few tea bags, an invoice book and toilet paper. Bob gave nothing away and was not prepared to provide toilet paper other than for himself and his staff of two. He was such a miser it is a wonder he did not insist on his staff using the paper on both sides! The burglars left empty handed; they had made a bad mistake by breaking in to Bob's place. The welding unit and cutting torch were still by the safe when we arrived the next morning.

Bob's office was next to mine. Each day midway through the morning, he would disappear into his office and shut the door for his morning 'tonic,' pour a drink from a bottle of port or sherry he kept in a box under his desk, and stir in a raw egg. On one occasion he had forgotten to lock his door and had gone out. I looked in. There were three eggs in a box, and I took these away and boiled them in the kettle for ten minutes. Then I put them back. Next day I made a point of being in my office when he went for his tonic. I heard the cork being drawn and the wine being poured out. Then came the click as he tapped the egg on top of his glass, followed by another click, a bit louder this time. Then I heard a much louder crack, an outburst of swearing and then my name being called. "What the hell have you been doing, Ken?" I peeped around the corner trying - but failing - to keep a straight face. "What, me?" Bob didn't see the funny side of it and stormed out. I bought him six eggs to make amends, but it was a long time before our relationship was back to normal, and even longer before he again forgot to lock his office door.

Another of his money-saving ideas was to cut pieces of plastic to put into his shoes where the sole had worn through. Had he been really short of money I could have understood but this was not the case. With him, it was just miserly greed and he was often unaware that what he was doing was making things worse. For instance, he would ride round for miles in his old patched up Ford Cortina looking for the filling station with the cheapest petrol, probably using a gallon in the process. One day when he went for his lunch, he left his cheap old working shoes with the plastic insoles to dry by the stove. I pushed them a bit nearer the fire and the plastic melted.

I always stayed open on a Saturday afternoon for tyre customers. One Saturday in winter when I was about to lock up and go home a lady walked into the garage. She had a worried look on her face. "Can you help me? I'm with my elderly mother and we are locked out of our car." By that time I had worked all day and was ready for home, but what could I say? She told me the car was a Ford Cortina, which was a relief. I had once watched a policeman open a Ford with a wire coat hanger, pushing it past the doorpost then hooking it over the locking button and flicking it up. I could do the same. I collected a coat hanger and went with her to the car which was parked outside the railway station in the centre of Harrogate. When we arrived an old lady was sitting on the wall. She stood up and, though she looked frozen, smiled and greeted us. "You are our saviour," she said. It felt good to be able to help until I looked closer at the car. At that time Fords were so easy to break that some owners resorted to sawing the tops off the buttons. Someone had done this with the lady's car making it harder if not actually impossible to use the wire to hook under the button.

The two of them were relying on me. They were cold, it was late and they wanted to go home (as did I). Fortunately, I had brought a few tools and my 'second chance' packing tape. I prised the door open just enough to push in the packing tape with a loop on the end. I hooked this over the locking button and pulled it tight. I then tugged it upwards but it slipped off. I had another go, then another but each time the same thing happened. I moistened the tape to get a better grip and leaned on the door to take some pressure off the lock but nothing worked and I ran out of ideas. What made things worse was that I could see the keys lying inside on the floor where the driver had dropped them before getting out.

It grew dark and my hands were cold as I tugged repeatedly on the tape. Then without warning it happened! I heard a click as the button sprang up. I took hold of the handle and opened the door reaching for the keys with a huge sigh of relief. I was their saviour after all. I felt pleased as I looked at their smiling faces. The older woman excitedly fumbled to get her handbag open with hands that were numb with cold. She fished inside and drew out a £10 note which she offered. I could see that they were not rich by their clothes and the old car, and I certainly didn't want to be paid. I told them to, "Get off home and call at my garage when you need new tyres for your car."

I buy out Bob

Bob Knowles decided to retire and sell his garage. I had the choice of buying it or finding another place to sell my tyres and cars. I had developed a tidy business with a good reputation and people knew where to find me so I didn't want to start again from a new location. I decided I would have to buy the garage. The price kept going up as others made offers but eventually Bob and I agreed a deal and shook hands on it. The deal was expensive but I could just about manage to find the money with help from the bank.

But next day matters took a turn for the worse. Bob came in and asked for more money, not a small amount either but £5,000. He could not look me in the eye and gazed at the carpet as he stammered out what had happened. He had been phoned during the evening and a new potential buyer had made a much bigger offer. "But we shook hands on it, Bob, and you have always said your word is your bond." I told him I had arranged a loan and could not get an increase. The conversation went this way and that and he was as difficult as ever. But gradually we came to an agreement of sorts; I would meet the extra £5,000 but I would have a number of months in which to pay.

By this time we had a lot of equity wrapped up in our Ornhams Grange house. As far as I could see the obvious thing was to sell up and move to a smaller dwelling. This would release capital to put towards the purchase of the garage meaning any loan could be kept manageable. But Julia would not agree. Some time before she had said, "You know Ken, we live together but we're not married. Ornhams Grange is yours and I just live here with you. We have a good solid partnership that I feel will last; neither of us are interested in marriage, things are good as they are. But I feel like I have no security. What if we should change or something happens to you?" I understood her concerns and replied, "Julia, we'll go tomorrow to the solicitor and arrange for the house to be put in our joint names. This will give you half of the equity in the house." At that time Ornhams Grange was valued at about £140,000 and our mortgage was small. The joint owning arrangement had been set up, and now, some years later she was refusing to put the house on the market to help me buy the garage. "I love this house and if you move it is without me," Julia warned. What could I do? Perhaps I should have said, "I'm moving with or without you." But I was in love and decided to find another way. I borrowed a larger sum against the house, which Julia was pressed into going along with, and in that way I became the proud though nervous owner of Yewdale Garage.

I was pleased with the outcome. We still had our nice house, I owned my business premises and my businesses continued to do well. Though I had a large loan from the bank, the assets stacked up well against the borrowing. Property appreciates in value and I felt I would be able to get by through hard work. For a number of years all went well until the crunch!

Brian the County Court bailiff

Years before as I built up my business in Ilkley in the 1960s I had been in the right place at the right time. When it collapsed in the mid 1970s it was partly due to me, partly down to a man I had employed to run the contracting side and partly a result of the way bank interest escalated. Well here I was now in 1993, in the wrong place at the wrong time as interest rates began to rocket. I've been here before, I thought. The terms of my bank loan were that I would repay at the bank base rate plus three percent. Due to economic policies I have come to understand, the government allowed the official rate to scale fifteen percent to control inflation. For me this meant I was now being charged 18% each month. Instead of reducing, the outstanding amount was growing. When I took out the loan it was the absolute maximum that I could borrow on the profit that my business was generating, and the absolute maximum monthly repayment that I could handle. So the minute the repayments went up I was in trouble. At the same time property values plummeted. Again, as in the 1970s I felt the noose tightening around my neck with the pressure from the loan sharks at the bank. I worked hard to keep my businesses afloat but court summonses for non-payment began to arrive through the letterbox. The County Court bailiff became a regular visitor to Yewdale Garage and, in fact, he became a customer for my tyres and someone I got to know quite well.

The bailiff, Brian was his name, was okay. He would arrive with a writ and say, "What about this one Ken, can you pay something off to keep them quiet?" Another time he said, "This is a new one; I can hold it until next week." If I spotted him walking up the forecourt I would hide under the desk or run into the toilet but he would find me and we would have a laugh - though as far as I was concerned there was nothing really to smile about. What was worse was that creditors called at my home during the day when I was at work and some were not as nice as Brian. They would hammer on the door if Julia was home and would try to intimidate her. When I arrived home she would be quite distraught as she was not as resilient as me. Just like two decades before I was again playing for time. Everyone told me that interest rates could surely not stay so high for long but would fall, and the loan would become once again manageable. I started to sell off my personal possessions, some of which were things I had managed to hang onto during my past difficulties.

I had a collection of guns that I had owned and treasured for many years. I decided that they had to go. One of them was a special English 12-bore shotgun made by Lindsley Brothers, gunsmiths of Leeds. The firm still had a shop in Leeds and I went to see them. They offered a ridiculously low price but I was in dire straights and needed the money. I had owned and cared for that shotgun for forty years but I was now forced to sell it for a fraction of its true value. Next to go was my jewellery. Years ago when business had been good, I had bought a few items of gold: a chain, a bracelet, Krugerrands, sovereigns and various other items. Even though I knew the jeweller, John Masons shop was in the next street to my garage and he bought tyres from me, he offered only a rock bottom price. I had to accept as the cash that came in bought me a few more days.

That precious time flew by and again the question arose, what can I sell? One of the only things of real value left was my number plate, 5KW. This had been with me through my earlier business collapse and I had fought to regain it from the Alan Morgan managers who had acted like they wanted to grind me into dust. The plate had been on many different cars over the past quarter century including in better times Porsch Ferrari and BMW, what it now represented for me was survival. But matters grew worse and worse until a sale became inevitable. Things had deteriorated to the point where it was more important to keep the pot boiling, stay in the house and have Yewdale Garage as a springboard from which to earn a living. So the number plate was sold. Don't ask how much I was paid for it as I don't want even to think about it, and really in the scheme of things it made precious little difference. Imagine what it would be worth now: enough to buy a house I shouldn't wonder!

If there was one possession even more important to me it was my diamond ring and I was adamant that this wasn't going under the auctioneer's hammer. It was not worth a fortune but, like the number plate, had survived my previous financial crisis and meant a lot. It was in the late 1960s that I had bought two diamond rings, one for Wendy and one for me, from Paling the jewellers near Ledgards' Garage in Otley, and had paid cash. More than anything it reminded me of those earlier days when business was booming and I always had at least £1,000 on me. When I met my friend Barry Taylor in the pub after work he would reach round to my back pocket give it a squeeze and he could tell by the size of the wad what kind of day I'd had.

A daily struggle

Well, all that had gone now for the second time of asking. Day-by-day it was now a struggle for financial survival. I concentrated on my tyre business and rented off other parts of the garage. This helped pay my constantly rising loan commitments but it led to unforeseen problems. I rented out the back part of the garage to a man who renovated vintage cars. When I went round to see him one day there was what looked like a lovely old MGB up on the lift. He hadn't noticed my arrival as he was preoccupied underneath the car, poking body filler into a hole where the chassis had rusted away. When finally he noticed me he didn't seem embarrassed and finished filling the hole before stopping to talk. I went back later for another look and saw him brushing on underseal to hide the 'repair'. He had done a good job of camouflage and I could not tell where the hole had been. But it showed me the type of man he was and, sure enough, worse was to follow when my tyre stock started disappearing. He always worked Sunday mornings when I was at home. But he tripped himself up because the tyres that went missing all met the sizes that would fit his cars, mainly 14-inch tyres for the MGBs. He was not my tenant for long.

The next person to rent that part used it for a paint and body shop for his car repairs. He was a Frenchman, called A, and had lived and worked in Harrogate for a number of years before starting on his own. At first I thought A was quite different from the previous occupant: he was good at his job, pleasant and paid the rent promptly. I was pleased with the arrangement until one month-end when I went round to collect his rent cheque and got quite a shock. The door to his part of the garage had been left open but no one was there. I called his name but there was no response, so I went inside and looked around. He had obviously gone out to deliver or collect a car. As I walked back towards the door I passed close to the meter which measured his electric consumption from my main supply, something did not look right: the glass on the front was not quite in line. When I looked closer I saw that the seal put on by the Electricity Board had been broken and the screws loosened to allow the front panel to be moved slightly. I noticed also that though he had left the garage lights on the wheel of the meter was not going round; a small strip of celluloid similar to a camera film had been jammed in to stop it. He was stealing my electricity, the bastard. Our deal was rent plus electricity at cost, and while I was struggling to pay the bill he was enjoying free juice! Again, I said au revoir.

I rented out the forecourt complete with a small office to someone involved in car sales. I was pleased to get a little more income but this arrangement did not last long as the man who sold the cars turned out to be a gambler. After he sold a vehicle he would disappear around the corner to the nearby bookies in Westmorland Street. It was not a surprise when his business soon turned up its toes. The next man who came along to sell cars did not like to pay his rent and always made excuses when it was due. I could see that he was selling cars and making money so I waited till he went home one night and changed the lock on his office door, taking out and replacing the latch barrel. The next day was a Sunday and the phone at Ornhams Grange rang mid-way through the morning. The voice on the other end was irate, "I can't get into my bloody office Ken."' he said. I replied, "Who's office?" He got the message and paid the rent on time after that but didn't stay long. Finally, I was lucky and at last met a straight car dealer, one of a very rare breed. His name was Bob Nash and he always paid on time. I liked his company and we often had a drink together after work.

Meeting Bob was an isolated ray of sunshine when nothing else was going for me. As the noose tightened, interest rates did not come down and property values continued to decline. I was slipping further into debt and found it difficult to get supplies from the tyre wholesalers, having to pay cash on delivery. Only one man continued to help, a real friend called Malcolm from Knaresborough Tyres, but sadly he would also lose money when the crunch came. While the then Tory government sought to squeeze down inflation by high interest rates, I much prefer the Coalition's policies of today (2012) which keep rates low. Certainly, this is the lesser of two evils. I spoke to David Crowther, my long-standing accountant and friend from the 1970s, who said, "You have to face facts and rather than get further into trouble you should seek the protection of the bankruptcy court." He put me in touch with a man in Leeds who specialised in giving advice on bankruptcies. I went to see him and put my cards on the table. He looked at the figures before saying that by trying to keep going so long I had dug myself a bigger hole. "You will have to declare yourself bankrupt. It is the only way out and it will get them off your back." After the meeting I stood up to leave and said, "How much do I owe you?" He looked at me and smiled as he reached out shook my hand and said, "Nothing, have this one on me and the best of luck."

There were thousands, maybe even a million or more people in the same situation in the country at that time, but you can't help but take it personally. I had done all I could. I was not sleeping well and was bringing home my troubles. Drink helped me to get to sleep but not for long. I'd wake and lay there in the dark early mornings going over and over my problems. This of course disturbed Julia and led to friction between us. It was not her fault. Her clothes business was still doing well and out of it she paid many of our living expenses but a barrier came down between us. I moved into another bedroom thinking, "Is this the beginning of the end?" Sadly it was, as our relationship started to break up. The future looked bleak and I could see no way out.

CHAPTER SEVEN

BANKRUPTCY
1994

There was a newspaper cartoon that appeared several months after the US elections in 1992 showing the previous President, George H W Bush, wearing a dress and tied to a railway line in the style of silent film melodramas. Bush had been beaten in the previous year's elections by Bill Clinton and political pundits agreed that what did for him was the poor state of the US economy. The cartoon appeared in 1993 by which time there were signs of a dramatic recovery, but the train in the drawing had already run over Bush, mangling his chances just as the hero, named Economic Recovery, was galloping up to the rescue. Bush says with full sarcasm, "Gee, thanks a lot!" The point being that things improved too late for him, as they did for me too.

The move to close down my business operations came in 1994. The last few years of high interest rates meant that I couldn't pay my debts and my loans. The falling value of my properties meant I couldn't borrow more to meet my obligations. I was squeezed in a vice until there was nothing left. There was no help and the court-appointed receivers were prowling around like birds of prey. I had taken advice and registered at the Bankruptcy Court in Leeds, and now all the procedures had been completed. The idea was that at least I had a measure of protection, but as things turned out this was nothing like what I had hoped for. Eventually I was to lose my business and my home. To say my spirits were low is an understatement: I was devastated. All my life I had worked hard and tried to do the right thing, but here I was at 59-years of age and broke ... again! A very nice lady at the Court had given me forms to fill in and even helped me do so, but all I felt was embarrassment. In such circumstances you are a real loser and the nicer people are the worse you feel, and the harder you have to fight not to show it.

My final visit to the Bankruptcy Court was in late 1994. Now all the arrangements were completed and I would soon be hearing from them.

I walked out in a daze into bright Autumn sunlight. I could not get the thought out of my head, "59 and bankrupt. Will there be enough time left in my life to recover?" I felt light headed as I set off walking along the road through a small shopping precinct. It wasn't quite Ilkley in 1977 but my foot-steps sounded the same and the weight on my shoulders was as great. In the distance I could hear music and made my way almost automatically towards it. I approached a crowd of people gathered around a group of musicians playing country music from the Peruvian Andes. I stood there listening for a long time, feeling intoxicated. I don't think I had heard anything like it before. The group were playing traditional pipes, guitars and flutes, and since have become well known as APU. They are three brothers who come from the old Inca capital of Cusco and now live in this country. Their's is a mix of old and new Andean music with spellbinding rhythms and I for one was caught up in it, standing for what seemed like ages listening to them. Before I left I bought a copy of their CD, Music from the Andes, and still play it on occasions. Whenever I do my thoughts go back to that time. Perhaps you have heard them too?

The bailiffs move on Ornhams Grange

There was no one to talk to. You can't go into a pub for a drink and say, "Today I went bankrupt. How was your day?" But the wheels had been set in motion and it was not long before we received notice to vacate the premises as the buzzards began to gather. It has taken me a long time to get round to writing this chapter. I have thought about it, then written about some other part of my life, while I kept this on the back-burner. But it must be done even though it still hurts. What came next was one of the most difficult single days of my life, when the vultures came to Ornhams Grange to pick the last of the flesh off our bones. We had been given notice to quit the house and were dreading the arrival of the court bailiffs.

The night before had been almost never-ending with my mind whizzing over everything that had happened, and periodically settling on how happy we were when we first moved in Ornhams Grange. Julia and I had been so excited we could hardly sleep. Now on what was to be our last night in the house we could not sleep but for a very different reason – anxiety and remorse. That first night we were so happy in each others arms, now twelve years later we were in separate rooms!

There was no need for an alarm call, we were up early. A big van we had used over the previous weeks to move out most of our possessions was parked in the driveway. We still had a few things to gather from around the house. Julia felt very bitter about the way the court had allowed the creditors to hound us and she insisted on moving some items that otherwise we might have left, like the heavy cast iron gate at the entrance, the wooden gate leading from the garden into the field and some shrubs that had special significance. But she decided that the grape vine would have to stay.

I dug up a small tree we had planted to mark the spot where we buried our old dog Bessie, the Black Labrador that had come with us from Greenhow. Standing by Bessie's grave I could see the shrub had put down strong roots, just as we had over our twelve years of living at the Grange. I stood up straight to ease my back and take a final look around; everywhere I looked carried our stamp. I had trained the honeysuckle bush, growing big and strong by the wall, to hang like a saddle over both sides of the brickwork. When it was in bloom I could not resist the lovely smell, around dusk I would often wander out and stand by the bush becoming intoxicated by the fragrance. At the other side of the wall, sheltered in the corner, was our grape vine. It had never thrived given our northern latitude and the grapes grew only to the size of a currant and most of that was pip. I looked at the vegetable patch where we had worked so hard and were rewarded by the heavy crops growing well in the rich, sandy soil. Over by the front door under the eaves where the porch adjoined the house, I could see bits of straw from the remains of a spotted fly catcher's nest. For the previous two or three years a pair had nested there right under the porch. I often spied on them from the lounge window. They could be very patient; the one that was on food duty would perch on the edge of the porch in the evening looking for a meal, his or her eyes much sharper than mine. There would be a blur as it launched and flew round in a small loop before returning with a fly in its beak to feed the brood, then return to its perch. This would go on for hours.

I heard a car pull into the drive and shook myself from my thoughts. There was one car, then a second and eventually a damned convoy of them. I finished digging up Bessie's tree, wrapped it in plastic and carried it to my van. The bailiffs were there getting out of their fancy cars, three men and a woman all well-dressed no doubt from the proceeds of unfortunate people like Julia and me. They had assistants but no police or security men, presumably expecting us to go quietly. Everyone is entitled to earn a living but what kind of people are they that get rich from the misfortune of others. I despised them.

I felt really pissed off when I saw them in a huddle with papers and clip boards ready to view their plunder and then decide who would get first choice before it went to the market. I was wound up inside thinking of how hard I had worked, worried and stayed awake at night. If I had been feeling sorry for myself and Julia a few weeks before when leaving the Bankruptcy Court, now I became angry. Everything had slipped through my fingers. Maybe it was a good thing that my guns had been sold because I would have been tempted to fire a blast over their heads to scare the shit out of the scavengers. But there were no guns and it took only a moment for me to regain my control. In reality, it was only me who could be blamed, not having insisted on selling the house when it would have meant a smaller loan.

Ignoring the bailiffs, we put the last items in the van in silence. Not a word was spoken as I drove out of the yard without even a glance at the intruders. I turned left down the A1 and away from what had been a lovely and for most of the time a happy home. I could not avoid a last glimpse out of the corner of my eye knowing this would haunt me for the rest of my life. I still have bad dreams about the place and writing this chapter has brought much back to me.

Now they take the Garage

A few days later another court-appointed receiver arrived at the garage. He was quite pleasant at first but had a job to do and since his office was near Huddersfield he wanted to get it over and done with quickly. This meant he rushed things and was careless; after all who was he to give a hoot. There was so much equity from the house that the receiver could easily get what was owing to the loan sharks from that, meaning he ended up selling the garage for a song. I was left with nothing. The man who bought Yewdale Garage - stole it in fact - offered to rent it back to me if I wanted to continue selling tyres. I stayed for a while to get a little money together and dispose of a few things, but the sight of his wife calling for the rent, book in hand, turned my stomach. I could not bring myself to pay a man who I felt had profited from my misfortune, so I walked away.

There was no reconciliation for Julia and me and we went our separate ways, Julia to a flat in Starbeck and me to a caravan site in the Bilton area of Harrogate. My elder sister Freda lived in a residential caravan on the same site and told me of one that was for sale. It was old and run down, and the rain leaked in during storms, but it could be purchased cheap, patched up and made into somewhere decent to live. I bought it and started the job of making it habitable.

Another loss

On our site, caravan owners were not allowed to keep dogs so Julia had Bella during the week and I had her at weekends. This worked well as I loved taking the dog on walks around the River Nidd. Then one day Julia rang to say that she had taken Bella with her to a barbecue. They ate corn on the cob and Bella had been chewing the husks and had swallowed some causing a blockage. She had been taken to the vet who operated to remove them. He thought that she would recover but the next day poor Bella died. When Julia rang to tell me she could hardly speak for sobbing. She felt responsible as Bella was in her charge and she also knew how much I loved her. Now I had the painful job of burying Bella. I collected her from Julia's flat, carrying her away in my arms. Other people's dogs often smell bad to me, but Bella had a nice odour, I brought her to my caravan and dug a grave in a strip of grass by a hedge under the trees. For once, I had little strength. I felt gutted and confess that tears fell on the soil and spade as I dug. Tree roots made it harder toil but I wanted Bella to be in a nice sheltered spot where she would never be disturbed. It took a long time to cut through the roots and get the hole big enough. I was not going to bundle her in but wanted to make her as comfortable as if she had been asleep. Eventually it was done and I spread her bed on the bottom and gently laid her on top, then covered her with her blanket and laid her dish beside her. Last of all I put in her lead. I would not be needing it for another dog as I had decided there was not going to be one. Bella would be a hard act to follow. I stood silent for a moment and tried to remember the last time I had cried. She was a wonderful dog, a thinking dog and we were very close as only dog lovers will fully understand. But I guess I was also crying for all that had gone wrong. When my financial problems had driven a wedge between Julia and me, Julia did not welcome me home as before. But Bella was always there sitting on the back step, gazing out towards the road, waiting for my arrival. In those difficult times she was this man's best friend. I covered her first with fine soil as I didn't want stones to land on her and, eventually, she was gone from view in a mound of soil. I placed bricks around the border and thought of putting a photograph of her on the tree as they do by graves in Italy. But I kept it for my bedroom where it stands to this day. I had lost my business, garage, home and partner, and now I had lost my dog.

I still see Julia quite often and we remain friends, but Ornhams Grange is never mentioned and when I pass the house on the A1 I look the other way. It is a reminder of me falling off the housing ladder for a second time, and ending up living alone in a leaky old caravan.

CHAPTER EIGHT

WORKING FOR OTHERS
A new start and a fresh direction

At the age of sixty I could have felt the game was up. My first round of business ventures in the 1970s had failed and now twenty years later a second had gone the same way. Though I had been a victim of circumstances beyond my control any fault was down to me as I took on the huge loan instead of moving house. Now what was left, I had been down this road before and hadn't found it easy to bounce back when I was much younger. How was I going to cope?

Now this isn't a positive way of thinking, I told myself. I could live for decades. I had always kept myself fit, hadn't smoked except for the occasional cigar and drinking was under control. Thanks to a lifetime of hard, physical work in the outdoors I was healthier than most of my contemporaries. I thought, "To hell with this, I am going to change course. I am going to do what I want to do, and keep out of debt" My small private pension could be drawn any time after my 60th birthday. "Draw it as soon as you can," said my Accountant David Crowther. "Who knows how long you will live," he added somewhat more so disconcertingly. So I did.

The first job was to improve my accommodation which was going to be a lot easier than the building work on the Old School House at Greenhow. I patched and painted the old caravan, then thought, "What next?" What would anyone do in such circumstances? What had I dreamed up when I was a little boy in Red Lane, Masham? Learn to fly; that's it. I am never going to become an airline or fighter pilot at my age but there has to be something that is practical. So, as I passed into my seventh decade I joined a flying school to learn to paraglide. I wanted also to do good work for others, so I made contact with a local charity volunteering to take humanitarian aid to Romania. I still had time on my hands and needed an income even if only a small one, so I took on part time work for an old friend Martyn Senior. In a few weeks I was back on my feet, not quite a changed man but one who had found a new direction. With my new-found positive outlook, it was now time to get on with the rest of my life.

One of my tasks for Martyn was to help him fit LPG (liquid petroleum gas) conversions to cars and vans. Gas was much cheaper than petrol and he had a line of customers queuing up for the conversions. I fitted the LPG tanks and helped out with everything else. At the time I had a petrol Transit van and decided to change it to run on LPG. I did most of the work and paid Martyn for the kit and his expertise in setting it up. We fitted a very large tank so I could go longer distances between refuelling. I was very pleased when it was finished as it was smoother and quieter than a diesel fuelled vehicle. I was hoping it would be much cheaper to run, but I was to be disappointed.

I had made friends with Chris Seals an instructor at the paragliding school and the two of us decided to go to Spain with our gliders to meet up with other pilots. We would go in the Transit van as it would be a good test for the conversion. It was not a camper van but at night we could sleep in the back in our sleeping bags. And even though it was early Spring and still chilly in Yorkshire, Spain would be much warmer we reckoned. We set off in a blaze of optimism and with a little grey cloud of LPG following us down to the Channel, across on a ferry and onto the roads of France pointing south. But it never became warmer. In fact, if anything it was colder in France and Spain than it had been in England. It was no fun at all sleeping in the back of the van. It was not lined out like a camper van. The thin tin panels gave little protection from the cold outside as we huddled in our sleeping bags. One night I thought I was going to freeze to death as the inside iced up while we slept. The new fuel was no consolation either as the engine ran cold was thirsty, and we were on constant look-out for filling stations. While these were fairly plentiful in France, when we arrived in Spain we often could not find any LPG at all. Luckily, the Transit was still able to run on petrol so we used that in Spain – and paid the higher price.

Eventually, we reached the south of Spain and the temperature started to pick up and our holiday began to look as if it would take a turn for the better.

But it came too late for Chris who had a severe attack of homesickness. There was nothing for it but to turn around and go home. We picked the most direct route we could find on the map, straight through the mountainous country to Madrid. It was a long drag climbing up through steep hills to the Spanish capital. The van had no power and a head wind made things even worse as it was a big vehicle. The weather grew colder again and we were back to facing long shivering nights in our sleeping bags. I was very pleased when at last we made it back to Harrogate.

I cursed the decision to convert to LPG. I think it works better on cars and light vans but bigger commercial vehicles need to run on diesel. So the van was put up for sale. Martyn was not happy at this as he had done me a special deal on the conversion and of course he was very biased towards LPG. We did not fall out, though, and I continued to work for him. There was soon response to the advert including one from a man in Scotland who was very keen and said he would come down the next day with the money. Well, I could not argue with that but my experience of the motor trade had left me a little sceptical. However, next morning there was a pleasant surprise when he phoned to say he was on his way and expected to arrive about mid-day. When he saw the van complete with the new conversion and the large LPG tank his face lit up. I was expecting some tough haggling but he was full of enthusiasm and accepted my price without question. He took out of his pocket £3,250 in new Scottish £20 and £10 notes and counted them out one by one. Now it was the turn of my face to light up. The notes were so new I could smell and even taste the oily printing as I wet my fingers to check his counting. I scribbled a receipt, gave him the documents and test certificate, shook hands and closed the deal. I filled the tank with gas and he drove away happy.

Suddenly, a black cloud went across my mind. I had signed the vehicle over to him and he had gone off with both van and ownership title. What was I left holding? £3,250 in forged Scottish notes? How was I to know? Was that why he was so eager to get the deal done? I felt a bit uneasy. When he first gave me the money the thought crossed my mind that I wouldn't know if they were forged, but what was I to do, ask him for a cheque?

The next day I drove around to the bank and before going in drew some cash from the ATM machine. Then I joined the queue for a teller. As I waited I took an English £20 and a £10 note replaced them with Scottish notes then paid in £80. With them tucked in the middle. The cashier flicked through them then tucked them with others into a drawer. She stamped my paying in book and said, "Thank you Mr Walker. Have a good day." I turned and walked out looking more casual than I felt. I was not home and dry and there would be further scrutinising done later in the day at the bank, and I waited for a call. I knew that if you pay counterfeit notes into the bank they would be confiscated and you would have a lot of explaining to do to the local constabulary. I didn't want that. But no call came and two days later I was back in the bank paying in a few more of the Scottish banknotes. Again, there was no call, so I started to relax, they were genuine after all and soon trickled away.

Because of my move to the mobile home at Village Farm, Bilton, I had cut my living expenses. The pension would give me an income and I would supplement this with other money-making enterprises. This would leave time for other things I wanted to do, principally travel and paragliding. Around these I devoted a large slice of time to charity work in Romania. All of this will be covered in this and the succeeding two chapters of this book, which need to be understood as different strands of my life which happened more or less simultaneously over a dozen or so years from 1995.

Tools of trade

First I need to go back in time to the final moments of my bankruptcy. I was closing the Yewdale Garage prior to its fire-sale by the receivers and had sold most of the items that the receiver had let me keep - plus a few items he did not know about. In bankruptcy a man is allowed to keep his 'tools of trade' to enable him to make a living. In my case these were the tyre fitting machine, the wheel balancer and various hand tools used in the tyre business. To raise a little money I advertised them in the Yorkshire Post. I had several enquiries, one from a foreign-sounding gentleman from Keighley who soon arrived with a car and trailer, and three assistants. He came into my office, while unseen by me the others dispersed around the garage. He came from Pakistan, a part of the world where you haggle for everything you buy. His favourite phrase was, "Mr Walker, what is you last price? " My experience of the car trade stood me in good stead and I was able to ensure we arrived at a fair deal for the equipment. One of the advantages of dealing with people from his part of the world was that when you finally agree a price they always paid cash.

While we were in discussion in the office, I was aware his entourage were keeping out of my sight. Luckily my loyal helper Kenny Cowan had been keeping an eye on them, and he suddenly appeared in the doorway and motioned me to follow him into the garage. When I drew close he whispered, "One of them has taken our pneumatic air gun and put it into the back of their car. I saw that and there may be other things disappearing too." I looked across the garage to the place on the wall where the gun used for speedy removal of wheel nuts always hung. It was missing. Kenny, was a man of few words – unless he was selling a car that is ... but he was wide awake and pointed to the culprit. I immediately confronted him. He gave me an innocent look, shrugged his shoulders and held out his hands palms up in the international gesture to indicate he didn't understand.

Clearly there was no point in arguing with him. I walked back to my office where the first gentleman was hovering. I ignored him while picking up the telephone and pretending to dial a number, saying down the receiver in a loud voice, "I want to report a theft. Will you send an officer round to Yewdale Garage as soon as possible? If you can spare two it would be better as there are several of them." I was interrupted by the Asian gentleman. "No, no, just wait a minute," he said. Changing into his native language he bellowed out into the garage to his assistants. After a flurry of words the meaning of which I could guess, one of them rushed to their car and returned holding the gun. Kenny took it from him and gave a quick check to make sure nothing else had been secreted away. I went back to the phone and made another pretend call, this time cancelling my request for police assistance. After that, it was a simple matter to close the deal on all the equipment. I was handed the cash while they brought around their trailer. As they climbed into the car to leave we had a final check to make sure that nothing else was leaving with them.

Meeting Beryl

When I was still at the garage one of my customers a fellow called Dave told me that he had joined a singles club, which met weekly in a hotel on the outskirts of York. It was reserved for older (or should I say more mature) people. "Would you like to come along?" he said. Well, Dave was what you might say a bit rough, but I liked the idea and as I could never walk into such a place on my own it was important to have someone to accompany. "We can go in my car," he said. Dave was a jobbing builder and his car was also his work vehicle with tools piled on the back seat and everything covered in cement dust. It was more of a shed than a motor vehicle and was not an auspicious way of meeting members of the opposite sex.

Going to the club was like turning the clock back to my days of attending dances around Masham in the early 1950s. On the way to the hotel we stopped off at a pub for a pint to give us extra confidence. Thus emboldened we parked at the back of the hotel, well away from other vehicles to reduce the chance that any would-be conquest would see 'the shed' before he was ready to break the news. He put on the hand brake, reached over to the glove compartment and pulled out his false teeth. These were given a quick wipe on his sleeve and were then popped into his mouth, giving me a huge smile in the process. "That's better. I must look my best and there might be some grub," he said, while I dusted myself down from the cement dust. Inside the hotel, he said, "I wonder if I am going to find my rich widow tonight." He wandered around before stopping to talk to two women at a table. I followed and spoke to one of them, a lady with an attractive smile which was nearly ruined by an awful pair of white-rimmed glasses in the Dame Edna Everidge style. We chatted for a while and she was friendly, but I felt awkward and like a fish out of water after so many years with a steady partner. Dave and I circulated among others in the room until it was time to go.

The following week this same singles group had arranged another meeting, this time in a Bradford hotel, with the object of listening to Cajun music. We had made a nice enough impact and were invited to go along. This time, I insisted we went in my car. The music was fabulous but there was little chance to get to know anyone.

Two weeks later we were back in York. Dave continued his search for a rich widow while I looked for the woman with the white rimmed glasses who I had found friendly and who had stuck in my mind. At first I couldn't see her, but then I realised that the glasses had gone and she was now wearing contact lenses. It was a very pleasant surprise. She looked far more attractive and I decided to get to know her better, offered to get her a drink and stayed close. She said her name was Beryl Alban and she taught at an infants school near to her home in Wetherby. Like me she was on her own, though in her case this had come about through the tragic death of her husband Eric from cancer in 1993.

Beryl had been born in April 1943 in Newton-le-Willows, Lancashire. She met Eric at the local Grammar School. They then went on to train as teachers. After qualifying they married in 1966. Their daughter, Shirley Amanda Jane Alban, was born in September 1967. In fact, Shirley came to play an important role in my story when she suggested to her mother that she write the story of how her parents met, which started me thinking about putting my own tale down on paper. Beryl pursued her career as a school teacher and when we met was responsible for the reception year at a primary school in Alwoodley, Leeds.

Beryl and I hit it off from the start though we came from different worlds. We started meeting regularly – and still do. She keeps her space in her home in Wetherby and I have mine in my mobile home in Bilton, but we have stayed close sharing each other's lives ever since. And I, for one, have never regretted a day of it.

Celebrating New Year with Beryl - 1998/9

Van and car dealing

My years of dealing in second-hand cars did not go to waste as I carried on buying and selling vehicles. I concentrated on vans, but also traded in plant equipment and the occasional car as a way of keeping busy and earning a little money. Unwilling as I was to rent commercial property after the debacle at Regents Parade, I found I could use space beside my mobile home at Village Farm for cleaning and minor repairs. As before, the places where I bought most of my vehicles were at the auctions, a habit inherited from my grandparents that had stayed with me over the decades.

Although I never earned great sums, this dealing brought in useful amounts and I was able to combine my many years' experience with engines which went all the way back to our little terraced house in Red Lane, Masham. There my father would get me to identify the different feeler gauges by touch to impress his friends though I was probably not more than four or five. When we lived in Cambridgeshire during the war I would be pulled out of school to work on laid-up cars dad had bought. By the age of ten I knew how to change the oil, strip a carburettor, change and reset plugs and points and tune an engine. This knowledge had repaid dividends when I bought my first motorbike and rebuilt the engine. Now, I rediscovered how much I enjoyed doing the work. So it was really like combining a way to earn money with a hobby; my grandfather's words, "Have a hobby that pays," came back to me. Though the mechanical work was good fun, I didn't enjoy the wheeler-dealing as much. Once I had a vehicle ready for sale it would be advertised. Many of those interested would be also involved in some form of commercial buying and selling, and many were crooks of one sort or another, as I had said before. Some would try to con me. Two or three would arrive together and try to intimidate me. I did not like it and in the end my attitude towards finding a compromise solution probably meant I missed out on bigger profits.

All ran well until around the turn of the millennium in 2000 when I lost out big time due to the finagling of insurance companies, proving that it isn't just motor traders who cheat. I had converted a VW minibus into a camper van, taking out the seats, and having it fitted out with beds, sink, cooker, curtains and all the necessary fittings. I came to an agreement with a motor dealer friend to offer the camper for sale on his forecourt at Killinghall alongside his vehicles. Though it was clamped for security, thieves came in the middle of the night cut off the clamp and stole it. It was never recovered. My insurance company refused to pay because it had been taken from commercial premises that were not my own, and my friend's insurers likewise refused compensation because he did not own the vehicle. I lost out on about £7,000 and that was that for me with motor dealing. From now on, I thought, I'd find something else to supplement my pension.

Cutters from China

In 2004 Beryl and I went for a Down Under holiday to visit my old National Service friend, Stan Thompson, who was living in Adelaide, Australia. There was a story behind this as he had visited my wife Wendy and me 45 years before. Like me he was driving buses, though his routes were all in Cumberland. At the time Wendy and I were talking about emigrating to Australia and our enthusiasm had a great effect on him. When he went back to Whitehaven we lost contact but unbeknown to us he had gone home made plans and emigrated. In the meantime, we had started a family and Wendy was having second thoughts about leaving elderly parents,(well into their fifties)! So we never went. All this is recounted in my first book, *Nothing Easy*. Contact with Stan had been lost but the wonders of the internet had put us both back in contact by 2004. "You must come out and stay with me and my family," he wrote ... and so we did.

It was a great holiday and I have to say I felt real regret in never having gone like Stan to what is a beautiful and exciting country. I am sure that with my practical and rural skills I would have prospered. Towards the end of our holiday I went with Stan to a garden centre and saw Chinese-made garden tools being sold at very low prices. Once I was back in Yorkshire I turned on the computer to locate Chinese suppliers of garden tools through the internet. There are plenty of them and they are very keen to sell to you but want orders for container loads. I was never going to be able to manage this sort of quantity and carried on shopping around, eventually finding a supplier who would ship a small order of 10,000 secateurs at a go. Again, it was a matter of money up-front and my caravan had again to serve as a warehouse. By late 2005 I was in a new business and I dropped the animal medicines.

Selling secateurs was a good business. Such was the low cost of the products and the low overheads under which I operated, that I was able to sell the tools very cheaply. At first it was a matter of standing around at car boot sales, but then garden centres in the area became regular customers. Later, I formed a website and took orders over the internet. I placed more orders with firms in China and carried on making a modest but useful income to, the present day.

Sri Lanka December 2003

"Hello is that Ken Walker? Gordon Brown here." I had not heard from Gordon for some time He asked me what I was doing. "Nothing much." "Well, I have just the job for you" he said. "If you're interested in a trip to Sri Lanka come and see me."

First off, who was Gordon Brown? Well, not the man who was to become the Prime Minister in 2007. I had known this Gordon Brown since the early 1960s with his brothers he owned first an agricultural equipment company, and then expanded into a trucking and plant hire business in Otley. Thirty years earlier he had been my main local competitor when we both hired out JCB diggers and excavators. He often tried to pinch my customers and drivers. But in later years any rivalry vanished and we became good friends. Gordon was one of three brothers but he was the most entrepreneurial and had been the leading light and responsible for their meteoric rise in the construction industry but like me, he had known life's ups and downs, though his ups had been higher than mine and his lows were not so far down. Companies had come and gone, but by the late 1990s he was doing well again, trading as Weston Plant at Pool-in-Wharfedale near Otley, assisted by his wife Liz, son Simon and daughter Tina now more of a family business. His main activity was trading in construction equipment, both new and second-hand, buying and selling all around the world.

I had been with Gordon to a few construction equipment exhibitions helping on the stand and enjoyed it but this one sounded exciting, a part of the world that I had never been to. "Can you go to Sri Lanka tomorrow?" My hearing is not good but did he say Sri Lanka, and just as casual as saying Leeds or Skipton? "I want you to supervise the loading of a shipment of excavators? The excavators will be brought to the UK by cargo ship and I need someone I can depend on." "Could I? I certainly could," I assured him. This was a great opportunity to see a part of the world I had never been to, yet had always wanted to visit. He gave me a run down on what I would have to do. As usual, it was 'all go' with Gordon. He never seemed to plan much ahead: what he wanted, he wanted straight away. So the following day I was on my way. It was a long trip. Leeds Bradford Airport to Manchester, then on to Dubai for another change of aircraft before the final leg on Air Lanka down to Colombo, the capital of Sri Lanka. This was December 2003.

Colombo felt like another world. Everything was so interesting and a complete change of culture as I looked out from the taxi on the way to the luxury Ceylon Continental Hotel. I had seen a little of the world but nothing like this and I was fascinated. Gordon's son Simon had stayed there the week before and I booked in to the same Hotel. The scenic views were magnificent. My room looked out over the sea, calm and blue, with just a few breakers gently rolling in and lapping the shore. There was not a cloud in the clear blue sky. It was hot with a gentle cool breeze blowing off the sea. The air felt good and revived me after my long hours of travel. I walked around the hotel being greeted by the staff, who were attentive and helpful. There were tall, dark, slim, beautiful women in long, brightly coloured dresses waiting to answer your questions. I ate a very good meal in the restaurant, followed by a single beer, then retired to my room and read for a short while before falling asleep.

The next day I tried to speak to my contact, a Korean gentleman called Mr Park, who was never on the number Gordon had given me and didn't call back. I tried for a long time before giving up, leaving a message and the hotel details. He'll call me when he can, I thought, as I opted to explore the town. Outside the hotel there was a row of smart taxis for the convenience of hotel guests, while further up the road, almost out of sight, was another row of smaller taxis of an entirely different sort. These were the little three-wheeler 'put-puts' you find across Asia, and were much cheaper. Instinct told me these would be better, and though I was on expenses, I thought riding around in one of these would be more fun. One of the drivers stepped forward and asked if I would like to be shown Colombo. He was polite and I took a shine to him. I liked him even more when he told me how much he'd charge for a two hour tour. His name was Zampata and he said I could always find him on this stretch of road as put-puts were not allowed closer to the hotel. "Mine is the only green one so you will easily see me," he added. Thereafter, I used him to get around every day I was in Colombo.

Ken with the taxi driver Zampata, Colombo 2003

I climbed in the back while he straddled the scooter and revved up, white smoke puffing out behind leaving the air thick with the sickly smell of two-stroke petrol. He drove along the coast road to the centre of the city, giving me a commentary on history and culture, and pointing out places of interest. There are many different religions in Sri Lanka with a mixture of temples, ashrams, mosques and churches on almost every street. We stopped off to see a magnificent Buddhist temple covered with intricately carved figures and a little further on we called in to visit the famous Murugan Hindu temple. Zampata took me to a bazaar where they sold precious stones of every type and colour. There was no doubt he was on a bit of a commission from the stallholders but that didn't interfere with my enjoyment, as I was not in the market to buy.

However, I did purchase something as we left. Sitting on a box by the entrance was an old man

Hinau Temple Colombo, Sri Lanka

selling stamps, old postcards and coins. These were pinned on a piece of old cardboard beside him. The postcards were covered with cling film and looked tatty and worthless but I looked at the prices being asked. The whole lot wouldn't have bought a first class stamp in UK, and the old man certainly looked like he needed the money. I was about to put my hand in my pocket, when Zampata whispered in my ear, "You don't have to pay the marked price. Make him an offer." Frankly, given the low cost anyway I couldn't bring myself to do this but bought the whole display at the price marked, and added a little something extra, which brought me a wrinkled grin from the old man. I still have the card. Some of the old stamps date back to the time when the country was coloured pink on a map, occupied by the British and called Ceylon.

I bought many packets of tea in lovely presentation packs to take home as gifts. They are very proud of the quality of Ceylonese tea introduced by The British in the 1960s. There were many reminders of the British. We went to a museum to see relics of British engineering –including an old Aveling Barford Steam Road Roller circa 1900. It

Old Aveling Barford Roller

had not steamed for many years and stood with other road making machines out in the open courtyard of the museum, gently rusting away. Zampata took me to see the monument that had been erected to commemorate Sri Lanka's independence, granted on the 4th February 1948 soon after neighbouring India had become an independent nation.

The traffic was heavy in the centre of Colombo. This was the case all day and much of the night and not just during rush hour. The congestion was made worse by the absence of traffic lights, roundabouts or any other control at intersections. This gave way to a general free-for-all. If Zampata needed to cross one of the busy roads he just threaded his way through six lanes of slow moving traffic tooting his horn, as did almost everyone else. Remarkably, everyone seemed to remain good humoured - unlike in Britain, where the much less frequent blast from a horn might be accompanied by a two-fingered gesture. Zampata explained that in Sri Lanka they toot the horn to say, "I am here; I am here," rather than "Get out of my way." What a wonderful outlook but it did make for something of a din! Sri Lankan attitudes on the road are calm and conciliatory, and no one tries to carve up or rush to close a space. The system works in such heavy traffic and while driving in the city is slow, it still flows.

Finally, we did come across one set of traffic lights, at which we stopped. A large lorry pulled up alongside us, its wooden body painted red and brightly decorated with artistic figures and designs. I recognised the throb of a Leyland 400 diesel engine, a thought confirmed by the great front wheel so close to me I could almost touch the Leyland badge in its centre. I looked up at the cab and was surprised to see the door was missing. The driver wore only a pair of shorts, his left hand on the tall gear stick, his right on the steering wheel. Two bare feet hovered over the clutch and accelerator. Those controls were so familiar to me. It was an old Leyland Comet, the same type I had acquired for my transport fleet in the early 1970s. I had driven thousands of miles using those very same controls, though never with bare feet. In the UK, old Leyland wagons such as this were rusting in scrap yards after having the engines removed to be sold for power boats. Here in Colombo, there were many still in regular use, while we were buying only foreign-built trucks.

Mr Park doesn't show

I started to worry that I had not heard from Mr Park. I managed to get a message back to Gordon Brown and explained my predicament. After checking, he sent a note back saying that after struggling himself to raise his contact, he had finally managed to speak to him and I would be hearing before too long. All I had to do was to supervise the loading of the Caterpillar earth moving machinery onto a cargo ship when it arrived, make sure everything was secure and note down the serial numbers before coming home for Christmas.

So I remained patient. Eventually, I was able to reach Mr Park on the telephone He was a fast-talking South Korean and it was difficult for me to know exactly what he was saying. As far as I could tell he apologised for the delay, said it was none of his fault, then reassured me that the overdue ship would arrive at any moment. It would stay in port for just two days so I need to keep my time flexible and be ready to respond when called. I asked him where the equipment was being kept and he told me that it was in a secure compound lower down the coast, but added that on no account was I to visit the place. My suspicions grew. Something was not right about all this and I felt I owed it to Gordon Brown to check things out. On my own initiative I decided to look for the compound.

I went and collected my camera, before walking up the hill to the put-put taxi rank. I was in a strange country and was about to take on something that could prove to be a little dangerous, or at least foolish. What I needed was someone I could trust. Sure enough Zampata was there. I explained to him that I wanted to find this compound, adding that I had neither address nor location. Resourceful as ever, Zampata told me he knew how to find out and convened a meeting of the large group of other put-put drivers. After a short and very lively conversation in Sinhalese one of the drivers called for quiet. They all simmered down as he pointed down the coast, explaining to Zampata how to find what we were looking for. Zampata turned to me, raised his eyebrows and smiled. "I can't be sure but one of the drivers thinks he knows where the earth movers are being kept. But if he is right it is a compound that is being guarded by the military. Why would they need to do that? It is close to a new road that is partly completed and where the machines were being used until recently. Work came to a standstill when the contractors ran out of money." It all sounded dodgy.

I jumped into Zampata's put-put. He revved up and we shot off towards the coast road leaving behind a cloud of smoke and one or two disgruntled taxi drivers, as Zampata had been waiting his turn halfway down the line but had jumped the queue to take me.

It took over an hour and I don't know if Zampata deliberately took me through the poor, run-down areas to let me see the poverty in the country. He knew that I was interested in seeing all aspects of life in Sri Lanka and not only the tourist areas. We wound our way through the dusty streets of the industrial area down by the port and finally found what seemed to be the right place. He pulled up at the side of the road and we got out to look around. There was a high wire fence surrounding the compound and through I could see Caterpillar machines lined up in neat rows. There were armed soldiers and police on the gate and patrolling the area. Deciding that I was in for a penny, I walked up to a little wooden shack that appeared to be the office and decided to bluff my way in. I had been spotted as I arrived and I guessed no one thought I could be particularly important as I had arrived in the back of a put-put. This seemed to help. I spoke to the most important looking man in inform, putting on an air of authority, while being careful not to overdo it and remain polite.

"I am from England and have been sent to look over the machines in this compound, check their serial numbers and inspect their general condition." The uniformed officer reached out and shook my hand, saying he would have to speak to his superiors before he could let me into the compound. He walked across to the telephone and spoke to someone in Sinhalese. After a few minutes he broke off to ask who had authorised my visit. I replied, "Gordon Brown in the UK," adding that it had not been possible to give prior warning as they only found out yesterday that I was here on holiday and asked if I would undertake this assignment at short notice. He took his hand off the mouthpiece and returned to the conversation in Sinhalese, his free hand moving back and forth between me and the distant machines, By his expression I think he was having a tussle with whoever was on the other end of the line but I did hear the name Gordon Brown mentioned more than once. Eventually he put down the phone turned to me and almost smiled. At the same time he instructed two of his men to escort me to where the machines were lying on the far side of the fence. At that point Zampata bravely came forward to join me but was immediately turned back and pushed roughly back outside. I walked towards the machines, escorted by a guard with a rifle on either side.

In my notebook I wrote down the number of machines and the serial numbers. The machines were a mixture of loaders and bulldozers but did not have cabs as in UK, but only a little canvas canopy over where the driver sat to shield him from the sun. I noticed more guards standing by the machines and others by the perimeter fence. They were certainly being well protected. Then I saw some white United Nations signs. When we got back to the gate

I thanked El Capo and we left. It was now evening and with Zampata raced back to the hotel as fast as the put-put could manage. This time we went by a more direct route.

With the time difference between Colombo and Otley, Weston Plant would be now opening for business. I called Gordon and asked him to ring back to save phone charges. He called immediately. I explained my meeting and my cloak and dagger work in finding out the location and the connection to the United Nations. I apologised if I had done wrong but felt I ought to check things out on his behalf. Nothing, I said, seemed proper. I added details about the huge United Nations-sponsored projects being carried out in civil war-torn Sri Lanka to try to revive its economy, which I had learned from Zampata. The question of who owned the earth moving equipment and who had the authority to sell it to Gordon Brown hung in the air. Gordon listened intently. His first comment was that I had acted correctly and he explained he was pleased with the important information I had told him. "Ok," I said, feeling greatly relieved. "What do you want me to do now? Christmas is approaching and I am told that the docks will shortly close down until after New Year which is still two weeks away. The machinery will not be loaded before so I think it will be some time before anything further happens. Shall I stay or come back?" Gordon thought for a moment, then said I should return to Yorkshire. We would look at things again in the New Year.

A test match in Colombo

I found that it would take a couple of days to sort myself a flight back to the UK. Meanwhile, I thought, I might make good use of the free time. I had seen on the hotel noticeboard information about a trip to Kandy and the Elephant Orphanage at Pinnawala. I made enquiries but learned that the next trip would be in a few days and could clash with my flight. However there was something else interesting going on at the same time which I could fit in: a cricket test match between Sri Lanka and the visiting England team. Though I'm not a great cricket fan I thought this was an opportunity not to be missed. With Zampata's help I managed to get a ticket and he dropped me at the back entrance to the Sinhalese Sport Club Ground where I bought a sun hat to protect my pate.

England were batting. As I made my way into the stand I looked at my ticket for a seat number. On the corner it read Lanka Bell Pavilion 21. There were no numbered seats only rows of wooden benches packed with very happy locals as England were being well and truly thumped. I walked towards the far end of the stand searching for somewhere to sit when I noticed a group of who I took to be England supporters. As I made my way towards them, there was a huge roar from the crowd and the group I was approaching jumped up from their seats and joined in the celebrations. I looked across to the pitch where I could see the stumps splayed and an England batsman – Mark Butcher I think it was - walking, head down, back towards the pavilion. All around the ground there was ecstatic applause. What sort of England supporters were these, I wondered? As things quietened down I picked up their accents and realised they weren't English at all, but Australians, and, of course, they were all supporting Sri Lanka. If they spotted me I was in for some real mickey-taking, so I did a quick u-turn and went back to sit with the local Sri Lankans who at least offered me some sympathy.

I was impressed by the enterprise of one young man. He had strapped on his back a large plastic tank, the kind you see used by council workers to spray weeds. A pipe with a tap on the end led round to the front where he had a tray of plastic cups. Through the pipe he was dispensing a local beer, which I can tell you was very good and cheap. I watched the game and really quite enjoyed it, although England were to lose by an innings and 215 runs and with it the three-match series, having drawn the first two.

Zampata picked me up in the evening. On the way back to the hotel he told me about his put-put taxi. Some years before he had purchased a Lambretta scooter and with a friend had converted a wagon on the back. They had cut a trailer in half, fabricated the rear part with two wheels and seating for two passengers, then welded it together, finally fitting a hood to keep off the sun. The reason it was painted green was because that was the only colour they could find at that particular time. It worked well for him as this was the only green put-put in that part of Colombo and his taxi always stood out.

At last, it was time for my flight and Zampata took me to the airport and helped with my bags. We shook hands for the last time. Over the few days I had been in Colombo we had established a real bond. All through my stay he was kind and helpful. He clearly enjoyed being a taxi driver and most unusually seemed embarrassed when asking for payment so I always topped up his asking price. I never did return to Colombo – Gordon realised the excavator deal was fishy in the extreme. In the New Year he told me the deal was off. We heard that the machines were later loaded on a ship in Colombo, before being taken off at another port and as far as anyone knew had remained in the country. Possibly someone had parted with money when the ship first left port, but they are unlikely ever to have taken delivery. Everything was dodgy about this deal. In time, I read about other corrupt practices with United Nations equipment earmarked for aid schemes.

In December 2004, almost exactly to the day a year after my flight home from Colombo airport the Boxing Day Tsunami struck Sri Lanka, devastating much of that lovely country and taking the lives of some 35,000 people. Colombo was affected badly. I watched the TV news and caught glimpses of the places I had seen the year before, but now wiped out. I will never know if my friendly taxi driver Zampata survived, but I do hope he did.

CHAPTER NINE

CHARITY WORKER
1996 - 2001

So, back to the mid-1990s. As described, I had occasional work from Gordon and eventually a few business ventures … vehicles, animal medicines and secateurs on the go. Together, these and my private pension provided an income and living on the caravan park at Village Farm kept my expenses modest. With this financial cushion and time on my hands my mind turned to some of the things I had always wanted to do. Foreign travel headed the list, whilst I felt that I had been in some ways unfortunate there were many more in the world much less fortunate than me maybe I could help, combine the two while my legs were still strong. I had been following media stories about volunteers from Britain who were taking supplies to the then troubled countries of Eastern Europe. This caught my attention.

In 1996 my younger sister Connie was living in Bingley and often looked in at the local charity shops. Thinking I might be interested, she put me on to one of the helpers who had recently returned from humanitarian trips to Bosnia and Romania with a local charity. Nora, the lady in question, told me about her work and painted a bleak picture of long journeys, travelling day and night, being held up at borders, getting lost and even being arrested, but adding of the pleasure of helping those in much more trouble. It all sounded exciting and was just the sort of challenge I wanted. "Where do I sign up," I asked? She directed me to JOY (Jubilee Outreach Yorkshire), an ecumenical Christian charity based in Shipley.

One of JOY's founders and the mainstay of its management was the formidable Dr Kathy Tedd and it was to her that I spoke next. After seeing TV broadcasts of the terrible suffering

Dr Kathy Tedd

of thousands of needy orphans in Romania after its revolution in 1989, Dr Kathy and others had set up the charity, opening shops and starting a system of delivering aid, supplies and equipment to the country. This had been extended to other places in Eastern Europe, though Romania remained the key focus. Kathy had resigned from a well paid job at Airedale Hospital to devote her energies full time to this project. As I later learned, she was a born-again Christian and described to me the work of the charity. "We go to Romania once a month with food, clothing and medical supplies, and support a team of workers who travel out there to renovate schools, homes and orphanages. And we have self-help groups of determined Romanians with whom we work in concert on major projects," she explained. "What about you, Ken, what are your skills?" I found this a difficult question to answer. Put on the spot I realised I knew a little about a lot of things but I had no real area of specialist trade. "I was for many years involved with transport, construction and demolition. I can drive almost any kind of vehicle and have added to my mechanical knowledge more recently running a garage business," I told her.

"Good," she said. "We need experienced drivers to get our supplies across Europe and as it happens we have a project to convert an old stable block into accommodation for street children. The roof needs taking off; could you do that?" "Yes I'm sure I can," I replied. "Then you are welcome; the trip will cost you £260!" I was taken aback by this. I was to give up my own time, endure discomfort along the way and also fork out for the trip. Kathy was nothing if not forthright, laying down the rules that had to be observed by anyone volunteering to help. "That's the way we operate. We send out a big van loaded with supplies. It has an extra row of aircraft seats and six volunteers go on each trip. All meet the expenses for fuel and other necessities themselves. There will be food in the van, but you will need to buy some of your own. We take turns driving, snatching a little sleep in between. When we arrive we stay with families, most of whom are members of the local Church. You are welcome to join us?" I thought of the orphans. All had much less than me; in fact, as I was to find out, having absolutely nothing at all is a hell of a lot less. So I filled in the forms, booked my seat for the next trip and prepared myself for a new experience. This is going to be different!

The harbinger of JOY

Since the Second World War Romania had suffered under one of the most repressive Communist states. From 1967 to 1989 it had been led by Nicolae Ceaușescu, who had virtually bankrupted the country while brutally repressing dissent. Finally, the people had enough and a revolution ensued. In Romania the over throwing of the system was far more bloody than those that happened elsewhere in the communist system. It ended in the execution of Ceaușescu and his wife following a televised and hastily organised two-hour court session. Thus ended the regime but it left in its wake many casualties in the population. Worst affected of all were children, particularly those considered as orphans by the state. Under Ceaușescu abortion and contraception had been forbidden which had led to a rapid increase in birth rates. Something that accorded in some way with his philosophies. But it resulted in much misery. Many of the children born to single girls were abandoned in state-run orphanages, which also housed disabled and mentally ill people. All were subjected to institutionalised neglect and abuse. As Western media gained access to the country in the wake of the revolution the scandal played across TV screens and in newspapers. It awakened strong feelings in Britain and prompted many people to give up their time to go and help. For the next seven years I became one among these volunteers.

While I packed my bags for that first trip I guessed that many things would be in short supply. What little extra could I take that would not take up space in my luggage? I had heard somewhere that you could not get paracetamol in Romania so I bought a few boxes. Although well intentioned, my information was out of date as I was to discover. There was plenty available and at prices cheaper than in the UK.

More practically, I sorted out some demolition tools to take such as nail bars, wrenches and tyre levers. Most had been left over from my previous business ventures. The day before we set off we gathered in Shipley to load the big Mercedes van, working to the strict supervision of Kathy Tedd. It was vital to pack things properly to get maximum use of the space and only Kathy could do that properly, or so she thought. She reminded me of my father! We loaded tinned food donated by Morrisons supermarkets, beds and medical equipment scrounged from local hospitals, and other supplies of medicines and antibiotics close to or past their expiry date (like much of the food). As explained by one of our party who was a retired chemist, using date-expired medicines and antibiotics was not a problem, as they do not go off but just slowly lose strength over a long period. While our hospitals, pharmacies and shops would have to discard them, they were welcome in Romania.

Off to Romania

Next day it was an early start. I left my car at my mother's house in Bingley and sister Connie took me to Shipley to join the rest of the crew. There were three women and three of us men, one of whom, Dave, had been before, so he was team leader. The party were a mixed bunch, most with different ideas for doing things but all were extremely well-intentioned. This was a good introduction for me as subsequently I saw others who looked on going to Romania as more of a holiday. When sorting out the driving arrangements Kathy always asked people if they could drive, not what they could drive. Some had only driven a car, which was to lead to occasional problems that required me to solve.

We were on our way by 8.30am and hadn't been going long before we hit the first snag when the door mirror on the passenger's side fell off. This was going to be problematic on the Continent as it was a right hand drive vehicle. We improvised by taping on a small mirror from a ladies compact which had to serve until we could get a replacement. It called me to the fore which helped break the ice and by the time we reached the ferry port at Dover we were all friends. Everyone was excited by what to most of us was a new adventure. Three people sat in the front and three behind on the aircraft seats. We arranged ourselves in the front so that one drove, one followed the map and the other watched for road signs. The three in the back slept or rested. The ferry company P and O gave us concessionary tickets, though this meant crossing as freight in a queue of lorries. This took longer to board but once we were on the ferry we headed for the truckers' restaurant where we could also take advantage of good food at lower rates. It would be our last chance of a good meal for a while.

The route from Calais was north to Lille, then across to Brussels, turning south-east and on into the night. Liege-Cologne-Frankfurt-Regensburg, heading for Vienna and passing close to Linz, the birthplace of Hitler. Round the outskirts of Budapest and on to the Romanian border at Hegyesha-lom-Bors. Our first port of call in Romania was the city of Oradea. We faced certain difficulties. One problem was currency. On the journey we handled five or six different currencies in those pre-Euro days. Another issue was to come in dealing with officialdom when we reached Eastern Europe. When we approached border posts in the West we would most likely find them deserted, but the situation was much different when we reached the former Soviet bloc countries.

The only stops that we planned to make were for diesel, toilet breaks and to change drivers every three or four hours. The toilet facilities at many of the filling stations were dreadful. We had to borrow a key, taking turns in a single toilet that seldom had any paper. As we found on this first trip, an important thing to take with us was toilet tissue. One toilet near the Hungarian-Romanian border was a little wooden hut with a pole across a hole in the ground.

On that first trip we were forced to make an unscheduled halt. It was night when the fog on the road between Vienna and Budapest became so thick it was impossible to see. There was nothing else for it but to pull into a lay-by where we slept until 5.30 am. I was the first to wake with the rising sun glaring through the windscreen. We had an early breakfast, cereal and tea brewed at the roadside and were soon on our way again towards

Budapest. The new ring road around the city was not yet open so we had to drive through the centre of Buda and then across the bridge to Pest. It was a nightmare. There were few signs, many of the roads were narrow, the city was just waking up and the rush hour was beginning. We went around in circles. Though we knew we had to cross the Danube, when we were doing so for the second time we knew we were lost. I was not team leader but made a suggestion. We needed to go east-south-east, so I figured out that if we drove just to the right of where the sun was rising we should hit the road. Not everyone agreed and as we argued the toss we crossed the Danube for a third time. I had always wanted to see the magnificent Hungarian parliament building by the side of the river but three times within an hour was too much. This clinched the argument and I took over behind the wheel, keeping the sun on my left. Just when I expected someone to say, "We are still lost," I saw a sign for Szolnok and the road we wanted. A cheer went up and I felt quite pleased with myself.

We travelled across the vast Hungarian plain of fertile land, dark brown soil, with corn and tall sunflowers as far as the eye could see. Whichever direction the sun was coming from the sunflowers would be gazing up at it.

Crossing the border

In those days when you arrived in the old Communist world things started to deteriorate fast. They had lived in a different world and would take a long time to adjust to ours. The roads were poor, the systems were antiquated but the hardest to deal with were the border guards. Delays could last for hours and the problems were often deliberately caused. Kathy insisted that we never bribe police or customs officials but that is how they had lived for years under the Communist regime. Hungary was improving and the officials, while not overtly helpful, did not cause too many problems – though they clearly resented all the aid going to Romania. But the change on the Romanian side was stark. The guys in uniform sat around the customs shed listlessly smoking, eyeing us suspiciously with none going out of his way to help. On later trips we were often told to unload the full contents of the van and, though I hated doing it, I did offer bribes of food, cigarettes and coffee. On that first trip we were relatively lucky, having to take just a few things out of the vehicle. But it still took an age to process us. At last, we were waved through and the second major culture shock struck home. The previous part of our journey had been through Hungary on roads that were in the process of being improved and had clean picnic areas. There an effort was being made. But suddenly we were now bumping over joints and gaps on Romania's ancient concrete patchwork roads and everywhere there was rubbish blowing about. In the distance was Oradea, the border town. The Iron Curtain might have been lifted but when you entered Romania the first thing that struck you was the grey curtain of the remnants of failed, corrupt Communism.

I had never seen anything like it in my life! Everywhere were blocks of grey dingy flats, a monument to Ceausescu's misrule. Apparently, he wanted everyone to live in a modern, centrally heated flat and had the old style traditional homes bulldozed to make way. A lot of the flats had been pre-manufactured in factories and when assembled on site had never been put together correctly. Many were crumbling at

Typical block of dingy, crumbling, grey flats

the corners from poor quality concrete and there were patches of damp on the walls where the plumbing was leaking. I noticed central heating pipes that were not correctly joined together as in the UK, but were welded onto radiators. Hot water piped from power stations miles out of town was often cold by the time it reached peoples' bathrooms. I was told that the system had never worked properly.

In Oradea a new MacDonald's had recently opened and this became a regular stopping point for us, more for the clean toilets than the burgers though we took advantage of both. I love to people-watch and I looked out of the window and gazed at the folk at the nearby tram stop. It was rush hour and all the people looked glum. In fact, many of them seemed half-dead, beaten as if their lives were not worth living, their faces as grey as the flats they were on their way home to. I did not see one smile. Even the trams were painted a dull orange and rumbled along lines that looked flat and worn out. The occasional horse and cart trotting by became a sight we would soon get used to.

After MacDonalds we felt refreshed and set off again with still a long way to go, deeper into Romania on ever worsening roads. We passed through Cluj Napoca, the third largest city in Romania. Cluj had been once a very important place when it was called Kolozsvar and was part of Hungary. After World War One, the town along with the rest of Transylvania, had been grafted onto Romania even though many of the people living there were ethnic Hungarians. As we approached, we noticed the road was lined with stalls selling blankets, sheepskins, sheets and covers with fancy coloured embroidery all blowing in the wind. Many stalls displayed the locally-produced, fine white ceramics, which I later brought back as gifts for friends and family.

We travelled up into the hills then down into Korund, fast becoming a tourist spot, again with roads lined with market stalls. Ours was one of the first British aid parties of 1996 as the roads had shortly before been blocked by snow. Even now as we climbed higher there was still snow on the verges and in the dense pine forests. Occasionally, we would pass a cart loaded with a huge tree so long it was pulled by two horses at the front and a cart at the back like an articulated vehicle. I was told that in the rural areas if they needed timber for building they would just go into the forest cut down a tree and cart it away. We were advised not to drive outside the towns after dark as there were so many horses and carts with no lights.

Our final destination was Targu Mures, a city of about 120,000 people in the centre Transylvanian province of Romania. We looked up our contact, an enormously resourceful American lady called Michelle, who worked for a US religious charity with which JOY operated in concert. She was wonderfully welcoming, and had become used to volunteers suddenly arriving from England. She let us stay in her small flat, the six of us rolled up in our sleeping bags so close together it was difficult to get to the toilet during the night without stepping on someone. The next morning I looked out of the window of Michelle's flat. Within sight was a large factory and out of its tall chimney poured continuous clouds of thick, yellow, sulphur-looking smoke.

I was told it was poisonous and could well believe it. From far around in the countryside the first thing you saw of Targu Mures was this yellow plume.

The Abos family

We delivered our medical supplies to a local hospital. As we unloaded I noticed a small pick-up truck parked by the rear entrance, painted white with green crosses and bearing in English the words, 'Emergency Ambulance'. It did not even have a hood over the back.

Our next task was to take food to a nearby orphanage, where three of the team stayed to help and the rest of us set of for Miercurea Ciuc, a small town about a hundred kilometres by road to the east. Before we set off, I tried to buy a replacement mirror for the van in an auto supplies shop they could not help but sent me to a plumber who went to a great deal of trouble cutting one out of a much larger house mirror. While waiting I browsed in one of the nearby big stores. In those days, there was a severe shortage of consumer goods, with just a few items spread out thinly on the shelves mostly food-stuffs. I looked at bottled fruit and pickles, many out of date by as much as two years. There were a few glass ornaments and fine white porcelain, lovely and cheap, but little else.

I returned to the plumber who had made a good job of cutting us a new oglinder, the Romanian word for mirror. With this fitted we set off up through hills, then down to a green and fertile plain where in the centre stood Miercurea Ciuc. This was less industrialised than Targu Mures largely because what industry there had been had run down and closed. It was early evening as we approached and a thin blue haze from house fires hung low over the town. The only tall buildings visible were church towers and spires.

Like most of Transylvania, Miercurea Ciuc was populated mostly by Hungarians, many of whom were rediscovering their Roman Catholic faith. We were met by Father Isvan, the local leader of the Hungarian Catholic Church, who was accompanied by a young boy. Members of the Church had agreed to accommodate us in their homes, he told us. One of the crew called Dave and I were allocated to the Abos family, who took us to their new, not quite finished house. We were offered a bedroom which the family hadn't started to use but which only needed the electricity wiring up and a lick of paint. But I could see that in getting the place built the plumbing had been rushed, and the toilets and drains were often blocked, which caused a bit of embarrassment. Still, the Abos parents, Alexandra and Maria, and son Ede were lovely people and we quickly settled in. Alexandre, an ethnic Hungarian, met his wife Maria, a Romanian, at college during the time when Ceausescu had sought to integrate the Hungarian and Romanian populations by moving students around the country. For the most part, Romanians live in the south and east of the country, and the Hungarians in the west and north. I asked Alexandra and Maria about life under Communism. Alexandra would not speak of the past, but when we were on our own Maria would sometimes tell me a little about those times, the grinding boredom under Communism where the working lives of most people largely involved killing time, drawing a wage packet from one week to the next. I realised that fear had closed their mouths in former times, but also I had an inkling that there was something else in their background that Alexandra did not want to talk about. He was intelligent: 'switched on,' as you might say. But what he might have been switched on to during the height of the Communist era I never discovered.

They now both worked for the local authority in the municipal building in the centre of town and had prospered more than most in Romania. Their new house was built and paid for by themselves. I couldn't help but ask myself how this was, wondering if they had been prominent members of the Communist party or secret police. I made friends with their young son Ede, a bright lad who spoke good English. He showed me round the town and occasionally we played tennis together then called for ice cream on the way back, We also shared the same birthday.

One evening after our meal I sat chatting with the Abos couple late into the night. They wanted to learn about England and I was keen to hear about Romania. The Romanians give you a small glass of palinca, a very strong, rough plum brandy which you are supposed to drink straight down. If you sip it they think you are not enjoying yourself, but if you sink it in one mouthful your glass is immediately refilled. That evening the longer we chatted the more glasses I had and though I did not feel at all drunk, when I stood up to go to the toilet I felt as if I only had one leg and it was at the wrong side. I collapsed in a heap. When I regained my feet I was not much better and had to be helped to bed. The following morning I felt dreadful and my head ached until late afternoon.

Converting the orphanage

You will remember that Dr Kathy had earmarked me to help convert a stable block into accommodation for homeless street boys. I was anxious to look over the project and the next day we went round to look at the stables in the grounds of the huge old house where Father Isvan lived but we were then told that there was a problem: planning permission had not been given. So the roof would have to stay on for the moment and the street boys remained homeless. Other volunteers from England had come to help but nothing could be done until we received the official go ahead and things move slowly in such places. While waiting we helped another project which involved painting and decorating an old house that was being converted into a home for unmarried mothers.

On our way back from town we passed an old gypsy woman in the traditional bright coloured long dress. I wanted a picture so we stopped spoke to her and showed her my camera, she soon got the message, held her hand out palm upwards then rubbed her thumb and forefinger together. We agreed a fee, up front she was not going to be caught out but Dave made a bad mistake letting her see how much money he had and she kept poking her fat fingers into the wad pulling out more notes till he got the message and closed his hand. She was like most of her clan, sharp when they see money.

For our meal on our last evening before starting the return journey to Yorkshire Maria told me we would have lamb. I had not seen much meat in my time in Romania and I thought it would be a nice change from the normal boring food. I have to say that traditional cooking in Romania is not very appetising with lots of pollenta cornmeal and cabbage. So I was looking forward to the change even though lamb is not my favourite. Earlier in the day Ede said to me, "Come outside Ken and I'll show you the lamb." I followed him to the back of the house and there huddled up on the grass was one of the most pitiful sights I have ever seen. A tiny lamb, not more than a few weeks old, lay trussed up with a bewildered look on its face. Alexandra came out of the house with a long knife in his hand, and told us to go inside. I had already lost my appetite. That evening the table was set for our special meal with palinca brandy for starters. I was wary after my earlier experience but thought it might at least help me through the lamb course. I was conscious of the fact that this was a special meal for them as they seldom ate meat, and thanked them sincerely for all the trouble they had gone to.

The next morning we made an early start, picking up our three crew members in Targu Mures on the way back. We had a tiring but largely uneventful return to Shipley, calculating that we had covered 5,500 kilometres in the round-trip.

Wheelchairs for Oradea

"Are you up for another trip?" Kathy asked when we arrived home. I had found the whole thing really interesting and unhesitatingly confirmed my availability. It wasn't long before another call came. This time my role was to help an elderly couple from Bingley called Alan and Barbara who went out every year, renting the vehicle from Kathy and doing their own thing with their own contacts. They asked me if I would like to go with them to drive and help once we arrived. I agreed. Though they were nice people and chose to go at a more leisurely pace than the JOY parties, stopping in hotels overnight, they were both very pedantic. If I was driving at two or three miles over the speed limit one of them would prompt me, and we covered most of the journey strictly within the rules.

Alan was a retired chemist and was invaluable for his knowledge of drugs and medicines. The couple's main interest was to deliver wheelchairs, some of them battery operated, older or redundant models which they collected from Yorkshire hospitals and nursing homes. Alan would service and repair them, often cannibalising parts from one to get another working. On this trip we had six that Alan had worked on during the year and put back into good working order.

When we reached Romania our first delivery was to a man in the border town of Oradea who had been trapped by a packaging machine when working in a factory. His legs had been badly crushed. We parked outside the block of flats where he lived and he came down on his crutches to look at his new wheels. I don't know what happened to him in the accident but it didn't look as if much had been done for him since. His legs were buckled, one shorter than the other, his right foot pointing out at two o'clock. His friend and Alan helped him into the wheelchair, he looking at the controls before getting hold of the knob and gently moving forward. He had obviously used this type of chair before and his face lit up as he took off around the yard needing no further instruction. His family were so pleased and insisted on us going inside for tea and, as usual, regardless of the time of day out came the palinca.

Our next delivery was again to a block of dingy grey flats. This time we took the wheelchair up to the third floor, fortunately the lift was working, they so often are not. The door was opened by a woman who looked a bit surprised. This quickly passed as she saw the wheelchair, then a broad smile creased her face. We were invited in and I was impressed with her home which was beautiful, bright and clean. It can sometimes be very deceptive when you look at the outside of these blocks. There were two other people in the flat so I looked round to see who the wheelchair was for and then saw sitting on the sofa a pretty young girl, her jet black hair hanging down to a white frilly blouse neatly embroidered with tiny flowers. Her short blue skirt reached to just above her knees, but her legs stopped just below. There were no lower parts to her legs. She looked shy and I, too, felt embarrassed as I did not know where to look or what to say. She had such a pretty face and had I known more of the language I would still have been speechless.

Inside the front door there was quite a large hallway. Alan set up the wheelchair and connected the battery. The girl's mother came forward with her daughter in her arms and placed her in the chair. Alan took hold of her hand and placed it on the control knob. Instructions were relayed and we all waited as her frail white hand pushed the knob forward very gently. The wheelchair moved about six inches then stopped. She looked up at us and if only I had my camera ready what a picture! Her face was flushed with excitement. Then the same again forwards, then backwards. She loved it. They would have problems getting it in and out of the block of flats, but I could see the pleasure she would have after spending her life being carried everywhere. Alan gave instructions on how to recharge the battery. Maybe that would be soon as she had not stopped and was now managing to negotiate in and out of the rooms without bumping into anything. After drinking tea we left them with one very happy little girl.

The other wheelchairs were delivered to a care centre for the elderly in Oradea, before we headed south to Targu Mures, making several calls on the way to deliver blankets, medicine and clothing. We booked rooms in a hotel in the centre of town. As they did not have a secure car park we took the vehicle to an open area near the International Hotel, where some enterprising soul was charging truckers to park overnight. A young man guarded our vehicle all night for just £2.

Our Hotel was quite large in a prominent position in town but there were few guests, at breakfast only one other table in use and no chance of an English breakfast, cold thinly sliced ham, cheese, a hard boiled egg thick slices of grey bread and a large pot of week tea. It would certainly not have excited many Western tourists. Even kids backpacking around the country would have been put off by the dingy brown walls of the dingy brown hotel. Though it was almost empty now there were signs that it had once been busy. The carpet and tables showed signs of use, there was a stage at one end of the large dining room and a stale smell of cigarette smoke. What intrigued me most was that every table had a well used ice bucket on a stand at the side. Maybe a few years before when the Communists ruled this had been the meeting place for the region's hierarchy as the head quarters was close by. I could imagine them wining and dining while many lived on so little. We could hardly complain as we paid just £7 for bed and breakfast.

Doctor Maria

After visiting the orphanage in Targu Mures the next call was to deliver some medical supplies for a local Romanian, Doctor Maria Petho. She was involved in establishing a centre for handicapped youngsters called Clever Hands. By the time we had unloaded and talked for a while I was beginning to feel unwell. All my life I have been blessed with sturdy good health but the bad toilet facilities on our travels at last had an effect. I had avoided using them since leaving England but now I had no choice, and for the next couple of days I would have to stay where there was one close by. Maria kindly invited me to live at her flat while Alan and Barbara continued with their deliveries. Maria was a wonderful woman who worked long hours at her surgery trying to help an endless stream of sick people. She had very few medical supplies and was always pleased and grateful for whatever help she had from us. She did all this on a £40 a month salary.

Her life was made even more difficult by her alcoholic husband, who was in and out of hospital and needed constant attention. Due to my enforced rest I came to know him quite well. He was crazy about fishing and in the rare periods when he was sober that was about all he did. He was also a nice man to talk to in those brief moments. I was ill for three days before Maria had me back to normal with some special Romanian medical concoction. It transpired that I was one of many who had been ill and it was traced back to infected watermelons grown on a sewage farm. They tasted good and were cheap, but after three large slices it was clear that I had paid a higher price!

Alan and Barbara came back to pick me up. When we said our goodbyes Maria went to her China cabinet and took out a lovely tall vase, wrapped it in paper and presented it to me. I was quite overcome. She had let me stay in her home, cared for me and now she gave me one of her own possessions. Maria was a wonderful woman. The journey back to the UK was quite leisurely and for once I was thankful to keep to the speed limit.

The charity shop

I was now getting more involved working with the JOY charity. At the time I had a large Transit van and used it to collect donated goods from all over

West and North Yorkshire. One regular collection point was at Malton police station where an officer worked hard in his spare time to collect clothes, children's toys, hospital equipment, stretchers, zimmer frames, walking sticks and anything else he thought would be useful. There would always be a full van load to bring from Malton back to Shipley. Dr Kathy would divide donated goods into items for Romania and some for sale in JOY's charity shops. Anything that still hung around I would take to car boot sales, which became a regular Sunday morning outing for me. On one occasion we had been given a lot of children's cuddly toys. They were clean, just like new, so I put them in plastic bags and hung them around my stall at the car boot event. A customer pointed to the one he wanted. I thought he was buying a present for a grandchild and I discounted my usual £1 price to 50p. He paid me then took the toy out of the bag and threw it onto the ground where his dog grabbed and shook it like rat. I wished I had charged him the full price.

When others at the car boot sales came to know I was working for a charity they would bring me their unsold items at the end of the day, so that I sometimes left with more than when I arrived! On another occasion we were given dozens of boxes of mohair knitting wool from a shop that was closing down. Knitting is not as popular as it once was but some of the older generation were good customers. One lady in particular could not resist buying some and every week went away with a box. She was old and her eyesight was failing, but she never missed a week, guided by her daughter. When she opened her purse to pay me I noticed that it was not bulging with money so I always gave her a good discount.

I met many interesting people at car boot sales. Many of them were anxious to support a charity, though there was always the odd scavenger just looking for something for nothing. I snapped with one. The item he picked up was marked at 50p but he offered just 10p. "I got out of bed at 5.30 this morning to help a charity raise funds for the poor in Romania," I told him. "If that is the best you can do put it back where you found it and don't bother." He did.

My third trip to Romania loomed. Dr Kathy rang me, "We have permission to start the demolition of the stable block in Miercurea Ciuc," she said. "And I want you to be the team leader." I must have impressed her. With being team leader went the added responsibility of holding the purse strings for the fuel, tolls and any other running expenses, as well as keeping currencies separate as we moved from one country to another.

Again there were six of us and off we went across Europe. This time we had two trainee nurses to help in a hospital, a plumber, a joiner and an ex-soldier to help me with the demolition work. During the night somewhere in Germany we changed drivers and it was the turn of our ex-army colleague. I had tried to ensure that only those drove who had experience with bigger vehicles and according to him he had driven everything, including tanks. He took over and I settled in the back for a rest. My mother may have rocked me to sleep as a baby but the rocking now was keeping me awake. I sat up and looked over the driver's shoulder. He couldn't keep the van in a straight line and would drift one way, over-correct and swerve the other. I told him to pull over at the next opportunity. He climbed out grumbling and told me again what he had driven. I gave the driving to another and we set off down the Autobahn. The next day our soldier was given another opportunity to drive, this time in daylight, but he was only slightly better. It turned out that his eyesight was very bad. He didn't like this to be known and bore me a grudge for the rest of the trip.

Customs at the Romanian border were a problem and after a log delay I did something I had avoided until then, bribing an official with a large container of coffee. As he took it from me he shrugged and pointed at his mate, "There are two of us". I had no choice but to part with another. Eventually, we arrived at Targu Mures where our American friend, Michelle, welcomed us as warmly as ever. We unrolled our sleeping bags in her flat and enjoyed a good night's sleep after so long on the move. Next day we delivered supplies to a hospital, an orphanage and a doctor's surgery. The last drop was for a nearby village, which was along a narrow road close to the hills and was unsuitable for a large van. So we waited for someone from the village to come in a car to collect their items. They were late. We had wanted to push on to Miercurea Ciuc that afternoon but this delayed us, meaning we had another night at Michelle's. This turned out well as there was an orchestral evening in the Town Hall. Friends of Michelle's from the US had spare tickets and invited us, and the evening proved to be a special treat. The building had been newly renovated and was a great setting for the music of Mozart, Schubert, Wagner and Strauss. The Communists may have made an absolute mess of most things but they had always supported musicians and the orchestra were magnificent.

In the morning we were on the road early for the drive to Miercurea Ciuc, where we were in for another surprise. The roof had already been taken off the stable block and its timbers and slates were neatly stacked at the side. We were supposed to have done this but a local builder, who was also a member of the Church, had made a start. At the time I felt this was fine but as I discovered later this would turn out to be something of a problem, which was dropped in my lap to sort out.

We had not been there long when my little gypsy friend arrived. How Yolanda always knew within a few hours when we were in town I will never know but here she was her pretty face covered by a big smile she was always ready to help, spoke a little English was helpful and knew the area but though she looked so attractive when you got close like all gypsies she had a strong smell of stale wood smoke from their central heating system!

There was no standing around as there was painting to do inside a large hall that had not seen emulsion for years. The whitewashed walls just sucked up the paint, gallons of it. Fortunately, it had been donated by a local company in Shipley and we had plenty.

My skills with the overlocking

We were shown some German and Dutch projects. A workshop had been set up for homeless boys to learn carpentry. Here they made everything from jigsaw puzzles to tables and chairs, and the lads appeared to be really happy. We purchased from them lots of wooden items to bring back and sell in our charity shops. There was also a machine shop where young unmarried mothers rescued from the streets made up bedding sheets, cushions and children's clothes. The sewing machines were brand new and had been sent from Germany. The girls did not have much material to work with but, I thought, I can do something about that on my next visit.

I'll jump ahead to explain. My friend Julia Nadal had lots of leftover material, oddments and roll ends, from her former clothes making business. She was happy to donate this to the cause and I took the material with me on the

next trip. The girls in Romania were delighted when I walked in with arms full of rolls of lovely bright coloured fabric. I noticed there was no one using the overlocker so I sat down at the machine and asked for material. You'll remember that I became something of an expert at this under Julia's tutelage when we lived in Ornhams Grange. The girls gathered around as I put a piece in place and pressed the pedal. The machine buzzed into action. I was accorded a round of applause, before the inevitable photo session with the girls all wanting a picture with me at the machine.

Eventually our work was done and we prepared for the trip home. We rose early, loaded the van and said our farewells. But when I turned the ignition key there was only a click. Until then the van had been so reliable. I soon found the problem as the accelerator rod had fallen off a worn ball-joint. It would be difficult to fix as the connection needed flexibility when the accelerator was pressed and it could not be wired up. Then I had a brainwave and wrapped rubber bands which would hold the rod in place while allowing the necessary movement. It worked and we were on our way after a small delay. All the way home the van ran normally, but I could picture the rubber bands stretching as I pressed the accelerator pedal and wondered what would happen if they were to let go when we were in dense traffic. Fortunately they survived the journey, though I felt very much on edge.

When we arrived in Shipley I dropped the crew at various points near to their homes. One of them, Dave, was met at his garden gate by his boy friend. I felt like telling him of the time Dave and I had slept together but restrained myself. What had happened was at one of our stops there was a shortage of beds and it was agreed that two men would sleep together in a double bed. I don't recall how it was decided but Dave and I had the short straws. I suspect we were both uneasy but made the best of it, lying on a tiny strip at either side of the bed with a huge gap in the middle as no mans land.

Sleeping with Sister Therese

Travelling to Romania was becoming a regular feature of my life. My fourth trip, with bundles of material from Julia, also had on board a special passenger, an Irish nun called Sister Therese. This trip was again to present with an unlikely sleeping partner – Sister Therese herself. "She is a bit scatty but I think you'll like her," said Dr Kathy. "She had previously worked as a nurse in a hospital in Targu Jiu, in the south of Romania, and would like to visit her friends with financial aid raised by the church in Ireland." I pictured a woman dressed in a black and white habit, with us having little in common and me having to be careful not to utter the occasional swear word. I could not have been more wrong.

We met in Shipley the day before departure to pack the van under Kathy's strict supervision. I was team leader and looked at the other five members, three women and two men, but couldn't identify the nun. Then a woman in jeans and a woolly jumper spoke to me, "Are you Ken?" she said in a broad Irish accent. "To be sure. And you must be Sister Therese. I didn't recognise you," I confessed. "Well, I don't go travelling in my habit. I feel much better in normal clothes." Thus started a very special friendship. She was not a bit starchy and we travelled miles together. Some years later when she had returned to Ireland I went with a friend to visit her and she made us welcome, wined and dined us, and gave us a bed for the night. More about beds later!

The drive out followed the usual pattern. At the Romanian border we saw a charity group from Hull being forced to take everything out of their van by the customs men. No doubt, they had the same instructions as us to avoid paying a bribe. This was their learning experience.

Going through hilly country deep in Romania our driver went too fast around a hairpin bend and we slid across the road into a deep pot hole with such force that it burst the tyre and buckled the wheel rim. This was another occasion when my mechanical knowledge came in useful and we had the wheel changed and back on our way in no time.

A detour was made to deliver tinned food to an orphanage in a tiny village in the hills miles from anywhere. But the delay to fix the wheel and the detour to the village meant it was getting late. We kept to the rule that we did not drive at night in the country areas, so we looked for somewhere in the little hamlet to stay. The orphanage was already full but a woman who worked there offered to put us up at her house. She had one tiny spare bedroom with two small beds. The rest would have to sleep on the floor in the living room in sleeping bags. This was good enough as we were used to such conditions but there was a discussion about who would have the beds. Someone suggested the two oldest, who were Sister Therese and me by a mile, born in the same year and now well into our 60s. The two beds, probably bought for children, were close together in the same tiny bedroom. Was I to sleep with a nun? I looked at Therese and she looked at me, each waiting for the other's reaction. "I don't mind," we chorused simultaneously. She was a wonderful woman and didn't make a fuss about it, though I don't think the Pope would have approved. I kept out of the way until she was tucked up and either asleep or feigning, then I crept in my tiny bed and enjoyed a good night's rest. Later, when it was mentioned that we had slept together it always raised a laugh. She was a good sport.

Eight thousand pounds

Next day we reached Michelle's apartment in Targu Mures and unloaded a few items for her. We had something to eat then Michelle, always so lively and full of fun, said, "Do you guys fancy a drink in the Cadillac Club?" None of us knew the Cadillac Club but we understood drink and together replied, "Yes." All except Therese, who decided to sit this one out. The club was a short walk through a very poor area round the back of the station. It was a dingy place, badly lit with cracked walls and peeling paint. Several shady characters stood at the bar with beer bottles in their hands, and one or two others were in the shadows watching us. Michelle ordered Bergen beer. Time for a confession! I needed a beer to steady my nerves as around my waist in a money belt I had £8,000. And here I was in a Romanian nightclub with a small fortune in cash. Not a good idea, I told myself. The cash was the deposit on a building Kathy had agreed to help finance.

I thought I might feel a bit easier with my back to the wall so I eased to the end of the bar and stood sipping my beer looking out into the room. No one knew I had the money, not even the crew but I kept thinking of Dr Maria, the Romanian doctor who earned just £40 a month. I had strapped to my stomach the equivalent of sixteen years earnings. I guessed that half the men in the bar would cut my throat for what was round my waist. I bought a round at 30p a beer, and took a swig of my second bottle thinking I had to keep calm. My friends were playing pool, the girls drinking beer faster than the men and all having a better time that I was. One of the locals came up to talk to me. I had to fight the reflex of putting my hand to my belt, forcing myself to relax. Many Romanians, brought up on a diet of pirated copies of Dallas think those in the West are all millionaires. He knew a few words of English and I spoke a little Romanian. Romanian is a Latin based language and I was able to draw on my knowledge of Italian and their similarities.

Michelle came over. "Come and be my partner at pool," she said. I was feeling a bit more relaxed after two bottles of Bergan beer and followed her to the pool table. We played several games drank another beer and eventually it was time to leave, just about 1 am.

What were we going to find outside in a poor quarter of an extremely poor country? To our great surprise, when we walked out into the street it was blocked by bleating sheep, hundreds of them slowly going past followed by the shepherd. Michelle spoke to him and we gave him a bottle of beer that he gratefully accepted. Apparently they were taking the whole flock, sheep and lambs to the abattoir where it is easier to separate them. Lambs are kept for slaughter and the ewes return to start all over again.

The shepherd had with him a couple of Romanian Mioritic sheepdogs. I had to look close to see the difference as they were about the same size as the sheep, with long shaggy coats the same colour as the sheep. It is hard to tell them apart and, apparently, that is the idea as it makes them better at protecting the flock at night from wolves or thieves when they bark and raise the alarm. The flock was going our way so we joined at the end with the shepherd and I just trusted in those same dogs to help protect me from thieves. I was very relieved when we made it back to the safety of Michelle's apartment.

We delivered our medical supplies to various places around the town. In the centre of Targu Mures was a set of traffic lights where the main roads doglegged across each other, the congestion made worse by roadworks. Vehicles being stationery or moving slowly for long periods presented an

 ideal opportunity to the window washer boys, who would jump on the bumpers with a bucket in one hand and a sponge in the other. No amount of protest would deter them as they were keen for work and needed the money. On a previous trip I had taken a photograph of one as he cleaned the windscreen, a tall boy

who looked like the gang leader. I stuck it in the middle of the windscreen and waited for him to show. Sure enough, he climbed onto the front of the van and started washing as we waited for his reaction. When he eventually saw the picture he was so surprised he almost fell off the truck. He smiled and pointed a finger at his chest repeating, "Me, me." I gave him the picture along with another that turned out to be of his brother. He was thrilled and we had a free wash.

At the same lights was a much sadder sight. A woman spent most of every day wheeling a crippled boy up and down in an ancient wheel chair begging at the car windows. It was sorrowful to see the poor lad sitting lopsided in his chair, scantily clad in dirty clothes to show him at his worst. One arm was only a stump below the elbow, his skin was dirty and weathered from the time he spent in the chair through summer and winter. It was difficult to guess his age. He was only the size of a boy but when you looked closer he could have been older, maybe even in his thirties. Perhaps he was the main meal ticket for the rest of the family. We always gave her money.

We set off for Miercurea Ciuc through small villages, many of which had gypsy encampments on the outskirts, a collection of tumbledown shacks with rubbish strewn around, dirty-faced kids and horses tethered on the surrounding wasteland. One village we passed through was very different. On the outskirts were smart new detached houses. But they were very obviously gypsy dwellings with elaborate, Indian-style ornate tinwork around the windows, doors and roof. These were the better-off gypsies. The largest house belonged to the local leader or Bulibasha as he is known. Among them there was a great deal of one-upmanship to have the flashiest home.

Horse and carts

Going through the Romanian country areas in those days what struck you was that there seemed to be far more horse-pulled carts than motor vehicles on the road. Often you would see a mare pulling a cart with a small foal trotting at her side struggling to keep up. That was the way they trained the foals. I had seen something of this before, in war-wrecked Germany in 1954 while I was on National Service. But Germany had moved on while here in Transylvania they still used the cart though most had been modernised!.

Gone were the iron wheels replaced by old car wheels and bald rubber tyres sometimes with the inner tube looking out. Occasionally I saw them being drawn by water buffalos guided by young boys with sticks. On Sunday mornings we would see horse-drawn carts carrying families dressed in their best black clothes on their way to church. I was impressed by how the Romanians had kept their faith despite repression through the Communist years.

The gypsies had their own distinctive carts, covered in large round canvas sheets like wagon train pioneers in old Western films. They would travel in them across the countryside for their gypsy meetings, just as those in the UK would gather for events such as the Appleby Trot. As they journeyed through hilly country they would chain the carts together on the long steep parts and get them pulled to the top by a tractor. On the way down, they fastened a huge boulder at the back to drag behind and serve as a brake. At the bottom of steep hills there were piles of these boulders left behind.

Sister Therese and I left the team in Miercurea Ciuc and drove to Targu Jiu, a moderately-sized town a couple of hundred kilometres away in the south west of Romania, which we reached through winding country tracks. Therese proved to be a wonderful travelling companion; she observed her religion but did not push it on others. We chatted away munching on the contents of an ever-present bag of sweets. She was very thoughtful and attentive. Occasionally, when we stopped for coffee from our flask, stray dogs would appear and she would find something to feed them. I have seen her in a car park surrounded by as many as eight or ten mangy-looking creatures, loving and feeding each of them equally.

We arrived in Targu Jiu late in the afternoon. The main road leading to the town centre had gypsy horses tethered along its verges and in the central reservation, where the grass was only as wide as the length of a horse. The horses grazed peacefully, paying no attention to the traffic passing close by on either side. Therese knew her way around having lived there for three years, and directed me to her friends' house where we would stay. The family was Romanian, and consisted of husband Tio, wife Dana and two daughters. Tio was an out-of-work geologist, a well educated man whose unemployment was a tragedy both for the country and himself. With plenty of time on his hands he showed me around the town, which had started life as a fortified Roman garrison settlement. We found we had something in common as we were both philatelists. Before we left he handed me his book of stamps. "Take any you like as a gift from me," he said. It was a modest collection with nothing particularly expensive, but it was the thought that was valuable. His kindness was typical of most Romanians. On his insistence, I took six stamps. I didn't like leaving gaps, though, so when I returned to the UK I sent him several of my own to compensate. Therese made her visits to old friends distributing aid raised in Ireland and we set off back to Miercurea Ciuc.

On the way we followed a different route which took us through a 'black village'. I stopped the van just to stand and stare. I had seen grimy pit villages in South Yorkshire and Wales but never anything like this. Everywhere you looked was blackened by soot. When I tried to rub it off it did not move, ingrained in the stone by many years exposure to smoke. I wondered how many lungs it had stained and how many of them were still breathing. Then I noticed the culprit, a long row of low factory buildings with a group of short chimneys poking out of the top about fifteen feet above the ground. Fortunately, they were no longer working. I could not understand why the chimneys were so short as this would have meant the village being engulfed in smoke when there was no wind. I have no idea what the factory had produced, maybe tyres, but I did hear that the Russians sent some of the dirtiest work to their satellite countries. Maybe Romania got the short straw on this one.

After we had finished in Miercurea Ciuc we set off to return to the UK. On the long route home I noticed that the main roads in Romania and Hungary were gradually improving. This was the result of grants from the European Union and most of the resurfacing was being done by Italian contractors. Compared to my first visit driving was becoming much easier but with it came the increased risk of breaking the speed limit. Policemen would appear with radar guns looking more like old torches, crying out, "Radar, radar!" It seemed inevitable that I would be the one to be stopped, and so it was on that return journey a policeman pulled me over. He obviously had a sense of humour as he told me, "This is no Hungaroring," referring to the new Formula 1 Grand Prix racing circuit in the country. I said, "No, but I was a racing driver and drove there." This was only half true as I had never been on that circuit but it did appear to impress him.

In these circumstances you can't argue but you can negotiate. I followed him to his little tatty Dacia police car, he pointed to the passenger seat and I got in beside him as he took out his pocket book. Stuffed between the pages were some loose sheets torn into squares I think the Police in Hungary seemed to feel safe fiddling with Western Europeans. "70,000 lei is your fine for exceeding the speed limit," he said scribbling 70,000 on one of the loose bits of paper. I screwed up my face. "We're a charity returning to the UK with only enough money for fuel." He pondered for a moment looking from book to paper, then crossed out the 70,000 and wrote 50,000. I took out a bundle of small notes with only two large ones among them and made hard work of counting, keeping some to one side that I told him were for diesel. It worked. He reached across and pulled out the two 20,000 notes and pushed the rest back to me at the same time screwing up the paper he had written on. I would not be getting a receipt!

He waved me off with the word, "Naroc," meaning good luck. The last thing I saw of him he was pushing the notes into his back pocket. When I got back into the van there was a chorus of voices from our crew, "How much did it cost?" I scowled as I answered, "40,000 lei," about £3.50. We had got away lightly. There was laughter as I once again pressed my foot to the floor, homeward bound with one eye on the oglinda,

There was another incident before we made it back to the UK. At one of the Hungarian checkpoints we had to queue as usual. By the side of the road was a large lorry park, with an awful racket coming from one of the vehicles. As we had time on our hands we went over to investigate and were horrified to find the trailer packed with old horses, not in stalls but just herded in loose. It was a very hot day and one of them had collapsed. It could not get up and the others were causing mayhem. The driver was nowhere to be seen. It was a dreadful sight and some of our crew were moved to tears. One lady, a member of the RSPCA, was very upset that she could do nothing to help the poor thing. The vehicle had a Polish registration plate and I guessed the horses were going to somewhere to be made into salami. Apparently Polish buyers used to go to Romania where there was a plentiful supply of worn out old horses, and no one much cared as they were going to the knacker's yard anyway. But that clatter of hooves rang in our ears for many miles and the RSPCA woman remained badly shaken all the way home.

It is unlikely that she ever made the trip again. In such circumstances it is difficult to control your emotions, but I have to say it did not deter me. I was perhaps less shocked by how they treated animals seeing what had been meted out to humans. Frankly, I enjoyed these treks to Romania, it was a challenge with different problems each time and though we were still in Europe Romania was a world apart. I had now completed four trips and was to do another six, and I had as much enthusiasm as when I started.

Building Surveyor

Kathy was again on the phone and sounded agitated. "Can you come and see me at Shipley, we have a big problem with the stable block?" I whizzed over. She had just received a huge bill from the Romanian builder for work on the block, which was due to be turned into accommodation, and did not know how she could pay. Worst of all, she did not know what work had been done and why it added up to thousands of pounds. Despite being normally tough and organised, this time she looked and sounded beaten. The conversion was to be done using only voluntary labour from the UK, but the Romanian church-goer who had taken down the roof, had been drawn into the whole project and now wanted paying. Having met him I had no doubt about what had happened. The builder had more or less taken over the project, no doubt encouraged by his friend and pastor Father Isvan. The project, still unfinished, was now at a standstill until he was paid. "Will you go and do a survey and assess the value of what he has done, while I try and find some money?" Dr Kathy asked me.

I wanted to help the Charity wherever possible but this was a task beyond my competence and I told her it needed a qualified building surveyor. "But we don't have one," she said. I knew a bit about construction but pricing was a specialist job especially in a country such as Romania. "Don't we have anyone who knows more than me?" "No one is available and we must move fast." "Ok," I said. "I'll go." The ball was now firmly in my court. I had made a commitment and would need to give it a lot of thought.

Luckily, there was someone who I could turn to, my son Jonathan. He was a builder and a very good one at that. He suggested I get hold of a Loxhams Guide, a book used by building estimators giving prices for labour and materials on all types of work. I bought a copy but found it difficult to follow. Years before when I was in business I had paid someone else to do this for me. What had I let myself in for?

Our trip out to Romania was uneventful until we reached the border. We had all kind of medical supplies in the van, including injection needles. Romanian rules were constantly changing and a new regulation stipulated that syringes must be kept separate for inspection. They were listed on our inventory but when the customs official asked to see them, no one knew where they were packed. Our fear was that if we unloaded the whole contents in the customs shed we would never get everything back in to the van. After about three hours of pleading with various officials they decided to put a seal on the van's back doors that could be removed only by customs officials when we got to Targu Mures we were then able to continue on our way.

We arrived at our destination late on a Saturday which meant the doors would be opened only on the following Tuesday, as Monday was a bank holiday. All we could do was make the best of the delay. Our American friend Michelle knew the area well and offered to be our guide; nothing was ever too much trouble for her. Knowing my interest Michelle took me to a newly opened stamp shop. Private enterprise was creeping back and small businesses were springing up. The woman shopkeeper had some lovely stamps and I bought about £60 worth. She was so excited and told us it was more than she normally sold in a month. I also bought several collections of old stamps in books from an antique dealer. Later, I inspected these purchases.

Some of the stamps were from before the First World War when this part of Romania was a province of the Austro Hungarian Empire. There were not so many from the 1950s or later, as the State decided it did not like stamp collectors who may have used this as a cover for communicating with the West. I knew that in Russia some poor collectors were sent to the gulags. What a system of government!

Michelle took us to the Orthodox church in the centre of town where most of the ethnic Romanians who were religious worshipped. Outside it was dreary but the inside was beautiful, though in a garish way. The walls were covered in painted icons and there were lots of carved woodwork in gold, black and red. We walked through the park opposite the church. By the seats there would be piles of sunflower husks where some poor person had eaten their meal. We passed another smaller church where an old man sat on the steps begging. He made a sorry sight in a tatty old suit holding a wooden crucifix in one hand; the other being held out in hope of a few notes. He stared at the ground in a humble manner as if he felt ashamed. I gave him a small amount but he did not look up, just mumbled what I assumed were thanks.

Cold Valley

Begging was everywhere. Whenever Michelle walked down the road she was besieged by children. She was a well-loved figure and they wanted to be seen with her. She sometimes worked at the gypsy camp at a place we knew as 'Cold Valley'. Once I was there with her and a little girl rushed up. Michelle looked down at the girl's bare feet. "Where are the new shoes I gave you yesterday?" she said. "My mother is keeping them for me." Michelle turned to me and said, "Her mother will have sold them, probably to buy drink. How can you help such people?" Cold Valley was an eye opener with dozens of shacks on the hillside cobbled together out of wood, tin and even cardboard.

Michelle took us to the make-shift school room, sparsely equipped but laid out in an orderly fashion with little children, all under eleven, sitting at rows of small desks. The teacher was a Hungarian gypsy and a leader in the community. When we arrived he stood in front of the class at a keyboard playing what sounded like a hymn. He was singing and they had a microphone but no stand, so a little boy stood at his side holding up the mike. The children all joined in and it was wonderful to hear their little voices, frankly bringing a tear to my eye. A teenager came into the room pushing a badly handicapped boy in a wheelchair. I was told later that they were brothers and almost inseparable with the older boy pushing his disabled sibling everywhere. The boy in the wheelchair looked across at me and smiled. The chair was guided over to where I was sitting and was parked by my side as he reached up to shake my hand. He kept hold, all the time smiling as we sat listening to the singing.

Michelle's US charity had organised prizes of small bags with sweets, pencils and writing paper as rewards for regular attendance. The teacher locked the door and they were all excited as he started handing out the packets. Suddenly there was noise outside with someone banging on the door. He rushed back to the door and told whoever was there to go away, but they did not and the noise grew worse as a crowd started to gather. Obviously, word had got around that something was being given away and larger kids, mainly teenage boys were turning up to get their hands on whatever was available. It looked as if they would break the door down so the teacher gave up, opened it and they flooded in. They grabbed as many packets as they could, and we were powerless to

stop them. I saw one lad take three packets, hiding them inside his shirt. Eventually, all the packets were gone and the teenagers disappeared leaving just the prize winners behind. Luckily the teacher had secreted enough away to give them to the younger pupils.

As we left, we walked towards the main road along a track between the rows of flimsy shacks. I noticed a new building project and was intrigued, so I went for a closer look. The normal practice for the gypsies in Cold Valley was for them to patch up old houses rather than build new. But here on a small plot between two old houses was a man putting up a new home. He had collected off-cuts from the timber yard and nailed them together to make the frame work. Now he was cutting turf in neat blocks and stacking them against the woodwork to form the walls, obviously trying to make his new home insulated from the cold winters. I complimented him on his tidy work. He was not one of the more prosperous Roma you would see strutting round other parts of the town showing off their wealth. Those men liked to wear black or dark brown suits and leather trilby hats, gold chains and bracelets. They looked smart though many bore battle scars on their faces. Their women looked even better in long, brightly coloured dresses and head scarves, many with gold trimmings and coins attached.

We had not walked far along the main road when we met a very different little gypsy, one that I had seen many times. The poor girl wandered round the town with her tiny baby in arms desperately searching for someone who could help. She approached anyone who looked as if they were from the West or a charity worker. Apparently the baby had been borne with a very soft skull and it had not set after the normal time. I don't think anything could be done for the poor thing but she clung on to the hope that she could find someone. She always came to us holding the tiny thing close to her breast in clean white cloths as she herself was. As she looked at you she would say little but her sad face and lovely dark eyes said it all. On one of my later trips I saw her walking along the street on her own.

While still waiting for the customs men to open the seals on the truck I accompanied Michelle on a visit to one of her American friends, who was with the Peace Corps. We went for a pizza at a newly opened restaurant. At that time food in Romania was quite cheap and the restaurant offered us excellent pizzas and plates of chips with grated cheese on top, the way the locals liked them. An old lady came in selling flowers. She was small, thin and stooped, with a bright scarf tied round her head and a long coat almost reaching the floor. I bought some flowers and on later visits came to know her quite well. Whenever she spotted me her smile would spread a little wider and she would rush over and plant a toothless kiss on my cheek, much to the amusement of the rest of our crew. She was a mystery. I could not decide if she was very poor or a shrewd old woman making a good living. She sold many flowers and most buyers gave her a generous tip.

As we left the restaurant I noticed two bicycles parked against the wall near the door. Fastened behind the seats were small cardboard boxes with 'Pizza Delivery Service' written on the sides in English.

The stable block takes shape

Finally, it was Tuesday. We were at the customs compound early but were told there would be no activity until after lunch. So I went for a hair cut and beard trim. The elderly barber fussed around me, powdering and snipping. I was a little nervous as I watched him strop the cutthroat razor and thought his hands were not as steady as they might have been. After he finished I felt a little sore, but when I looked in the mirror I could see he had done a good job. He then opened a little cupboard and took out a bottle of cherry brandy pouring me a glass and wishing me, "Naroc," good luck in Romanian. When I asked him how much, he put his hands behind his back and shook his head saying, "nimic – nothing". He was poor but sometimes those with so little show the most kindness. As I looked round I spotted a price list. Taking the largest price I doubled it and left the money under the mirror.

That afternoon we unloaded the vehicle under the watchful eyes of the customs officials and found the damned syringes in the middle of the truck. We had arranged for one of the hospitals to collect them, which freed us to go. But as I drove the van out of the compound I heard a squeaking noise and on investigating found that one of the front wheel bearings had collapsed. It would need replacing before we could travel any further and the new bearing would have to be imported. A small backstreet garage offered to do the repair and put in an order for the part, but it meant a further delay. Thank goodness, I thought, that it was a Mercedes van and the part would come from Germany, rather than from further away. In the end the bearing turned up in less than two days and the garage refused payment as we were from a charity. The owner was just like the barber and many others I encountered on my travels in Romania.

Finally, we were on our way to Miercurea Ciuc where I was to stay again with the Abos family, Alexandre and Maria. It had become my regular home when in town and I was always made welcome. Once I had settled in I went to look at the stable block. As I had been told, work had stopped pending payment. But what had been done was good. A new reinforced concrete floor had been laid, walls were built up, windows had been installed and the roof timbers were in place. It was a professional job but how could I possibly price it up? The builder appeared with Father Isvan. They were expecting me to hand over the money, but they were in for a shock as I explained that my role was just to check on the work to see that the price was right.

I had studied my *Loxhams Guide* on the trip to Romania and had learned the main points. First task was to estimate the amount of time the work had taken to assess labour rates. Then I would need to measure the amounts of timber, stone, bricks and concrete that had been used. I needed to visit a local builders' merchant to price other items and a specialist window and door company. This is where my friendship with Maria Abos paid dividends. She accompanied me wherever I went and did all the translating. It was still very difficult. All the time Maria continually reassured me that the builder was honest and he would never overcharge the church. But I needed proof.

I totted up the amounts and did my calculations on labour rates. At first I wasn't sure I believed it, but after re-checking the bill sent to Dr Kathy I found that it was spot on. Our friend had done a good job at a reasonable price. Apart from the cost of labour, as the charity had expected the work to be done by volunteers, the rest of the items had been bought cheaper in

Romania than we could have bought in the UK. Though the finished price was higher than Kathy had expected it wasn't unfair in any sense. I knew how good she was at raising donations and felt she would manage somehow, and in this I was proved right.

It was with great relief that I was able to tell the builder that I was satisfied and he beamed his thanks, while Maria started the celebrations amongst the church members. Before I left, the builder gave me a lovely wood carving of a monk made from the branch of a hawthorn tree. In the end, the building never housed street boys as had been originally planned, but became used by visiting church dignitaries from Europe and the USA. A few trips later I slept there one night and was amazed at how well it had been constructed and fitted out, all funded by the JOY charity and the good people of Yorkshire.

Mushrooming

Alexandre and Maria asked if we would like to visit the mountains to do some mushrooming. There were two of us staying with them, myself and a fellow volunteer called Dave. As we both had a country background we leapt at the chance. We heard that some of their friends would also like to go but none of them had a car, and the usual way to travel there was by horse and cart. The mountains, it hardly needs saying, were a long way off so I offered to take them in our van.

The road deteriorated not far from town and was soon a deeply rutted cart track winding its way up into the mountains through thick forests. It was not really suitable for our van but I enjoyed the challenge and took it slow and steady. The Abos and their friends, meanwhile, were having a good time travelling by motor vehicle, passing others from the town who were jostling along on the backs of carts. It took us an hour and a half to reach the mushrooming area and I daresay this was a fraction of the time it took those in horse-drawn vehicles. I imagined it would be almost time to return when they got there!

The track took us through a forest which opened onto a hillside. It looked like Switzerland with clumps of fir trees dotted about, wild flowers and cows grazing peacefully with the occasional tinkle of a bell. We wandered over the hills collecting the mushrooms which grew everywhere. Apparently, one rare type of mushroom only grows for a few days in the year and we had timed it just right to pick them.

Maria said she knew a place nearby where we could buy sheep cheese. I looked around the hillsides. We were in a very remote area with no sign of farm or shop for miles. "Follow me," she said. Not far off was a clump of trees which hid a hut the size of a garden shed. This turned out to be a one-man mini cheese making factory. Each spring the shepherd would come up into these high pastures with his flock and stay all summer milking the ewes. For him it was a lonely life until he could return to lower pastures and his home in the autumn, so he occupied himself by making cheese. As you might imagine he was delighted to have visitors and showed us the workings of his operation. We were offered samples to try. There were two different kinds, one fresh, soft and creamy, and the other older and set firm. I enjoyed them both and Dave and I bought some to bring home. The shepherd was well organised for his remote existence with a gas burning stove, a small fridge and a gas ring big enough to boil a kettle. He had a little narrow bed covered with blankets which doubled both for sleeping and sitting as there was no chair. His small table held two books and I noticed a large girlie poster pinned on the wall. I saw neither radio nor TV so he really had no contact with the outside world.

After thanking him we wandered back to where we had parked the van. Someone had brought a steel railway container up to the mountains, donated by a Swiss charity, and we used this as our canteen for lunch. Apart from our group, there were about a dozen other people and a fire was lit, over which was hung a large old iron cooking pot. This was filled with potatoes, carrots, onions, garlic, herbs and one or two things I did not know the name of, followed by something I did recognise: a sheep's head with its eyes staring skywards. It was left to simmer while we scoured the hills for more mushrooms.

Romanians love to go to the mountains in their free time and I can understand why. The place had a wonderful feel and they obviously feel comfortable there just as I do in the Yorkshire Dales.

In the early afternoon mushroom hunting stopped and we sat on the grass for our meal. After all the energy we had expended, the stew looked and smelled good. I took a dish and a thick chunk of coarse grey bread and joined the queue. The cook stirred the pot then poured a scoop onto my bowl, and I sat down to eat. As I have explained, mutton is not my favourite dish but I was hungry. I dipped in my bread and was enjoying it until my teeth bit into a lump of something strange, a bit of gristle which then burst! I pushed bread into my mouth and swallowed it all down as I realised what I had was an eyeball. I ate more bread and finished my plate, swilling it down with beer. When offered a second helping I politely refused. After everyone had finished I walked over and looked into the pot, which was empty except for the skull with long brown teeth. Both eyes had gone and I wondered who had the other one.

As I sat on a bench sipping the last of my beer I felt a little hand reach over for mine. It was a little girl who had come over to make friends. Her parents also noticed and came over to chat. The little girl's name was Suzie and she was three. I felt quite proud that she had chosen me for a friend. She was a lovely little thing with curly blonde hair and became my constant companion for the rest of the day. I made a note of where her parents lived and before leaving for England called at their house with some crayons and a book.

The mushrooming had been a huge success. When we arrived back at the Abos house Maria cut some into small pieces and strung them up in the garage to dry. Before I left she gave me some in a jar, they had a lovely smell and back home a constant reminder of our great day out.

Gliding in the Carpathians

When I first went to Romania I had just begun to paraglide and after the first few visits decided to take my glider with me to use in my spare moments. What started this was an incident when I was helping to fix the spouting on the stable block. I stood up to stretch and looked up to the hills. Out of the blue a paraglider appeared briefly in the distance then disappeared behind the trees. I was excited. I finished my work and drove in the direction I had seen the glider. But before I could find him, he found me! The pilot dropped out of the sky and landed in a field not fifty yards away from where I was driving. I stopped and rushed over to help him gather in his wing. His name was Lutz Levente and he spoke English passably well. He was a member of the local Somylu paragliding club. I explained that I was also a pilot. He was as excited as I was. There is an affinity between flyers. I was due to go back to the UK in a few days but agreed to meet him on my next visit. "Bring your glider with you," were his parting words.

On my next trip I did take my glider and stayed with Lutz for a few days while we went flying together. He introduced me to other members of his club, and I came to realise that the few gliders they had were old and communally owned through the club. Lutz explained how they acquired the few they had. First they hitched a lift through Hungary to Germany, where they did any kind of casual work that they could get. With the money they earned second-hand gliders were bought and they hitched a lift back home. I told them that I would try to bring some glider equipment from the UK.

When I was back in Yorkshire I placed an advert in the paragliding magazine Skywing asking for glider donations. Many pilots up-grade their equipment and others retire and are left with a glider that is soon outdated. In Britain there was not much of a second-hand market so old gliders usually end up in a cupboard or under the bed. I had a good response to the ad and collected eight gliders of varying vintage but all still in good condition. I had them checked over to make sure they were safe though I need not have bothered as for Romanians everything had a use.

When Dr Kathy asked me to take the next trip I was delighted as I would be able to take some of the gliders with me. As I have explained Kathy liked to manage the packing of the truck, but I managed to find gaps among the bags of clothing in which to tuck the gliders away. They really do pack up very small and light, just like a parachute. I anticipated what I would say at customs: that they were tents for the orphans' summer camp. But there were no problems. When I met Lutz and we took them to the club and everyone was delighted. There was no cost, I explained, as everything had been given free. The club leader, Barac, made good use even of the oldest glider, which he had cut up and made into flying suits, glider bags and wind socks. The best of what I had brought out, a Barracuda, he said was big enough for dual training flights.

Problems with train spotting

Lutz and I became close friends and we went flying together whenever we had the opportunity. One day on the way to Siculene, the small village near Miercurea Ciuc where Lutz lived, I had spotted a railway siding with rows of old engines. I wanted to have a closer  inspection and asked Lutz what he thought. "Go and have a look," he said. "It will be okay." Well the next day I did but it wasn't okay and I found myself arrested. The siding was huge and contained a graveyard of dozens of old railway engines, paint peeling off them and rust taking over. There was high wire mesh fencing all the way round topped off with barbed wire, but I found a hole. Once inside I looked at the rows and rows of engines, all very different from ours in the UK. I took a few photographs then wandered among them soaking up the railway nostalgia. I noticed the name plates and identification numbers were missing and doors hung open with their handles gone.

I was about to climb into one when I noticed movement at the end of the row as someone in blue ducked behind one of the engines. I only caught a glimpse but he looked like military or police, and I was sure he had a gun slung over his shoulder. I had walked a long way from the hole in the fence and he was now cutting off my return There was no escape and I felt a little nervous. Looking through the engine wheels I could see two blue legs slowly moving in the same direction. When I stopped, they stopped. I was being stalked by a man with a gun so I thought it was best to confront him. I walked back towards him and around the end of an engine, meaning to duck back if I thought he was going to fire. We came face-to-face only a few metres apart and I found myself looking down the barrel of his rifle. I looked for his trigger finger and noticed with relief that it rested on the guard not on the trigger.

I pointed to the engines and my camera, while he made a similar gesture with his rifle to a nearby building and motioned me to walk in that direction without saying a word. He banged on the door, keeping his rifle pointed at me. I noticed the blue-grey colour inside the end of the barrel which meant either that it hadn't been cleaned for a while or that it had been recently fired. Another guard appeared and then another. The one with the most gold braid on his cap took charge and started the questioning, while the other two stood watching me.

The officer didn't know a single word of English, which I reckoned gave me about a twelve word advantage. I communicated as best as I could that I was from England and worked for a charity. I mentioned Lutz Levente, but he either didn't know him or didn't understand. I tried to explain what a train spotter is, but here I started to get into hotter water as he started waving his arms about. Then I remembered my mobile phone – still a very rare sight in Romania. "Could I phone a friend?" I asked. I couldn't understand his reply, so I took that for a yes. It was with great relief that I heard Lutz's answer at his work number. I explained what had happened, making frequent references to the advice he had given me. "Could you speak to them?" I pleaded. Lutz was decidedly unsure as to whether this was a good idea, having had long experience of the local police. But finally I gave him no choice by handing the phone to El Capo. After a long conversation the captain began to cool down, and almost smiled when he returned the mobile. He told the guard to take me back to the hole in the fence. On the way I tried to make friends and asked if I could take a photo of him by one of the engines. Later, I realised this probably didn't help and anyway he declined. I crept through the hole and said, "La revedere," goodbye, while shooting off across the waste ground to the road. I gave him a wave and to my surprise he waved back.

I wondered if I had caused big trouble for Lutz, but when he came back from work he just laughed. He said that he thought it was okay to look in from the outside but hadn't expected me to get into the siding. Then he explained why the captain said I had been arrested as villains had been breaking into the siding to steal the brass, door handles, fittings and the aluminium name plates. In the end Lutz thought the police had almost found it funny that this strange foreigner would have gone to all this trouble just to take photos of the old rusting stock. What they put down to eccentricity had probably saved me from landing in worse trouble.

Lutz's sledge dog champion

Lutz had a lovely Dalmatian, impressive for its size and condition with a strong muscular back. "He is a champion," I was told. "How do you mean, do you show him?" "No. In the winter we have sledge dog race and he won last year." This was a big thing in Siculene, Lutz explained, when the snow lay thick on the ground. A small child would sit on the sledge, and Lutz's two year old son, Arcos, was the passenger the previous year. "My dog is very strong but does not like the cold and when the race is over he can't wait to get back indoors." Lutz's training method was to take the dog three kilometres out of the village in his car then make him run back. "He is never far behind.

By the time I have parked and walked to the door he is there. That's why he is so strong."

Dana, Lutz's wife, was a teacher. They had lived in Miercurea Ciuc in one of those dreary grey blocks of flats until moving to a traditional house in Siculene shortly before I met them. These traditional houses were narrow at the front where they faced the road, having tall wooden gates and a carved surround in the Hungarian style leading to a huge back garden where they grew vegetables in the rich black soil. This, for Dana and Lutz, made them almost self-sufficient. Some of their neighbours also kept a cow. Late one afternoon I watched the cows ambling down the road back into the village, each breaking off at the appropriate open gate like men coming home from work.

Some of my trips to Romania lasted several weeks then I would have a month or two back in the UK between them. As I prepared for another visit I learned that this time there would be a VIP passenger, Dr Kathy Tedd herself. Kathy went a few times each year but this was the first occasion that she would come with me. I had been warned by other volunteers that Kathy could be a bit tiresome as she was bossy and pedantic. She was, of course very religious, so all swearing had to be cut out. I thought I would not mind as underneath her tough exterior I found her quite sweet. It could be an interesting trip, as well, because Kathy would be visiting hospitals, orphanages, church groups and workshops that I had not been to.

All went well until we neared the Hungarian-Romanian border in the middle of the night and realised we were lost. As luck would have it, I was driving. "Stop," said Kathy. "Pull over at the side of the road. Turn off the engine, Kenneth, and we must all pray for the good Lord to guide us back onto the right path." In all my years of driving I hadn't tried this one before, though I had often used his name. I closed my eyes, Kathy said a few words that I don't recall, then added, "Right, Kenneth, off we go. He will guide us." We had only gone a few miles when I saw the sign for Szolnok. "In future, Kathy, I would like you to speak to him on my behalf as you have more influence than me," I ventured. She saw the funny side, smiling as we continued on our way

This trip with Kathy proved to be very interesting but saddened me at the same time. We had made progress in Targu Mures and Miercurea Ciuc, but some of the orphanages we visited this time were in a dreadful state. I will not attempt to describe some of them, but matters were so bad I still have pictures in my mind of rows of bundled up babies, the older ones sitting in their cots rocking to and fro with blank faces amid unclean conditions and awful smells. What I could never understand was the Romanian policy of separating young unmarried mothers from their babies. The babies would end up in these poorly equipped orphanages and the mothers in primitive hostels to the detriment of both of them. Kathy did help many and I felt sometimes she became stretched trying to provide aid. JOY was a tremendous organisation and she was a remarkable women, who apart from her bossiness was hugely resourceful.

Calling it a day

In 2001 as I passed my 66th birthday I decided to call it quits on my travels to Romania. When I first arrived in the country you could buy a bottle of the palinca brandy cheaper than the cost of a loaf of bread. It seemed a deliberate ploy under Communism as a way of keeping the people drunk but quiet. If Marx wrote that religion was the opium of the people, then under Marxism his heirs made alcohol a far more potent drug. Most of Romania looked grey – the houses, fields, forests and towns all seemed colourless. And there were queues every-where. I once noticed a long line of people all standing with an empty cooking gas bottle. Even-tually, a wagon drew up loaded with filled bottles and I compared the number of people in the queue

with the bottles on the truck. They would not all get one. Those that didn't looked miserable but no one argued, resigned to this being the way things were.

How had things changed in my six years of visits? It has to be said that life for many was still very hard. But things had improved. There was more colour about and the streets were cleaner. People had TVs and those who had worked abroad mostly had cars. Those drab old apartment buildings were still standing around but there was new construction work going on alongside nearly every road. Queues were less common sights and children seemed better nourished and clad.

My last visit to an orphanage was in September 2001, shortly before the World Trade Centre attacks in New York. While the others went inside I stayed with the van to keep an eye on things as there were many boys running around. I watched them playing. Compared to a few years before they still had very little, but now  they seemed much happier. I watched a small group playing table tennis. I have heard of improvisation and have often had to do a bit myself, but what I saw was truly impressive. The table tennis table was an old door straddled across two stacks of bricks, the bats were two small bits of broken planking and for a ball they used a small piece of polystyrene. How's that for resource-fulness? Going by the squeals and laughs I'm sure they were having as much fun as if they had the proper gear. I could not resist taking a photograph. Somehow they will cope, I thought, as long as they no longer have the dead hand of officialdom on their shoulders. Help them, but let them get on with it seemed to be the message.

I went inside and saw more of the orphans on their way to the kitchen for their midday meal. It was like a scene from Oliver Twist with the boys queuing in a long line. Each one was given a thick slice of bread the colour of the hallway walls and spread on top was a spoonful of similar colour mashed potato. That would be their main meal of the day. You never saw a chubby orphan in Romania, which reminded me of the work still to be done.

The next morning we travelled back to the border through some of the smaller villages, many of which had stork's nests on the house tops. Storks are large birds and build big nests on the top of chimneys or telegraph poles. Hungarian and Romanian villagers encourage the birds as they are thought to bring good luck. To attract them they fix a ring like an old cart wheel on top of a pole or chimney stack, and the birds use these as a base to make their nests on. It is a strange sight to see a stork standing on top of the nest on one leg surveying all around as a proper protected species due to the good fortune they bring. And that's exactly what Romania now needs, I thought as I made my way back to Yorkshire, a huge slice of good luck!

CHAPTER TEN

PARAGLIDING
(and other adventures for a man in his sixties)
1995 - 2006

Life usually has us tied down – family, work, business, overdraft and mort-gages. Ambition and obsession can be as restrictive. I hadn't realised at the time but going bankrupt in 1994 had actually liberated me. In the previous two chapters I have explained how I managed to make an income in the years following the closure of my businesses, and have given some of the flavour of my charity excursions to Romania. Now I want to write about how I filled my spare time with a range of exciting hobbies.

The idea of going paragliding was not new. My interest had started in 1978 when I had spotted hang-gliders flying off the cliffs at Filey on the east coast. Just standing and watching them was exciting and I was amazed at how they ran to the edge of the cliff holding the glider above them, launched themselves over the cliff top and then glide gently down to the beach below. That was all I saw them do on that day. I don't think anyone had then tried soaring. But my interest was captured and I thought this was something I would like to try. My brother-in-law Derek, Connie's husband, had made many parachute jumps and one of his parachuting friends had recently taken up hang-gliding. His name was Richard and he took me to a site near Halifax where I could watch him and others, as well as help him lug his heavy hang-glider contraption around. My sons, Andrew and Timothy, came with me. I was impatient to have a go and maybe this caused what happened next.

The wind was low, perhaps too low. It was not an ideal site, consisting of only a small strip of grass that ran down the hill between rocks. Richard nodded towards me, "Your go," he said. He harnessed me into his glider and gave me some basic instructions on how to pick up and point the thing. Then he added, "Run as fast as you can." I did as instructed, setting off at a sprint then pushing the bar forward as I felt myself leaving the ground. But I still skimmed the surface, rising just a dozen or so feet off the ground, so

183

I pushed the bar further forward. This stalled the hang-glider and I came back to earth with a crash, nose diving into the ground. My shoulders hit the A-frame with such force that it was badly bent, as was the front section. My body was severely jarred, and cracking noises were heard by my sons standing more than fifty yards away. They told me later they thought I had broken every bone in my body. Luckily, this was not the case; it was only my joints creaking! I was shaken but most of the damage had been done to the glider.

On reflection I realised that Richard was the wrong man to teach me and hadn't given any real instruction. Particularly, he hadn't said that when I pushed the bar forward to rise I should expect a slight delay. That's how I stalled the glider. It could have been worse had I gone further in flight as I didn't have much idea how to land. I was lucky to walk away from the incident. As we packed the kit away I offered to pay for repairs. Richard said he would let me know but I never heard from him again.

My next attempt to learn was a few years later at a flying school near Hawes in the Dales. Unfortunately, on the first day I slipped on the damp grass while carrying the heavy glider pack and tore a muscle in my leg. At the time I was heavily involved in running my various businesses and realised that any sort of injury could stop me earning a living. So I decided to put my interests in flying on hold.

Now's the time

As I sat outside my caravan at Village Farm in 1995 sipping Earl Grey tea I thought, "What's to stop me now. If I get hurt, well, so what? It would matter to me but it wouldn't change anything or affect my income. I'm free." I jumped up and ran inside to find a paragliding brochure I had stored away. There were lots of contact numbers in it and I rang different flying schools, eventually booking a course with Active Edge, an organisation run by the British champion, Dean Crosby, in the Yorkshire Dales. He was the best tutor possible and what better place to learn: I just love those Dales. This opened a wonderfully exciting new chapter in my life. I guess I am one of those individuals who need risky challenges having raced motor bikes and cars in my younger days. In fact, since I had given up racing I had long looked for something to replace the thrill. Flying through the air on a concoction of silk, nylon and hope sounded just the job.

Active Edge's base at Austwick near Ingleton was close to many flying sites. I was the oldest of the six who turned up for the course, and looking around I could see that I was no more nervous than anyone else. We were all in this together. I partnered with one, a man called Bill Scott, or Scottie as he was better known. Through the training

we became friends and later travelled together to Spain to fly. He was as keen as me and came in his taxi all the way from Washington, Tyne and Wear.

Ground handling was our important first lesson, which involved learning how to get the wing above your head and keep it there as you ran down a slope until your feet left the grass. You become airborne for maybe twenty to thirty yards, or if you were lucky as much as a hundred. The next problem was landing, once again running as fast as you could when you came in to land, your feet clipping the grass to synchronise air speed and ground speed. I think the term, 'hitting the ground running,' was coined for just this.

Take-offs and landings mastered, we moved ever higher up the hillside for short flights. The higher we went the longer we flew. Gradually we reached a height where we could glide for up to a thousand yards before landing at the bottom of the field. My first real flight thrilled me and I was hooked. I stuck with the training and after a year or so took my club proficiency test to get a pilot's license. It had not been easy. I was with much younger people who had more strength and were less cautious. Whatever else that's said about age it does make you more aware of danger. It takes courage to run and jump over the edge of a cliff and many young people just go for it. By comparison I gave it thought; well, for about three seconds before launching myself into the air. They say that to paraglide you must have the right combination of madness and guts.

It is most important to assess conditions and decide when to fly, however, and I adopted the precaution of never being first off the hill. I always watched others to see how they were handling the conditions – or how the conditions were treating them!

Weather is very important to paragliders as conditions have to be just right. Too much wind or too little and flying is cancelled. Wind speeds of from ten to twelve miles an hour is all that can be coped with by beginners, and even for more experienced flyers sixteen or seventeen mph is about maximum. This means that there is a comparatively small window for when it is safe to fly. After I qualified, I would drive out to various sites hoping I might get a flight that day but often returned disappointed. I have climbed to the top of Dales peaks such as Whernside or Ingleborough carrying a twenty three kilogram pack, only to find the wind had picked up, changed direction or disappeared altogether. It was a demoralising trudge back down. But when I did get to fly, the feeling was magic and made up for all the frustrations. Anyway, it was good exercise and I never really minded as long as I was in such a lovely place as the Yorkshire Dales. It is never a waste of time just to sit there on a hill and gaze around.

Allum Pot

Via paragliding I became friendly with Dave Elliot who lived near Settle and had been one of my first instructors. He was great at teaching and I always felt easier about flying when he was close. But he did like adrenalin rushes and was into all sorts of other outdoor activity like hill running, caving and climbing. I think his latest craze is diving. Whatever Dave took on he did well. He shared his interests with his wife Polly and she was as competent. Dave was a keen and experienced caver and a member of the local cave rescue team. One day when the wind was too strong for paragliding he said, "Have you ever been down a cave Ken?" "Yes," I said. "Mother Shipton's in Knaresborough." He laughed, "That's only a show cave. Would you like to go down a proper one here in the Dales?" I didn't have to think for long, "I certainly would". "Well, first we must give you some training."

He took me to a climbing tower in Ingleton to practice rock scaling and SRT, Single Rope Technique. Rope ladders were out. "This is the way we do it now," he told me. I was shown how to move up and down a single rope using a ratchet attached to my harness and stirrups for my feet We spent the afternoon practicing, ratcheting up and abseiling down. I was learning something new and enjoying it, and after a couple more sessions had the hang of it. "Right, Ken, now that you can go up and down a rope we will visit a real cave, but don't worry it will be fine for beginners."

This was Allum Pot near Horton-in-Ribblesdale. The limestone hills there are riddled with tunnels and caves where rainwater drains through on its way to rivers and the sea. The time not to go underground is just after it has rained, though some fools do often with disastrous results. Then cave rescuers like Dave would turn out to save them, having to risk their own lives in the process.

Allum Pot would be the first of many new and exciting adventures with Dave. We entered the cave and stopped to put on our caving waterproofs and harnesses. Along with us was another experienced caver and flying instructor, Chris Seals, who I later became friends with. We set off along a rocky stream bed, squeezing through tight passages, abseiling down ropes and eventually came to a huge cavern over 300 feet deep. Our passage entered into this cavern about half-way down the side. Directly above us we could just see daylight through the falling droplets of water and I could make out trees hanging over the edge of the entrance. Spray and mist filled the cavern, moss and fern-like plants clung to the walls and rocks. We scrambled down further to where many years ago a huge rock had fallen and wedged across the chamber. This was called the Bridge and sloped down to where it was wedged against the side of the cavern. The Bridge was narrow and its surface was uneven, wet and slippery. I hesitated, not knowing whether to walk or creep across on all fours. Eventually I walked trying to watch where I put my feet without looking past them into the depths below. A few days later I was looking through a book on the cave which advised cavers to exercise extreme care as a slip here would mean certain death. I was pleased I had not read it beforehand.

Dave and Chris were ahead of me. They had fixed a rope for the descent to the bottom of the cavern but I said this was far enough for me on my first visit. Telling me to stay where I was and get myself as comfortable as I could, they went ahead and were soon out of sight. I had to stand where the Bridge wedged against the cavern wall. There was only just enough room for my feet on the slippery rock. I watched the rope till it stopped moving as they went further down, leaving me feeling suddenly cold and alone. I had been sweating when I was moving but now I was getting chilled. I unfastened the 'cow's tail', a short length of rope, from my harness and swished it round my shoulders to keep warm, but it had little effect. Soon, I was shivering and my thoughts began to wander. Suppose they had a problem lower down and could not get back; I couldn't get out on my own to raise the alarm. They had been gone for just thirty minutes but it felt more like two hours as I stood shivering, cut off and longing for their return. I could not see down far as the rope curled round the rock but I kept looking for movement and listening. Eventually, after almost an hour, the rope twitched. I stared. Then it twitched again as in a cloud of steam Chris appeared, sweating profusely as he pulled himself up. Dave was not far behind. I felt a great sense of relief.

We set off on the way back across the Bridge and along to the first rope climb. I put on my harness, attached myself to the rope by the jammer then started to climb, heaving myself up with the foot stirrups, then sliding the rope through the jammer. At the top Dave helped me unhook the rope and scramble on to a ledge. We were soon back in daylight out on the open moor, and I had chalked up another interesting experience.

Spain; Montejaque

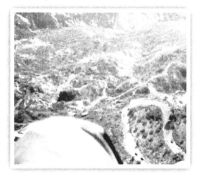

Dave Elliott often went to Spain to paraglide and I was invited along, though I would not be going as a pilot on this first occasion. He had already booked the trip for twelve people and I would have to fly out later on my own. I took a flight from Leeds-Bradford to Malaga, hired a car and drove along the coast road towards Marbella. It was a pleasant evening with the sun dropping down behind the mountains. I turned right off the coast road and up into the hills towards the town of Ronda, which was on the route to Montejaque where I was to meet Dave and the others. The road looked recently resurfaced as it wound up steeply through rugged mountains, but there was no sign of where I might stop for the night. By 8 pm I was beginning to feel uneasy at the thought of spending  the night in the car, something that was not at all attractive as the evening grew colder. As I rounded a sharp bend close to the top I noticed over to my left a small shack standing back from the road with a few cars parked outside. A dim light hung by the door in front of a weather-beaten sign that I was able to read when I drew closer, 'Restaurant, pension'. I drew up beside the other cars and breathed a sigh of relief.

The pension looked basic but they had a room it was clean and wonderfully cheap. I ordered beer and tapas before going to my room. When travelling in foreign parts it can be a worry not knowing where you will sleep and on many occasions I have had to rough it. But that night in the mountains once I was tucked up in bed I felt snug and was quickly off to sleep. In the morning I glanced through the window, which unfortunately looked straight onto a building site. A large extension was being built and I noticed they still used wooden scaffolding poles fastened with rope. About eight cats were basking in the warming sun, although in the shade there were still patches of white frost.

I set off towards Ronda, which was now mostly downhill as I discovered my night stop had been perched on the highest spot along the route. I had read quite a lot about Ronda, its history and spectacular setting, and stopped for a look around. I visited the old bullring which was the site in the eighteenth century of the birth of the modern style of bullfighting, where matadors stand on foot to confront the bull, armed with cape and sword. Until then they had fought on horseback. It is a place where Ernest Hemingway had spent a lot of time and there were more pictures of him on the walls than there were of bullfighters. I use this term, bullfighter, loosely as in my view it is no fight against a bull half dead by the time the picadors have finished with it. Many years before, I had been to see a bull fight and concluded that it was more of a slaughter than any sort of even contest. There was little entertainment for me in watching a poor animal being tormented to death. They have a much better idea in Pamplona where the bulls chase people through the streets.

Ronda sits on dramatic cliff edges from where I looked at breathtaking views of the valley below, the gorges and bridges, and the distant mountains. Though Grazalema close by it is the wettest part of Spain it is a lovely area for walking as I was to find out on later visits. It is also a wonderful site for paragliding and was the hometown of the semi-legendary Arab scientist, Abbas bin Furnas, who had experimented with flight in the ninth century.

I drove to Montejaque where I met Dave and the rest of the pilots. One of them had a tandem glider and I hoped he would take me up for a flight. But he was enjoying himself flying solo and left the tandem in its bag. Nevertheless, I had a very interesting week driving other pilots to various sites and recovering them from landing areas. It was very good weather and they flew almost every day. The social side was also very good as we talked day and night about paragliding without boring anyone else. We found different and interesting food, though one night we came across something that we did not like one little bit. Someone had noticed a little restaurant in a back street. It was more like the utility room of a private house but the food appeared to be good. What I had was a kind of tasty chicken stew. But it was all spoilt when someone at the far end of the table held up a large cockroach she had just fished out of her stew. Everyone stopped eating. Those with the same dish, myself included, stirred our stews to see if there were more. The woman of the house came to see what the problem was, but when shown the intruder she did not appear at all concerned and replied, "Well, it's dead isn't it?" That brought the meal to an abrupt end and we made for the nearest bar.

The next day was the most exciting of my visit. After the last flight of the day we met for a coffee before setting off on the fifteen mile trip back to base. We had four cars and I was driving one of them. The first two drivers set off like lunatics to race each and I couldn't let them get away, so I was quickly hard on their heels in pursuit. It was fabulous and I closed right up behind them. I couldn't pass as the road was narrow but when we made it back to Montejaque I was still right there. They were real boy racers and were surprised to find they couldn't shake off this old timer!

Nearly Snagged on Captain Cook's Monument

Paragliding became a real passion as my skill levels rose. However, one day I nearly came unstuck. One of the club sites was on the Cleveland Hills near Stokesley on a ridge that runs by the side of Captain Cook's Monument. The 'great man' was one of my heroes and had been to school nearby in the village of Great Ayton.

There were about six pilots on the hill when I arrived waiting for the wind speed to reduce. I sat with them, chatting to another pilot who had the same Nova paraglider as me, even the same purple colour. The wind's strength, measured by meter, was borderline for us but when it eased a couple of the more experienced guys started to fly, then my friend took off. He turned and came back, flying smoothly past where I stood. Now it was my turn. I walked to the edge of the slope and waited. Wind always goes up and down a little. When it eased I put up my wing and raced towards the edge, the wind caught me and up I went. In a few seconds I was three hundred feet above the edge of the escarpment and I settled back in the seat, easing up on the controls to go forward into the wind. But I didn't go forward! The wind was stronger than I had anticipated. I tucked in my arms and pushed the brakes up to the stops, while stretching out my legs to lower wind resistance. But it made no difference. I was not going upwards as fast as I had been, but I was not going forward either. Instead, I was gradually being pushed back, passing over people standing on the ridge.

I did not look behind as I knew what was there: the Monument surrounded by railings with sharp pointed spikes and behind that a wall and then a wood, equally dangerous for me. At that moment I was higher than the Monument but was slowly edging backwards towards an area where there would be no lift, and where I could drop like a stone. I had done all I was taught and had now run out of ideas. All I could do was to keep the glider pointing into the wind. It was not easy as the wind was gusting and changing direction. I had constantly to correct, because if I let the glider turn it would be a catastrophe and I would be blown across the moor out of control.

In front of me the distant hills were getting smaller when they should have been growing bigger. I continued to drift slowly backwards towards the Monument. Thankfully I was still about fifty feet above it but I was expecting to drop at any moment. I looked down at the ugly looking spikes and the lightning conductor on the top, all pointing up like spears waiting to stick me. I wondered how thick my seat was. I felt helpless but could do nothing.

Suddenly the glider gave a lurch, shook and folded. Fortunately, I had just passed the Monument. This caused the wing to collapse and I spun around and around, dropping much faster than I had been flying. I landed with a thump on the heather a few yards from the wall. By now others had seen me and ran across to help. They grabbed hold of my canopy and grounded it just as it was about to drag me over the wall and into the trees. I was helped to my feet, shaken but luckily no worse for wear thanks to the thick carpeting of heather. Even in the heat of the moment Dave Elliot's words when training me had come back, "Get your undercarriage (your legs) down to land." I had finished up less than forty-five feet from the Monument.

My friend with the Nova landed after forty minutes in the air and came across to see if I was okay. I asked him how his Nova flew so well when mine had gone backwards. He asked, "What model is your wing?" When I told him he said, "Well that's why. Yours is a good safe canopy to learn on, but mine is a later model and will penetrate stronger winds." You live and learn, as I had done in this case – just. It was definitely time to upgrade.

Marske by the Sea

A few months later I was anxious to try out my new Nova canopy. The weather had been wet for weeks which had kept me grounded. Now it changed, ushering in brilliant sunshine. I checked the forecast and wind direction then rushed off to Model Ridge, a flying site in the Cleveland Hills near Stokesley. When I arrived a group of pilots were waiting for the wind to come round onto the hill At the moment it was blowing at an angle not suitable for flying. I went for a coffee in Lord Stone's Café where I found Nigel, a friend from Redcar, fed up with the prospect of a wasted trip. He suggested we go to Marske-by-the-Sea, where he thought the wind direction would be right. Off we went, parking our cars at the bottom of the cliff and walking to the top. The wind was spot on, blowing in off the sea, a little on the strong side but still flyable. There was one problem, however, as the tide was in. This meant there was no beach to land on and we would have to maintain enough height during our flights to get back to the cliff top. The alternative was a dip in the drink!

I unpacked my glider, crisp and shiny with newness. I was anxious to try it out but did not want it covered in salt water. Nigel, an experienced pilot, was already walking to the edge ready to fly but found the wind too strong. He moved down the cliff a short distance, put up his canopy and took off, immediately gaining height. I watched him then did the same.

You have no time to think when the wind is strong. You have to shuffle backwards partway down the cliff to an area where it does not feel quite as strong then wait for the right moment when there is a slight lull and let go of the bunched up canopy, swivel round take up the slack on the controls and head out to sea. Once I was soaring I gathered myself together and eased back into the seat, then turned along the top of the cliff remembering the right-of-way rule when I met Nigel on his way back. I looked out to sea. The waves were crashing at the bottom of the cliff which reminded me, if I needed it, that keeping high was crucial. As I flew back along the ridge I ventured out over the waves which I found a new and breathtaking experience. On the next beat I moved out a little further and so on until I was quite far out to sea. The lift band does not extend far in front of the cliff. If I went too far in front of it I would lose height and would go down into the frothy waves. If that happened then, even if I survived the fall, I would be encumbered by the canopy and there would be little chance of getting out of the water.

I could not resist one more beat, taking me that little bit further out over the waves. My heart was now racing. As I turned at the end of the beat I looked back towards the cliff top and saw that Nigel had just landed, so I decided it was time to follow his example. I made a good landing on what was only a narrow strip with the cliff edge on one side and a barbed wire fence on the other. New canopy, new experience and I was thrilled. Driving home along the A19 I glanced at the speed indicator. I was unwittingly doing 98 miles an hour – all due to the adrenalin still coursing through my system. Slow down!

Spain, El Chorro and the scariest of walks

I have known fear on many occasions, several of them, it has to be said, on adventures with my paragliding instructor, Dave Elliot. My next story is one that was probably the most terrifying in all my life. By this time, 2000 I had become a regular on Dave's Spanish escapades. We had glided over many of the hills of Southern Spain where the weather around the lovely Ronda was more reliable than in the UK. Dave knew his way around, where to fly and from where the wind would be blowing.

The previous day we had flown from a mountain called Lejar and I had witnessed the very rare sight of Dave getting it wrong on a landing, sliding in on the seat of his pants where I had made a perfect touchdown just seconds before. In fact, I can't remember him making another mistake in all my flights with him. Twenty four hours later there was not a breath of wind. "I don't think we can fly today," he said. We were never stuck if we were grounded by the wind as he always had an answer: a hill walk, a cave, a canyon, one as taxing as the other. There were about ten in the group with Dave and wife Polly. "Have any of you been to El Chorro? It's an interesting walk through an old canyon." Fatefully, we were all up for it.

El Chorro is described on YouTube as having, 'the scariest path in the world,' something I did not discover until later. The path itself is called El Caminito del Rey or the king's little path, and clings to the side of a narrow river gorge running through a limestone canyon. The path existed because of a six hundred feet high hydroelectric dam further up the gorge built between 1914 and 1921, and is actually a concrete, two-foot wide cat walk around one side of the canyon wall which lulls you into a false state of security by starting low with a comforting rusty steel handrail. But as the canyon gets deeper, so the path gets higher and the handrail eventually disappears having rusted away. I remember wondering what kind of steel they had used. When I reached the point where the handrail had gone completely I instinctively lent inwards towards the canyon wall, my hands groping along seeking grip on the cold limestone. Dave was leading the way, skipping along like a mountain goat with Polly just as nimble right behind. I was trying not to look down, which was futile as I had to watch where I was putting my feet.

As we climbed higher the path itself started to deteriorate. It was at this time that I realised I had developed another phobia to go with my fear of fire; the new one was fear of heights, which had never manifested itself before. I was last in our line. I could have turned back but I'm no coward and thought the path had to get better further up. But it didn't. We rose hundreds of feet above the floor of the gorge. When those ahead stopped I saw that the path had all but gone, leaving just a twelve foot strip of steel like an old narrow gauge railway line to link two bits of crumbling concrete.

Dave spoke to reassure us. "The way to get across is to shuffle sideways leaning on the rock face." Two of the younger members of the party had become anxious so Dave demonstrated. Then Polly followed, also making it look ridiculously easy. One by one the others made it across with varying degrees of confidence. Then it was my turn. Dave could see by my face I was not happy so he came back to accompany me. We stayed close together as we shuffled onto the rail. I felt only marginally better as I was thinking of the extra weight the two of us were putting on that single length of rusty steel. I could hear the distant rumble of water and as I looked at my feet I could not avoid seeing past into the bottom of the gorge at the green and white water tumbling over the rocks.

When my feet touched the concrete again I felt weak with relief, though not for long. Dave spoke, "There you are Ken. You made it and don't worry, it will be easier going back." Going back, you've got to be kidding! That was in my mind but what I said was, "I thought we were on a walk through the canyon," adding emphasis to the word through. "Oh no," he smiled. "We carry on up here until we come to a bridge that is closed off to walkers and we have to return the way we came." I had summoned up what I felt was a superhuman effort so far negotiating a crumbling narrow spit of a path with no handrail, and then shuffling across the rail. I was going to have to do it again! I was gutted and shaking. But there was nothing for it but to press on.

A few of us were now suffering and our depression increased when Dave said, "Be very careful. The area we are coming to is most dangerous." For him to make a statement like that it must mean we were facing almost certain death. I saw what he had in mind. A huge rock jutted out from the canyon wall and the remains of the path wound round it. The concrete had disappeared for most of the way and all that remained was the single strip of steel. A rope ran around the rock just over head height. To continue you fixed a 'cow's tail' rope from your belt harness onto this as a safety line. This was too much for me. "I've had enough, Dave, in fact more than enough," I said. Two others agreed and also said they would not go on. "Don't worry," said Dave. "There's another route. Just go back a little way along the path and you come to a part where the canyon wall is not so steep and you can climb up the side to reach a track that runs parallel. It will take you to a tunnel which meets this path again further along." I felt slight relief.

The three of us set off, hugging the wall of the canyon. We found the spot for the climb and scrambled up. The higher track was a narrow channel that had carried a small workers' railway during the dam's construction. It felt good to be on level solid ground again. We found the tunnel and looked in expecting to see light at the other end but there was nothing but pitch black. We set off in single file. As it grew darker the surface became more uneven and there were pools of water and mud as deep as our knees that we had to stumbled through. Without torches we decided to link hands, groping through in utter blackness. I expected any moment to fall down a shaft. "What am I doing here? I came to Spain to paraglide, not struggle in mud and water holding another man's hand," I thought to myself. Eventually we saw the light at the end of the tunnel.

Dave, Polly and the rest had negotiated their way around the rock and were waiting where the track and path met. We climbed down to the path and continued on its failing concrete surface further up the canyon. It continued to worsen the higher we went, and most of us were now panting with effort and fright. Finally, we reached a small concrete and steel platform that acted as a viewing point for the dam, the gorge, the fast flowing river and the walls of the canyon. We could see much of the way we had come. Hundreds of feet below was a section of the Malaga to Cordoba railway line which runs through tunnels and on bridges. I learned later that this was the setting for scenes used in the film Von Ryan's Express. Several of us were in no mood to enjoy the view, though, and I realised that their faces, drawn with fear and fatigue, probably mirrored mine. I had to sit down close to something solid.

The walk up had left me exhausted and sweaty with fear. Getting back would be no easier and I had time to worry, "What am I doing here" and what if I can't go on? There is no way a helicopter will reach us. No one can carry me. The only way is to walk – or crawl. Can I do it on my hands and knees?" My head was swimming and never before or since have I felt so trapped. When I had been frightened before it had been momentary or at least was over in a matter of minutes. This had lasted much of the two hours' trek up there and was going to stay with me all the way back. The fear was debilitating and had weakened me as much as the effort of the climb. I thought of the way back along the narrow ledge with every step retraced and every terrifying moment relived. My upbringing stopped me showing my fear or talking about it with anyone in the same way it had forced me to go on when going back was the only sensible choice. I was particularly unwilling to discuss my feelings with Dave as he seemed to feel that everyone could do what he could do with the right encouragement. I didn't want encouragement; I wanted safety.

It was time to go. I staggered to my feet, the rest having replenished some of my energy. We set off, the one comfort being that each step was taking us nearer the end. The three of us who had gone through the tunnel did so again, once more holding hands as we groped along the wall with our feet slipping through the water. When we emerged it was into direct sunlight and I have never experienced such contrast from pitch black. Our eyes ached for minutes. We rejoined the path and the rest of the group, continuing back to the rail crossing, the worst part of the whole nightmare. Dave was waiting. "I'll go first Ken, you keep close to me." I had to go for it and turned sideways, put my hands on the rock face and shuffled along the rusty bar. Again, I looked past my feet to the grey rocks 500 feet below then back at the canyon wall inches in front of my nose as I crept along.

At the other side when the path resumed the group decided to pose for pictures. "Use a fast shutter speed Dave, as I am shaking and it will blur the picture." I said. Edging back we finally made it to where the path was intact and the handrail offered a measure of reassurance. "There you are," said Dave. "Ken, I told you it would be easier coming back." "Yes. On a scale of one hundred, the return was 99! And don't say it will be easier next time because never ever will there be a next time," I spluttered. And there hasn't.

Scores of people have died over the years falling from the El Caminito del Rey. This finally became too much for the authorities and the path was closed to the public in 2000, just months after I had climbed it. In 2011, the local government agreed to share the cost of restoring El Caminito, including building a museum and a memorial to those who have died.

I make a bad decision

Back in the UK, I flew whenever the weather conditions would allow. One day Beryl and I were on the ridge by Captain Cook's Monument. When we arrived the wind was stronger than we had expected. Pilots were waiting for it to drop but as the day wore on it didn't and many left. I was particularly keen to fly so I waited to see if the wind would ease in the afternoon, as it often did. Eventually, there were just three of us and the other two were experienced pilots. Then the wind eased just a little and off they went on their flights. It was still very breezy but I didn't want a wasted day and made myself ready. I laid out the glider then walked slowly backwards dragging it towards the edge. I waited for what I thought was the right moment, then heaved it up above my head. As I was doing so a huge gust inflated the wing before I was ready, taking it off across the moor, dragging me along the ground bouncing off rocks like a rag doll. I let go of one brake and tried with both hands to pull in the other side but could do nothing to stop it . I screamed with pain as I hit rocks. Fortunately, the other two pilots had just landed, cutting their flights short because of the gusty conditions, and saw what was happening. They came to my rescue, one running in front of the glider while the other grabbed the controls. This brought it to a stop. I was badly shaken and did not know which part of me hurt most. Beryl was quite distraught as she had seen it all. When they saw that I could stand without falling over the two pilots cleared off leaving Beryl and me to pack up the glider and carry it almost a mile back to the car.

I felt dreadful and ached all over but I realised it could have been much worse. My helmet was damaged where my head had struck a rock. The glider's seat was torn, though the back protector had done what it was there for and saved me from worse injury. My flying boots also had done their job of protecting my ankles, though my left foot was throbbing. I was bent but nothing was broken, thanks to having the right equipment.

It took an age to pack the glider into its bag. All the time I had to pretend that I was all right and not cause Beryl to worry. When the glider was in its bag the next problem was how we were going to get it back to the car, there was no way that I could possibly get the thing onto my back. Beryl took hold of one strap while I took the other, half carrying and half dragging it along. It was getting late and the light was fading as we struggled down the track stopping frequently and trying to boost each other's spirits.

Finally we made it. It was almost dark as we used the last of our energy to lift the glider into the boot. Beryl could not drive my car so, battered as I was, it was down to me. As I pressed the clutch the pain shot through my ankle and up my leg. How could I drive fifty miles home? Good question! Answer, because there was no alternative. I managed to make most of the journey in top gear so I did not have to press the clutch too often. Later, soaking in the bath at home with a glass of red wine I thought back over my bad decision to attempt to fly when the conditions were not right but luckily I got away with it.

Another visit to Park Rash

The place I most wanted to fly over was Park Rash on the edge of Coverdale. This had special significance for me as it had been the scene of two adventures, one, when Julia and I had driven that December night through deep snow to see her friends in Woodale, described in chapter two. The other was further back when I was seventeen and had crashed my motorbike in an almost totally deserted landscape. The bike had nearly slid over a sheer drop but was stopped by boulders placed by the side of the road. But it was badly damaged. I had patched the bike up, made a loop on the end of the broken throttle cable and reached down between my legs to operate it for the ride back home to Masham. This is a story in my first book, Nothing Easy. Park Rash is a glorious and wild part of the Yorkshire Dales, and one that not many people know about. I was eager to see it from above.

The problem was getting the chance. Not only had the weather conditions to be right but I had to pick a time when other pilots might be around as it is not a regular flying site and I would never fly on my own.

One fine day when the wind was in the right direction I made for Great Whernside, driving along a farm track to get as near as possible to the take-off point before starting the long walk. I had tried on many previous occasions without luck, but the weather was perfect and I could see a car parked by a wall at the end of the track. As I got nearer I recognised it as belonging to one of our club members. I looked up the hill, seeing two small figures close to the summit looking like little hunchbacks, misshaped by their back packs. My spirits rose. Could this be the day that I had waited so long for? There was just a gentle breeze here at the foot of the hill and the sun was threatening to break through light clouds. But I reminded myself that I should not get too excited as it could be blowing a gale at the top. I hoisted my fifty pound pack on to my back and set off to climb to the top of the two thousand two hundred foot peak. Everything in this world has to be paid for and the price to fly off Whernside was this long hard slog.

More than an hour later I staggered to the top. Just to stand and stare at the magnificent view took what little breath I had left. But it was not blowing a gale just about strong enough. The other two pilots had waited for me and as soon as I arrived they laid out their gliders and prepared to take off. We had a few minutes chat and agreed that conditions were just about as good as they could be. Soon they were in the air. I watched them fly out from the hill, slowly gaining height, and decided to follow suit. I kitted up. I am always nervous before I fly, just as I had been years before when I was motor racing. Here goes! My take off was smooth and there was plenty of lift as I moved out from the hill. I flew up and down the ridge a couple of times to gain height then turned right, in the direction of Leyburn looking for what I had waited a long time to see from this vantage point. I spotted the road from Leyburn coming across the moor on my right, dry stone walls on either side and a lonely farm house that I recognised surrounded by a clump of trees. I turned left and flew along the line of the road, going down a bit lower for a closer look. I was still hundreds of feet above the ground and it was not easy to tell the gradient but I could see quite clearly the hairpin bend where the gradient is one in three at the steepest part. This was it, the spot where fifty years before I had crashed my motorbike and rolled down the side of the road as my bike slithered along without me before smacking into the stone barrier on the bend by the sheer drop. I could never have contemplated on that spring day in 1953 that one day I would see that same place from the air. In fact, I would not have imagined that paragliders would have come to exist. It is also the place where I was stuck in the snow almost twenty years ago as mentioned in chapter two. While living in the past I had lost height just gliding along, I didn't want another crash! I turned back towards the hill, now looming high above me and flew along the side as close as possible to catch the up-draught. The wind was only light and I was concerned that I might not be able to get back to the top. I started looking round for a landing area lower down but patience paid off and a few stronger gusts lifted both me and my spirits, and after about twenty five minutes scratching close to the hill I was high enough to turn in and land very close to where I took off. I slowly packed away my glider then walked down to the car with a sense of real fulfilment. It had been another memorable visit to Park Rash and a milestone in my life.

New heights

There is a saying you learn when paragliding: "It is better to be down here wishing you were up there, than to be up there wishing you were down here." My highest flight was at Staggs Fell near Hawes.

As I drove towards the hill I could see about eight pilots in the sky, two of them were so high they were only specs in the sky. Obviously they were enjoying near perfect conditions. As the weather was good Beryl was again with me. Together we climbed up the hill. I unpacked my glider, harnessed up, then walked to the edge. There was a light wind blowing directly onto the hill which felt so good I took off straight away. As soon as I left terra firma I went up like a rocket, with the ground shrinking away below there was no searching for lift as it was everywhere. In no time at all my altimeter was reading five hundred feet above my take off spot and bleeping like crazy telling me I was still going up. I took a few deep breaths to help me relax and enjoy the view. In no time at all I could see the mountains of the Lake District and to my left the Plain of York, the Dales were below and to the south were the moors around Greenhow and Ilkley and the urban centre of Harrogate and Leeds beyond. It was like looking at my life story. What a great feeling. My altimeter was now reading over 1.000 feet. Pilots like Dean Crosby revel in conditions like this and fly for miles, but was I getting a little out of my depth? I looked down to the take-off area where I had left Beryl reading a book, her red anorak now just a little dot on the grass, and this made me realise how high I had flown. I cruised around for a while enjoying the views for miles in every direction still going higher but not at the same speed then decided it was high enough and turned towards Hawes to try and lose height but had to fly very close to the town before I levelled out then drop back along the valley to find another area where the lift was not as strong. Gradually I came down out of the clear blue sky, landing close to where Beryl was sitting. It had been exhilarating and I had enjoyed myself so much I took off again in the afternoon, feeling a little more sure of myself the second time and went up even higher than before. it was a most memorable experience.

I later learned that Dean Crosby had indeed taken off from Staggs Fell that very day and set a new distance record by landing somewhere near Doncaster.

Majorca – Gliding and Caving

I hadn't heard from Dave Elliot for a few weeks but no doubt he will have been planning another adventure and sure enough when the phone rang, "Hi Ken fancy a trip to Majorca?" "Yes Dave when?" was my immediate response, I have never yet been disappointed on travels with him, scared yes, often but never bored. He gave me the details and I agreed to go with him and wife Polly, they were meeting a group of Spanish cavers to explore a new cave but would also be flying and I could take the opportunity to visit an old friend Barry Taylor who now lived on the Island.

When we landed at Palma I telephoned Barry to pick me up and while I waited Dave went to hire a car. I said I would call him the next day to arrange where to meet. It was good to see an old friend after many years and we spent a pleasant evening going over old times in Ilkley when he worked for me as an excavator driver and we often had a drink together in The Rose and Crown. The next morning Barry dropped me off to meet Dave, He had arrange to go caving the following day with his friends who lived on Majorca but now weather permitting it was time for us to fly and we headed for the hills. Dave had checked the forecast and wind direction and knew where to go. It was early morning and we waited for the thermals to increase as the day warmed up. The take-off area was terrible, just a rocky patch on the side of a hill surrounded by thorn bushes. I had to run like mad, then quickly pick up my feet as high as possible as I skimmed the bushes to get airborne. Once in the air I flew up and down the ridge a few times but before I could settle down to a good flight I was dismayed to see on the take-off area six Spanish pilots unpacking their gliders. As a nationality they were known to be reckless and rarely took any notice of the rules of flying. When I saw them in the air I turned and made my way to the landing ground. I did not like a crowd, especially pilots who have little regard for others.

The landing area was at the far side of an almond orchard. The white blossom was out and looked lovely from above, but I made the mistake of doing an aircraft landing, gliding over the orchard towards the landing area but I was losing height much faster than I had expected and realised that I would not make it across the orchard. I started looking for a clear patch between the trees but there wasn't one. So I aimed for the smallest tree and came down through the light branches to the ground unhurt, but my canopy was snagged. It took two hours to untangle the lines while all the time I was worried about meeting the farmer, as I had broken some of the branches. Fortunately for me, there was no damage to my paraglider and the farmer didn't show up. I had just packed away when the Spanish pilots came in to land. They had a different approach to me, coming in high over the landing area then doing a spiral dive to the ground. This was interesting to watch but it was an approach I was not interested in trying.

The next day Dave had arranged to go caving. I did not fancy flying on my own so I agreed to go with him, though after my earlier experiences I made it clear I was along just for the walk. The cave was not marked on any map as a new shaft had only recently been discovered and its whereabouts were a closely guarded secret. Dave and his caving friends were very excited as this was something new. Eventually, we found a small hole surrounded by scrubby bushes and rocks, so well concealed you could have easily walked past. While the other cavers got their kit ready Dave fastened a rope round a huge rock close to the entrance, I walked over and peered down into the darkness where the rope hung, then went and sat down to read my book in the sun. "Are you not coming down, Ken?" I was asked. "No, I'll sit this one out. Anyway, I don't have the kit." Dave replied, "Well that's not a problem, I have a spare set!" "No thanks," I repeated. "I have a good book and it's a nice day to sit here and relax."

After El Chorro Dave was not going to put pressure on me. But one of the others, a lady called Jane, looked up from lacing her boots, "You know Ken, you could miss something very special, few people have been in this cave." She smiled and I felt myself weaken. She smiled again and looked at me waiting for my answer and I made one of my compromises. "Okay," I heard myself answering. As soon as the words were out I regretted them, but I couldn't go back on my decision. Before I knew it, I was wearing waterproof overalls, harness and a helmet complete with a new light.

The rope hung down over the edge of the shaft into darkness and one-by-one they hooked themselves onto the rope and slid backwards over the edge. I watched carefully to see how it was done. Then it was my turn. Polly helped me fix the rope and I backed over the edge. I slowly lowered myself into the darkness, my lamp flicking around the shaft wall as I went down. I eased the rope through my descender and as I went lower I felt a new and frightening sensation as my weight stretched the rope and it became springy. The ten millimetre rope, less than the thickness of my little finger, was just inches in front of my nose and I could not help wondering how strong it was. And another problem dangling on a single rope is that you spin round when you can't touch the side of the shaft.

I could hear Dave calling to me from the darkness below, his voice echoing up the shaft until I was level with the ledge part way down the shaft on which he and the others were standing. I swung myself over, and started to spin but Dave reached out caught hold of me and I scrambled onto the ledge, unhooking the rope from my descender and giving it a tug to let Polly up above know it was free. We went further into the cave and on the left the path sloped away into darkness. Dave was just behind me, "Keep to the right Ken, to the left is a bottomless pit." I hugged the wall on my right as we continued down. The slope eased into a gentle decline and opened into the most magnificent chamber I have ever seen. We lit candles around the walls

to better appreciate the remarkable sight. The decorations - cavers' way of describing stalagmites and stalactites - were out of this world. Because the cave was newly discovered nothing had been disturbed or broken off by souvenir hunters. We were among the first to see this place. It was like a beautiful, brand new cathedral.

After a photograph session it was time to leave. I climbed slowly back up the slope, keeping to the side as I didn't need reminding of the bottomless pit. Polly was first back up the rope, then it was my turn. I secured my jammer onto the rope, got my feet into the loops and swung out from the ledge. I ratcheted my way up the rope using the foot stirrups. It sounds easy but is actually hard work, and after a while I stopped for a breather. "Have a last look around," Dave called. "You may never again see anything like it." When I took hold of the rocky ledge at the top of the shaft my hands locked on, as I thought of the long drop hundreds of feet beneath me. Polly had to prise my hands free to drag me over the ledge and back onto terra firma. I will never see those sights again, but I do have the pictures.

Romania. Adventures in Sinaia

As explained, in between my escapades with caving and paragliding in the UK and Spain, occasional work with Gordon Brown and selling animal medicine, I would disappear off on charity trips to Romania. Once I had met Lutz Levente in a field outside of Miercurea Ciuc, I started taking my paraglider on every trip. Never ones to shirk from a challenge, Dave and Polly Elliot and a raft of other adventurers, arranged to meet me in Transylvania when I could get a few days off from helping the JOY charity.

The first destination we aimed for was Sinaia, a resort fast emerging as a popular spot for winter sports in the Bucegi Mountains, forty five kilometres south of Brasov. The resort had chairlifts working throughout the year, in winter for skiers and for walkers and paragliders during the rest of the year. It is very popular with Romanians with their love of the outdoors.

While waiting for our guide I took a walk along the main street and saw a dancing bear chained up outside a store. The problem was it didn't look like it had much dance left in it, sitting there tired, old and miserable. People were having their photographs taken by the side of him for 2,000 lei, about twenty pence. I looked into the poor animal's lifeless eyes, making it a very sorrowful sight. I am glad to hear that the keeping of bears by private individuals has been now banned in Romania.

Eventually our Romanian guide, Leonard, arrived. I had known him for some time through the paragliding fraternity in Romania, and the year before he had travelled to England to meet up with our club in the Dales. He was going to show us the best flying area in the Bucegi Mountains and we could take the chair lift to take-off area. As we set off in the chairlift up the mountainside I looked at the rusty cables running over the wheels of the equally corroded steel pylons. The lifts had been installed in the 1950s and like everything else had rusted under Communism. I wondered when they were last checked and serviced. I noticed the weight limit warning on the wall of the cable car and made a rough calculation of people and gliders. We were close to the limit!

I was the last out, heaving my pack onto my back and glancing down the valley to the dark green forest surrounding the town. Leonard and Dave were leading the way up to another lift, and then I realised that we were only half way up the mountain. Our final take-off site was to be near the top of Mount Omul, 2,300 meters or nearly 7,500 feet above sea level. Whew! I had never taken off from higher than the 700 metres, 2,200 feet, of Ingleborough.

The take-off area was a smooth grassy strip that sloped gently down between the rocks then suddenly disappeared over a ledge. I gazed at the spectacular hazy blue mountains all around us but when I looked down to the valley my stomach did a somersault. It was like looking at an Ordnance Survey map, just like that time I reached my greatest height in the Dales. The main road was a grey thread running through olive green forests to a town that looked the size of a 50 pence coin.

Dave can sometimes be very blunt, "Right, can you see the landing area?" the field was just a dot of green on the edge of the town. "Remember the golden rule, go straight to it with no detours. If you go down in the forest you are dead. If landing in the trees don't kill you then the bears will. And if the bears don't find you then neither will we. Remember the electricity cables and pylons on the landing field and the pipeline near the ditch on the edge. Look for signs of wind direction for landing, though there is not likely to be any. There is none here either, so you will have to forward launch and run like hell to get the wing above your head." Two of the other pilots were fairly inexperienced and they didn't look too reassured. As usual, I kept my feelings to myself.

"Polly will go first, then you Ken, so get ready." I tip-toed over to my glider thinking, "Dave is a good pilot and instructor. I trust him. If he thought I couldn't do it he wouldn't send me off." But hadn't I had a similar idea on the climb up the path at El Chorro? I wanted the toilet but it would have to wait, and I distracted myself by fastening the harness and checking and re-checking the buckles and lines. You have to concentrate hard at this moment as the most dangerous times are take-off and landing. Polly ran down the slope and took off a few yards before the rocky ledge, flying smoothly away from the hill. I picked up the front risers, one in each hand, waited for the command, then sprinted as fast as my nearly 65-year old legs would carry me. You only get one chance and there is no turning back for another go. I looked straight ahead at the other side of the valley. My steps felt lighter as the wing took over, carrying me over the edge and suddenly I was airborne, the great thrill taking away my breath as I settled back into the seat. I tried to relax as I floated out from the hill. Above me was the huge purple wing, twelve metres wide when fully inflated, swaying gently against the clear blue sky.

After a few minutes I felt as if I was not moving and checked the controls to make sure I was doing nothing to hold back. One of the worst things you can do is hold on too much brake as the wing needs to be moving forward to stay inflated or it will stall, collapse and drop to the ground. I was only applying a very small amount of brake to steady the canopy so I released them fully but it made no difference. I could hear the hum from wind passing through the lines and feel a slight breeze on my face, but I had no sense of movement. I was more than a mile above the forest and close to panic, I looked up and

down the valley and across to the range of mountains. I glanced again at the canopy, which was still fully inflated and rocking gently. Then I saw that my feet were moving very, very slowly past landmarks on the valley floor, just like when you look out from an aircraft window. Things were fine and I leaned back in my seat and started to soak up the view, which from a paraglider is unsurpassed.

I was higher than most of the surrounding mountains. After twenty-five minutes in the air I approached the landing area, the canopy giving an occasional lurch as I flew through thermals. I didn't try to stay in one to gain height as I was content with a nice smooth glide down. As I descended I couldn't see any bears in the thick, dark green forest but I was prepared to take the word of Leonard and Dave that they were there. Once in another part of Romania a ranger had shown me their claw mark, dug two inches into tree bark. Just as Dave said there was no indication of wind direction, but I kept a sharp eye out for the things to miss: power cables, pylons, ditches, pipelines, and a nearby builder's yard. I made for the centre of the field. With no wind it would be a fast landing. I pulled gently on the brakes to slow down, then about twenty feet above the ground I put the brakes full on, stalling the canopy and dropping onto my toes, an almost textbook landing. Then, weak with excitement and exhilaration, I spoilt it all by falling over.

There are some things in life you have to experience to understand, and this is one of them.

Polly was already there and the others joined us soon after. A gang of local kids came racing across, wide-eyed with wonder. They stared as if we had just landed from Mars, then helped us pack away our gear, touching and holding the glider material as if it had some magical quality. We always kept a supply of sweets, which were handed out to general acclaim. Among our fliers there were smiles all round as we shared our wonderful experiences.

That evening I pitched my tent next to Dave and Polly's camper van in the forest up a track five miles from town. After our meal and a bottle of Romanian beer we took a short walk, then I turned in to have a read before bed. It was so quiet in my tent and my mind wandered through the events of the day: the flight, the forest, the dancing bear. The thought of other bears and shady characters occurred to me. Can bears smell? Do they know where I am? What is the wind direction? I felt a little uneasy but yawned. Then I yawned again. The next thing I knew it was morning.

I fall off my feet

On a trip to Romania in 2001, Dave, Polly and other friends arranged to meet me in a place called Rimeta, a beautiful area in the hill country with gentle slopes covered with wild flowers and long grass. It is twenty kilometres south of Cluj Napoca and thirty five west of Targu Mures. Here, we enjoyed ourselves with flights from the lower hills and I had an unexpected adventure when I rescued my tent from a fast-flowing river, wading in freezing water up to my armpits. Then we made for higher ground at Padis, fourteen hundred metres or nearly four-and-a-half thousand feet above sea level. This was a popular camping area with Romanians. I imagined them journeying up there in the days of Communism by horse and cart, or in little Dacias, Romania's answer to the VW Beetle. It would have offered some solace from their awful system where they might enjoy a bit of freedom with palinca brandy, mountain air, mutton and mushrooms. It remained popular and that weekend I counted seventy tents pitched on the grassy area either side of the river bellow us. My tent, dry now from its dip in the river was pitched a little further up the slope, from there I could watch the goings on. As night fell

I'd see torches leading campers through the woods to answer calls of nature as there were no toilets at this camp ground.

Next day the wind was unfavourable so we walked to a distant ice cave. It was a long trek but when we reached the cave we were greeted by an interesting new sight. We walked down a slope into the mouth of the cave. About twenty paces in it opened into an enormous cavern. It was like entering a great freezer with ice all around and the deeper we went the colder it became. It is like this all year round.

The long walk back took us through woods and over streams, stopping off at a tiny wooden shack at which we bought my favourite Bergen beer. Back at the camper Polly made a nourishing and healthy meal, not much meat but plenty of beans, vegetables, fruit and yoghurt. We talked for a while after the meal then I said I would go to my tent. My feet were a little tender from all the walking so I had taken off my boots and skipped along bare foot down the slope towards my tent over damp grass. Without warning my feet suddenly shot from under me and I landed with my back hitting a rock. There was a sound like a rifle crack and I curled up in agony. Dave came and after a few minutes helped me to my feet. He ran his hands up and down my back and chest, "You'll be all right. There's nothing broken. You have probably torn the intercostal muscles between your ribs. They will be very sore for a while and only time will heal them." I didn't feel reassured as I had heard a distinct crack and was sure something was broken I also felt as if the jar had torn my insides from the rib cage.

That night in my tent was the most painful of my life and I reached my lowest point. I didn't sleep a wink. When I had to go for a pee I crawled out in agony on all fours. Paragliding is a dangerous sport and I had taken risks with caving and climbing. But here I was seriously injured just because of a slip on the grass. In the morning Dave lifted the flap of my tent. "How are you?" he asked. My reply was colourful. "Do you want to come out," "I can't." "I'll help, give me your hand." I offered my arm at the good side. He grabbed my hand and heaved me out with such force that I fell into his arms, nearly passing out with the pain. I clung to him, feeling faint. "You'll be alright. I always feel a bit dizzy in a morning myself," he said. Such comfort!

They took me to the camper van where I rested during the day while they went to find another cave.

There I stayed all day. When they came back I was no better. "Well," said Dave. "There's nothing they can do for you in hospital if it is torn muscles. We'll see how you are tomorrow." Another sleepless night convinced me that I wanted to go home. They had gone caving again and when they came back in the afternoon I said I had to get back to the UK. There was no way I was going to trust a hospital in Romania after all that I had seen when making deliveries.

My kit was packed away and Dave drove me the forty kilometres to Cluj Napoca, the nearest town with an airport. It took us four hours as we bounced over the pot holed track, each jolt sent a shooting pain across my back. Dave went with Leonard, our Romanian friend, and arranged a flight to Bucharest and from there on to Heathrow. It was actually a return flight as this was as cheap as a single. They booked me into a hotel for the night before they returned to Padis. Dave took charge of my glider and luggage and I carried only a book, my toothbrush and towel in a plastic bag.

I crept into my room but dared not lie down. I stacked all the chair cushions on top of the bed and propped myself up. After two nights without sleep I nodded off but when I awoke the cushions had slipped and I was laid almost flat and couldn't get up. I panicked. What if I miss the taxi? I had to lie still and gather my thoughts before making a move that I knew was going to be painful. I rolled on my side, slid my legs to the floor, then with a struggle sat up. The rest of the night I sat in a chair and dozed until I heard a tinkling noise way off in the distance. It was my early morning alarm call, but the phone was out of reach and had stopped by the time I made it to my feet. Before I could get to the bathroom there was a knock on the door. It was the hotel receptionist who knew I was injured and told me he was concerned when I had not answered the phone. He stayed with me while I gathered myself together and helped me to the hotel lobby to call a taxi.

I had been told many times to always ask the fare. As I climbed into the taxi I asked the driver in Romanian, "How much will it cost?" I couldn't understand his answer at all. Oh no, I thought, don't say I'm in with a rogue. I asked again and his reply once more eluded me. This continued and he started to get irate, saying the same things over and over, each time getting louder. He was obviously annoyed and drove at great speed in the early dawn, with my ribs sending out shooting pains as he swerved around corners. Then I noticed a little square meter by the side of the steering column with a row of white numbers and a slowly moving red one. He must have noticed me looking at the meter he pointed to it and repeated the first phrase. Obviously he had been telling me that the cost of the journey would be according to the meter. I felt a little embarrassed at my mistrust. At the airport I paid him a little more than the meter reading, but it only drew a faint smile.

The early morning flight to Bucharest was on a small twenty-seater aircraft. Changing for Heathrow at Bucharest was not easy as there seemed to be no one around to tell me where to book in. There were no signs and I had to walk from where I landed around the end of the runway to the main departure building. There I found departures for London. Fortunately, I didn't have long to wait and we left on time. To avoid having to go to the toilet I ate and drank little, but the person next to me did the opposite, eating and drinking everything he could get hold of. He was in the window seat so I had to struggle to my feet to let him pass when he wanted the loo. I couldn't stand in the isle while waiting for his return as I was blocking the TV screen, so the sitting and standing endurance test had to be repeated.

At Heathrow I walked very painfully through customs clutching my supermarket bag with my few positions. A very nice airport employee spotted the trouble I was in, the first person to have taken notice since I left the hotel that morning. "Can I get you a wheelchair?" she asked. I thanked her for her kindness but explained that it was better for me to keep on my feet. I rang Beryl and told her what had happened, downplaying my injury for the moment so she wouldn't be too worried. She said she would be at Leeds-Bradford Airport to meet me. The kind lady at Heathrow helped me to my seat on the aircraft.

When we landed I was one of the first through to the public area as I had no luggage. The first face I saw was Beryl's and my spirit rose for the first time in days. I was always pleased to see her but never more than then. I felt a flood of relief as I had been in agony for three days, travelling miles in misery, but now I would be in good hands and in her comfort zone. Beryl was shocked at the state I was in and shepherded me to her car, driving straight to the emergency department at the hospital in Harrogate.

We had to wait as the police had just arrived with two youths who looked as if they had been in a fight, and I thought how the same situation would have been handled in a Romanian hospital. Thank goodness for the NHS, I thought. A nurse took me to the x-ray department. After a while she came out and showed me the slides, pointing to an area of my rib cage close to my backbone. "Can you see these lines?" she said. "You have broken three ribs!" It was no surprise I heard them break and I had certainly felt the pain. "There is little we can do. They will mend by themselves but you need to rest." She gave me a prescription for painkillers, so far I had not had even an Aspro then turned me over to Beryl's care. That night I at last managed some proper sleep. Before nodding off l thought how lonely and desperate I had been, and really did think I could have died in those Romanian mountains.

Back To The Carparthians

I had left all my glider equipment and most of my clothes with Dave, who had taken them around to our friend Lutz Levente. The air ticket had a return portion that would have to be used within thirty days. I would have to mend fast, get back there, collect my stuff and return to the UK in the charity van. Thanks to Beryl's loving care I was soon feeling well, though I was still sore. But it encouraged me to book my flight back before the return ticket expired. Beryl, already convinced that I was mad to be still seeking adventures at sixty six, could hardly believe that I intended to return. But she saw that I was determined and did the best she could to help. I bought the biggest holdall with wheels I could find and flew to Bucharest. From there I caught the train to Miercurea Ciuc, where I met Lutz.

I stayed with Lutz for a few days. One evening after work he decided to go flying. His invitation to go with him I found tormenting. I remained weak and while much better, my ribs still hurt. "I'll carry your glider to the top of the hill and give you a push," he offered laughing. Now, it wasn't the best idea but I agreed.

I struggled slowly up the hill to the take-off point and it was no less a struggle for Lutz, carrying two gliders. But it was well worth the effort and we enjoyed two short flights. Later, there was a price to pay as I went to bed that night in some pain.

Dave and the others were still in Romania. He had decided to stay longer than originally planned. I talked to him and he asked me if I would like to travel back to UK with him and Polly in their camper van. There would be first a diversion to the mountains and I would have to sleep at night in my tent, but the daytime travelling would be easier than in the charity van. So I agreed.

I said my farewells to Lutz and his family and set off on another adventure with Dave – they are all adventures with Dave, as I am sure you have realised. There would be no more flying because of poor weather conditions but he wanted to visit the Fargaras Mountains of the southern Carpathians for a quick look around to find a spot for future visits. The main road leading there skirted the highest peaks but this was too boring for Dave who decided we would drive through the middle of the range, close to Mount Moldoveanu, the highest in Romania at 2,544 metres, or about 8,000 feet. The road itself was nearly as high at 2,000 metres (6,500 feet). We had to be careful as bad weather closed the road for six months a year, and we were two weeks off the closure date. Not many vehicles would now be using it and on the way up we passed only three cars coming the other way. At least the surface was good as apparently the dictator Nicolae Ceaucescu had used a shooting lodge up there. This was a drive strictly for daylight.

As we climbed towards the highest point on the road we were surprised to see that sections of the road were roofed with a large sloping concrete canopy to screen vehicles from falling rocks. The weather was getting worse with drizzly rain and mist. My passenger seat by the window gave a good view of the valley hundreds of feet bellow and there were no guard rails, not even on the steepest bends. The last section of road was through a tunnel that opened onto a grassy area very close to the mountain top, which was completely shrouded in mist. Leaning against the wall at the end of the tunnel was a solitary figure, an old man wrapped in a greatcoat fastened with string, bags on either side of him and singing his head off. What he was singing I have no Idea; what he had to sing about is even more of a mystery as rain was driving into the tunnel and he was catching the full force of it. We parked the van and walked over to him. His song sounded lively, possibly a patriotic or military tune which you could march to. He stopped singing and took apples from one of his bags which he offered to us. Though we didn't need any we felt he deserved something for standing there in the cold drizzle and bought two bags, telling him to keep the change. He was very pleased and burst back into song. Most of the apples were worm-eaten and we ditched them further on. But this was a strange interlude and the old man remained something of a mystery. We saw neither car nor bike, and there were certainly no apple orchards up there on the mountain.

Though the mountain top was only a few hundred feet above we could not see it for cloud and fine rain. We set off expected visibility to improve lower down but the fog thickened the further we went. It was not long before we had slowed to a crawl and the light was beginning to fail. It would be dangerous to drive in these conditions so we found a place to pull off the road where rocks would give us a bit of shelter from the wind which was now picking up. I would be sleeping in my tent, which I pitched in utter darkness, struggling to get the pegs into the hard ground. We ate in the camper van but I went to my tent once again feeling depressed. I couldn't ring Beryl as there was no signal, so I settled down to read. About 10 pm I crept into my sleeping bag but with the wind shaking the tent and drizzle turning to hard driving rain I was unable to sleep. As the gale tugged at the tent I felt uneasy about the pegs and knew that sooner or later I would have to go outside and check them. No time like the present, I thought, so I put on some extra clothes and unzipped the door flap. But as I did so the tent filled up with wind and nearly flew away. Only my weight held it in place so quickly I zipped up the door again and stayed put. At last there was a lull. I put on my caver's helmet with its light on the front, ventured out, checked the pegs and put a line of heavy stones around the bottom of the tent to anchor it down. As I crawled around the back I heard something that was quite unexpected: the noise of rushing water. When we had pulled off the road and pitched the tent in the fog we had not realised how close we were to the edge of the cliff. Water was now coming down the mountainside in a torrent, bouncing off the rocks, spray adding to the rain. I found the edge but could see nothing in the dark. My tent was an all-in-one type with the floor stitched to the rest of the tent. Had it blown over the edge I would have gone with it. After this discovery I added more rocks and carried inside the tent a couple extra to act as ballast. All this effort wore me out and though I could still hear the storm outside and the tent was shaking I settled down and slept well.

Next morning I was up early, the wind had dropped and it was a calm clear day. The sun was up, but blocked out by the mountains close by and it was still cool. I was now able to see clearly the area where we had hastily pitched the tent last night. I walked over towards where the sound of water was coming from then stopped suddenly, had I seen then what I see now I would not of gone inside the tent let alone sleep in it. Just a few meters from my tent was the edge of a cliff, I looked over the edge and saw that the drop was at least one hundred and fifty feet straight down to a mountain river. There was no sign of life from the camper van so I climbed down to the river at a place where it was not so steep stripped off and lowered myself into the fast flowing, icy water. It took my breath away even though I was only in for a few seconds. I rubbed hard with the towel and soon felt invigorated standing there naked and breathing in the fresh mountain air. As I climbed slowly to the top I saw that the camper door was open. Dave and Polly were up and preparing a healthy breakfast. I don't think they have a frying pan! We were soon back on the road, leaving Romania behind and travelling across Hungary, Austria, and into Germany where we made our next overnight stop.

It was getting late when Dave, who had driven all day, pulled over into a picnic rest area at the side of a busy road in Germany. It was easy for him as all he needed to do was park, put on the hand brake and then the kettle. He would lock the van doors, and he and Polly could go to sleep feeling secure. It was not so easy for me, though Dave always helped pitch my tent. But that night I felt unaccountably exposed and vulnerable more so than in the mountains of Transylvania. I looked around for a spot among the trees as close as possible to his camper, but everywhere there was an awful smell. It was now dark but as Dave and I checked with our caver's lamps there were no signs of anything that might be causing the odour and we eventually decided on a place for the tent. I ate with them in the camper then went to my tent and as usual read for a while before turning out the light. The next thing I heard was the sound of a large vehicle pulling up close by, its headlights momentarily lighting up my tent, then loud voices German voices. I kept quiet for a few moments before easing down the zip on the door flap and peering out. There was a coach parked a little way off and about twenty men standing among the trees urinating, steam rising into the night. Fortunately, none was close enough to splash my tent. I zipped up the flap, kept quiet and soon they were gone. Obviously this was a regular stopping place for men to relieve themselves and that was what caused the rank smell. That night in Germany on that trip was also the last time I was ever under canvas. That incident was probably the final straw: from now on, I decided I wanted comfort in a warm bed, preferably with Beryl beside me.

The next day we travelled out of Germany to Belgium, France and back to Yorkshire. Strange as it might seem, all the times I have driven back from the continent, whatever vehicle I was in had always seemed to run better once it was pointing north.

France, Canyoning

I may have finished camping but I had not yet quit the adventure trail with Dave Elliott. My ribs had healed and Dave called to say he had organised an expedition to the South of France and asked me along. My friend Chris Seals and I flew out to join him. We landed at Perpignan, hired a car and drove to meet Dave and the rest of the party in the small village of Rasigueres, where he had the use of a friend's house.

Dave gave us bad news. The area was normally reliable for flying as the wind, blowing from the north at that time of the year, made conditions ideal. Unfortunately, there was no wind. Although disappointed, I knew we would not be sitting around for long, Dave would dream up some other way to frighten us! Next day, we loaded our gliders into the cars and visited official flying sites hoping that the local experts would give us a better forecast. But the outlooks were all gloomy.

So we went to visit the Gorge de Galamus located in the Pyrenees, driving through on the dramatic two kilometre stretch of road in places propped on the walls of the Gorge, in other parts cut into the rock face. We stopped at one point and stood by a wall to look down at the river below. Dave turned to me, "You see that green patch in the bottom of the canyon? Well tomorrow we will be in it. "You will need a wet suit, Ken,". "Today we have taken the boring route by car but tomorrow we will take a more exciting route 'Canyoning'." We called at the next town and I bought a wet suit and a pair of cheap trainers.

Dave had done his homework and the next day we parked a car where we would come out at the bottom end of the canyon. We then drove in the other car the five kilometres back to a start point, where the river was little more than a stream. There were seven of us. Because of all the water I would have to manage without my glasses and packed them safely away. The plan was to follow this river, called the Agly, through the canyon. It was easy at first, clambering over rocks and splashing through pools. Then the walls became steeper, the river narrowed and the water grew deeper and faster. I am not a strong swimmer and feel happier when I can touch the bottom, but now that was no longer possible. We were in the Gorge proper, and came to a halt. The only way forward was down a thirty foot waterfall into a deep pool. Dave had tied a rope for us to slide down. He went first and as usual made it look easy, dropping off the rope before reaching the bottom and swimming clear. Others followed, then it was my turn. I grabbed the rope and slowly slid down with the water beating on me. But when I neared the bottom I was unable to swing clear and actually landed under the waterfall. The force of this pushed me under, everything went dark as the current thrust me back into a hollow behind. I surfaced and groping around found the back of the chamber and used this to thrust myself forward with my feet and launched myself through the waterfall and back into daylight, spluttering with all the water I had swallowed.

We floated around while those with waterproof cameras took pictures. Then we began moving further along the canyon into the deeper part, rocks high on either side. Though the water was deeper it was also slower moving and easier to swim through. I lay on my back and floated along letting the current do the work. I peered up at the canyon walls, now five or six hundred feet high, and at the little slit of blue sky at the top thinking maybe tomorrow I will be up there flying. This was another new experience, but I did feel uneasy again when the cold water started to seep through my cheap wet suit and I realised how deep the water must be. After a while the river swung round a bend and the canyon opened up. We were out of the steep section and were able to get out of the water and climb up the banking close to where the car was parked. So ended another of Dave's adventures, I have often been frightened on them but never disappointed and this one left me with a real glow of satisfaction.

USA, Phoenix, Arizona

Occasionally I would park my caravan at Killinghall, not far from Harrogate, on the premises of a friendly farmer called David Bellerby. I had known both David and one of his helpers, Roy Snuggs, for years. In fact, I had been friendly with Roy all the way back to my time motor racing in the 1969.

One day in late 2002 David and I were having coffee in his farmhouse when in walked Roy, during the conversation that followed Roy mentioned that his annual trip to Arizona was getting near, He went with his wife every year to visit a long term friend and that his wife was not able to go this year. I commented that I thought it would be a wonderful trip, If you are interested Ken I would welcome the company." I shot back, "Don't say something like that if you don't mean it Roy, or you will find me sitting beside you on the plane."

"I'm serious," Roy said. "And if you are too I will ring my friend Al in Arizona and square it with him. My wife Marge can ring around and get us a good price for tickets and it will be easy to arrange." So it was that Roy and I lined up for the British Airways flight that February in 2003. My paraglider, of course, was in the hold.

Roy's friend Al Yarlott lived in Phoenix, Arizona. Al was an American who had been stationed at the top-secret US military base at Menwith Hill near Harrogate. They had come to know each other when they worked together, Al in the US Air Force and Roy as a civilian worker. Al had returned to the USA some years ago and Roy and Marge would travel out to visit him every year – in fact, fourteen years on the trot. It was sad for Marge that she couldn't go this time, but her loss was my gain and before I left I had established contact with local paragliding clubs and instructors. What a wonderful thing is the internet!

It was dark when we came in to land at Phoenix, passing the twinkling lights of the outskirts then flying for what seemed like ages before we touched down at the airport. I had not realised what a spread out city it is. Later in the holiday when I was driving back to town I recall seeing a sign reading, 'City Centre, 23 Miles', and I was already in a built-up suburb. I suppose there's so much space in the US they don't need to pack people in as we do in the UK.

Al Yarlott's daughter Terry met us at the airport and drove us back to his house. I looked at the address on the outside of the house: 7937 West Flower Street. Did this mean there were 8,000 separate addresses on that street? It did. The problem wasn't just that there were so many houses, but that the numbers were rarely displayed and never visible from the road so finding which house you wanted was challenging. On a couple of occasions I had great trouble in locating Al's place when returning from trips. I have lived most of my life in villages where numbers are hardly necessary. A street with 8,000 houses on it is hard to comprehend.

Al met us at his front door but sadly he could not get past the doorstep as he was connected to an oxygen bottle that he carried around the house. He was in the advanced stages of emphysema and could not live without his supply of oxygen. Although he lived on his own, relatives and friends were nearby to help him, including his attentive daughter Terry. Nevertheless, he did all he could to welcome us. I have stayed in many places on my travels but never have been made more welcome.

Roy took the spare bedroom and Al pointed to a large sofa bed in a corner of the living room. "That's yours Ken. Spread yourself out and make yourself at home." I did as instructed. After our evening meal and a few bottles of beer, I settled in my corner noticing that above Al and Roy hung clouds of blue smoke. Roy had a bad chest and Al had emphysema but both were smoking. It was difficult to understand.

Al sat up through the night watching TV as he seldom went to bed. Spread out in front of him were boxes of pills. Whatever time of the night I awoke I would see him gazing at the screen, with the sound turned low so it would not disturb me. Occasionally, I would see him dozing but only once did he disappear to bed. Perhaps it was the drugs he was on. He did not look well but his mind was alert and we had some very lively and interesting conversations. Roy told me that before being discharged from the air force, Al had a high powered job. He had been in Vietnam at the time they had sprayed defoliant chemicals such as the notorious Agent Orange in the Mekong Delta, and he wondered if that had contributed to him having chest problems. He was doubly sure the air force were up to something bad as his service record didn't show his Vietnam stint. Maybe Al had been a victim of 'friendly fire' from his own unfriendly government, but the cigarettes didn't help.

I was keen to get out flying. One of the very best US sites is Torrey Pines in California, north of San Diego. I hired a car and drove the 360 miles to the west coast, booking into a local hotel before visiting the flying club. They made it clear I would have to attend flight school, to which I agreed. But they tried to get me to change some of the things I had learned in Yorkshire and I was not happy with this. On the way back to my hotel I managed to get hopelessly lost in back streets. At one point I thought I must have strayed into Mexico as everyone I saw looked Mexican and all the shop signs were in Spanish.

The next morning I was up early to get back to Torrey Pines but the weather was poor with low cloud and rain and the forecast was for more to come. It was clear I would have to return to Phoenix, but before I did I spoke to Marty, one of the instructors from the day before, and arranged to see him at his home club in Flagstaff, Arizona when he returned later in the week. I drove to Phoenix where my search for Al's house took almost as long at the journey from San Diego.

Dust devils in Flagstaff

I rang a guy called Dixon White who ran the flying school at Flagstaff. He told me they would be out flying, weather permitting, the next day. Al heard the conversation. "Don't hire a car, take mine," he offered. What a man! I come to his house as a stranger he welcomes me and offers me the use of his car. It was a rather ancient Ford Thunderbird, a big brute of a thing but I gratefully accepted his offer. The next day I loaded my glider kit into the huge car boot and set off for Flagstaff in high spirits on a new adventure. Along the road I saw intriguing place names such as, 'Dead Man's Creek,' 'Stinking Spring Mountain,' 'Death Valley Lake,' 'Devil Creek,' 'Disappointment Valley,' 'Red Horse Wash'. They really know how to name things around there.

As I approached Flagstaff I could see the snow capped peak of Mount Humphrey, its Observatory and the Snow Bowl. When I entered Flagstaff there was a sign saying this was Route 66, which followed the track settlers had used in the nineteenth century travelling from East to West. I couldn't resist driving along this for a while, just to be able to say I had. Terry had phoned ahead to book me a room in a motel that she had used in the past so I had no problem, once I found it! I slept soundly until my pre-arranged phone call early the next morning. It was to become a constant feature of the early mornings, "Good Morning Mr Walker. This is your early morning alarm call.

Rise and shine." I made an early start and drove out to the flying club meeting place just outside Flagstaff close to the cinder cones for an 8am rendezvous. There were a few other flyers and we were all grilled by Dixon White to see how much we knew. I was teamed with two other flyers who were over from Alabama for a conversion course from hang-gliders to paragliders.

One of the first things we were taught when preparing for take of was to look out for 'dust devils' These occur in the desert and are caused by sand being sucked up in a vortex by a strong, but localised wind eddy. If one comes whistling through we were told to ground our canopy and flop down on top of it, otherwise the devil can cause real havoc if it hits full-on. Your canopy might turn up miles away. This is taken so seriously that if there is a group one person is always appointed to be look-out. The flying area was on the edge of the desert in a volcanic region which had two large cinder cones, Merriam and Sheba, about nine hundred feet high. Dixon took us in his pick-up truck to the top of Miriam, the taller of the two, and left us there to fly down. I was in for a shock as I could not take off. There was hardly a breath of wind and the desert thermals came through with little warning and were gone as fast as they came. I was never prepared. I kept fumbling my turns, changing hands on the brakes and getting in a mess. Dixon took me to one side and told me my technique was wrong. "You don't have time here to change hands. You must do as we do: start with the risers crossed, then when you swing around fast they are already in the correct hands and you are away." It was not a very good start. I managed a few short flights but Dixon was hard on me and I struggled.

The next day things improved as Marty had returned from Torrey Pines and he took the two conversion pilots and me under his wing, so to speak. I worked hard, sweated a lot and most important of all learned the new crossed hands technique. After each flight Marty drove us back to the top of the cinder cone. While the other pilots were getting ready for take off I walked to the back of the cone for a pee when I suddenly heard a loud rattling sound. Now I am a bit deaf so if there was a noise it had to be fairly close. It took me a second to realise what it was but as soon as it dawned on me I moved very fast away from the area. Later, I could not resist going back for a closer look but heard no noise and saw no rattlesnake, he had gone. Maybe he didn't like being peed on!

The Painted Desert

I went flying every day even though the heat and effort was taking its toll on my strength but I persisted and got the hang of the new take-off method. The views were fantastic when we stood on top of Merrian the snow capped Mount Humphrey was behind us, while in front were miles and miles of the Painted Desert. As far as the eye could see were pastel coloured strips shimmering in the heat, ranging from the light brown of the desert floor up through strips of grey, pink, red, orange and lavender, eventually merging with the blue sky. Painted is about right. Dotted about the landscape were homestead settlements bought cheaply from the government years before. Many were now deserted though a few still operated as farms. The problem was that there was no water supply. The homesteaders had pick-up trucks with large tanks on the back and you often saw them in Flagstaff filling up with water. Their farms are referred to as settlements where they, "Carry their own water."

We had many flights. Marty was a great Instructor and he pushed the three of us hard to make us good pilots. But after several days things started to go wrong I was not landing properly. Marty would get one of us to fly as far as we could in a straight line and land, then the other two would be told to follow and try to land as close as possible. I was getting there all right but each time I fell over on landing. Dixon noticed and became quite annoyed with me. "You have a pilot's license but if you can't land properly on your feet I can't have you in my school." This hurt my feelings as I was trying hard. I was 67, more than twice their ages. But Marty and the two guys from Alabama were supportive. Marty suggested he would fly first and watch carefully as I came in to land and

try to spot the problem. When I first started at Flagstaff my landings had been perfect and it was strange that now I couldn't keep on my feet for love nor money. When I toppled again at the end of that flight, Marty came up to me smiling, "I can see the reason. You are pulling down harder with the right brake than the left at the last moment, and this is tilting your canopy at the point of touch down. Go back and do it again, but make sure you pull equally on the brakes." I did as suggested and made a perfect landing. When we analysed it we concluded that I had become so fatigued my stronger right arm was pulling harder than my left and causing me to swerve to the right and lose my balance on touch down. Incidentally during six days flying in the Painted Desert I lost over seven pounds in weight, though I ate very well, you would find it difficult not to in the US of A!

We enjoyed a few more days flying until the two pilots from Alabama finished their conversion course. Photographs were taken then we shook hands in farewell. I had enjoyed very much their company and a wonderful experience in the 'Painted Desert'.

At the end of the week it was time, too, for me to go. I decided to take in a visit to the Grand Canyon before returning to Phoenix. There is only one word to describe the Grand Canyon, unfortunately devalued by being over-used. It is awesome! To stand on the edge and gaze across the vast chasm was both breathtaking and spellbinding. I had waited so long to see it that I could hardly bear to tear myself away. When I eventually returned to the car I started the engine, stopped it, got out and went back for another look. I took a leisurely drive back, stopping off at other interesting places such as Walnut Canyon National Monument, the Prehistoric Indian Cliff Dwellings, Kokopeli, dating back to 1250 AD, and the Sunset Volcano Crater.

After the usual two hour search I finally pulled into Al's drive. I found it a bit easier this time, remembering that his house was the one with a fake owl perched on the roof to scare off the pigeons. His old Ford Thunderbird car had done very well and saved me paying for a hire car. I had taken care of it and was pleased to return it without even a scratch. While I had been away Roy had spent most of his time with Al talking of old times. They had done their sightseeing in earlier years but Al's daughter, the delightful Terry, was determined to show me a few more interesting places.

Americans love to come and see 'little old England', but now I had had the chance to see a part of their 'big country' with someone who knew her way around. Terry drove us to Sedona, Slide Rock and the Sonora desert, where the huge Saguaro cactus grows. Locally they are known as Arizona trees. We saw organ pipe cacti and others with such beautiful flowers they look out of place in the hostile dry environment. We travelled south to Tucson then on to look around the Pima Air Museum and the enormous aircraft storage area close by. Here, there are rows and rows of every kind of aircraft and helicopters looking like the place airplanes go to die. Typically American, it has become a tourist spot and they take you around on a sightseeing bus.

Bisbee, once a prosperous copper mining town with many big Victorian style houses, was the next stop. On the way out of town we looked at the huge thousand foot diameter open cast mine, the Lavender Pit. We took in places I recognised from old Western films and others, such as Tombstone, where the real Wild West had been played out. It was just like stepping back in time. In Tombstone there were bullets still stuck in the walls of the Bird Cage Theatre Bar and the OK Corral, which are claimed to be originals from the 1880s. We climbed up Boot Hill to see the graveyard where burial plots are marked by a pile of stones and a rough piece of wood for a headstone. I enjoyed every minute. On the day we visited there were more motor bikes in town than horses as Tombstone was hosting a meeting of the Harley Davison owners club. I suppose you can say these are modern day cowboys.

We set off for Phoenix through the mountains making one more stop at Fort Huachuca for a quick look at the military museum where the Buffalo Soldiers are remembered. On the way into town Terry stopped to buy parts for her computer and I bought my first digital camera in a place so big you could fit in several of our PC Worlds. Truly, this is the big country. Back in Phoenix we timed our return perfectly as Al and Roy had the barbecue fired up and two-inch thick stakes were ready for cooking. It was the last night for Roy and me, and we talked with Al long into the night.

Next day before we left for the airport, Al gave me a 1952 silver half dollar for good luck. It is in my pocket now as I write. I had enjoyed my visit so much on all levels. Al's hospitality was the best, and it was very moving to look back at him standing in the doorway, the oxygen bottle at his side, as we left in Terry's car for the airport. He smiled and waved his thin bony hand. Though I had known him for just a short time we had become firm friends. But I felt sure that I would never see him again and fought back a tear as we set off. I avoided looking at Roy as I was certain his thoughts were the same as mine. We had been back in Yorkshire only for a few weeks when the bad news came through that Al Yarlott had died. I was pleased that I had known him.

A flight in Australia

Stan Thompson was an old mate from my National Service days. I have mentioned how he, Wendy and I discussed emigrating to Australia in the late 1950s. He was sure we were set on it and arranged to go himself, expecting to see us there. But we never turned up, having changed our minds. In the early part of 2000 he and I made contact again via the internet and he invited me out. Stan had settled in Adelaide, Australia and like me he was retired. In 2004 Beryl and I decided we would go and see him. Much to Beryl's disapproval I took my paraglider, though this nearly became a wasted effort. I did not get much chance to go flying as, after all, that was not the reason for our visit It was to see Stan and he made it 'The Holiday of a lifetime' we enjoyed every minute of it being shown round that wonderful country where I had many years ago planned to live.

Nevertheless, I managed to get in one memorable day's paragliding on the coast at Tunkalilla, south of Adelaide at the tip of the Fleurieu Peninsula. It was a beautifully hot day. I found a site where there were other pilots and as it was too turbulent settled down to wait on the cliffs above the coast for the thermals to die down. Australia has some incredible sights. The sand along the beach was almost pure white against the blue green sea, which in turn merged into the lighter blue sky in the distance. There was not a cloud in sight. As I gazed out to sea I noticed numerous dolphins bobbing along just a little way out from the white strip of breaking waves. Finally, I made it into the air for a couple of short flights which were, incidentally, two of the last I was ever to make. That way they have stuck in my mind, for which I am grateful.

When the weather is very hot there many people go to the shopping malls to cool of rather than shop as the air conditioning is so good, even if you don't buy anything it is nice to stroll round in the cool while the sun blazes down out side. As we strolled round I noticed a rather attractive girl stood by a little table a few people had gathered round. Stan went up to have a look and I followed. Laid on the table were a few small branches about an inch thick and to everyone's amazement she was cutting them into short lengths with a small set of what turned out to be Ratchet secateurs and she made it look easy. Stan a keen gardener eased to the front for a closer look he would need convincing. She gave him a set to

try Stan picked up a length of wood and cut it into small pieces with little effort, he was surprised how good they were and so easy to use especially as he was not as strong now at 70 and losing his grip. He put his hand in his pocket, (It usually takes him a bit longer to get his money out!) And paid the girl, when we got home and tried them in the garden I too was amazed and took details from the package of the make and manufacture I am always on the lookout for a new Idea and realised right away that they would sell in the UK

When I got home I managed to find a company that imported the Ratchet secateurs that I had seen and I went down to their warehouse near Leicester bought a few boxes and some more garden tools to sell at car boot sales and on eBay. When they started to sell I decided that it would be much better if I bought them direct from China a lot cheaper so back to the internet and eventually I found a company in Shanghai that would deal with a 'small lot' small lot being 10,000! Normally they like to sell a container load but I managed to get what we agreed would be a Sample lot to get started! They came as a part lot in a container with other goods Paid for up front then I had to arrange shipping and wait.

Eventually they arrived, loaded on three pallets delivered to my caravan to many boxes to stow away in my caravan this time, more than 100 but my friend Charlie came to the rescue and took most of them to his farm to store them in an empty hen hut. I then got into business selling them on eBay, and sell they did I spent hours packing and posting but did not mind as it was a little 'earner that went on for a long time topping up my pension.

Glider for Sale

When Beryl and I visited Australia I was sixty-nine. Over the previous ten years or so I had enjoyed many fantastic paragliding experiences. We came back from Down-Under and the glider went unused for a while. Then one day in July 2006 I looked up into the sky on a lovely summer's day, with not a cloud in the sky and hardly a breath of wind.

"Come on," I said to myself. "You can still do it." I put my glider in the car and set off for Tow Scar near Ingleton. Three pilots were already in the air, flying smoothly along the ridge. A windsock told me that the gentle sea breeze coming from Morecambe Bay was smack on. I walked to the take-off area to sniff the air and prepared for take-off. I launched, turning sharply right along the ridge and feeling the familiar rush. I cruised up and down the ridge in smooth air for thirty minutes, flew towards the gate where my car was parked and made a near perfect landing. It was so exciting that I was trembling. I kept telling myself, "There's no need to worry, you can still fly," Little did I realise that this would be my last flight from, by coincidence, almost the same spot as my first ten years before.

Somehow it seemed I had fulfilled ambitions and had my fill of flying. There wasn't any need to do more. As they say, "Been there; done that." Instead of making the weather forecasts the highlight of my evening's TV viewing, and spending part of every day looking up at the sky and seeing which way the wind was blowing, I found other things to do. My friend Martyn Senior renewed my interest in motor bikes, selling me a vintage BMW, and I started going on club runs with him. Many of these were through the Dales and just by coincidence one day we went up Wensleydale and through Hawes where we stopped for ice cream. It was a perfect flying day and as I looked over towards Stags Fell there they were, six pilots drifting around in the clear blue sky over the hill. I felt my heart flutter as I gazed up into the sky. It was hypnotic as I thought back on the times I had flown there and the occasions when I had been in danger of being blown away, wishing I was down here. Well here I was, now wishing I was up there. The thought lasted for a few moments until Martyn called me back to the present by pointing at my ice cream dripping away. I didn't retire from gliding any more than I formally stopped caving or canyoning. It was just that I didn't seem to want to go any more. The paraglider sat in a cupboard, its technology getting old and out-of-date … perhaps like its owner.

More months passed and the urge to fly never returned. My seventy-second birthday came and went, then my seventy-third. At first I hadn't wanted to dispose of the glider as this seemed to be closing a chapter of my life, but eventually the old Yorkshire trader in me rose again and I realised if I did not sell it soon the glider would become worthless. I spoke to the man from whom I had bought it back a few years earlier and we struck a deal. It was a sad day to see it go as I had carried that huge back-pack up hills and mountains in many parts of the world, and the glider had carried me down with many a thrill and a few frightening moments along the way. But, well, nothing is for ever.

CHAPTER ELEVEN

MY MOTHER
Kathleen Walker née Robson

It was a damp April morning in 2004 and I was driving over Rombald moor down through Eldwick to Bingley in West Yorkshire to share the last few moments of my mother's life. It was a grey day and was to become sad to match the skies. Even though I knew it was coming I found myself unable to prepare myself for the death of my mother, and it is still hurts today.

My mother, Kathleen Walker née Robson, had lived a long life. She was almost 90 and had spent the last 32 years on her own after my father had died in 1972. She had never really recovered from his death and I suspect she looked at the remainder of her life as time spent waiting to join him. Earlier in their married life he had been dominating and threatening, as I had witnessed and her doing what she could to keep a quiet life – it may seem strange that she viewed her relationship with him in this way though he had mellowed over the later years of their marriage. She didn't say much but there would be occasional references to "Leslie," and her life with him. I remember one day her saying to me, "you know Kenneth there is never a day goes by when I don't think of your father, especially at night when I climb those stairs and go to bed on my own." I had a troubled relationship with my father and though I was sorry when he died, I remembered the hard times.

At the time my father had died they were living in Charles Street, Bingley. Though it was a house too big for her on her own, mother was reluctant to move. She felt comfortable and clung onto the past. It was not far from the town centre, convenient for shopping, our younger sister Connie was just a few streets away and Freda and I could get there in less than an hour without too much trouble from Harrogate. She had a friend, Sylvia, who lived on her own close by, Sylvia's husband also having died. Together they used to take trips north to the Border country, to Hexham and Alnwick, where my mother's family came from. It was on one of these trips that she bought *The Steel Bonnets* by George MacDonald Fraser which described the activities of the wild borderers from whom we were descended, families such as the Robsons, Hedleys and Grahams which piqued my interest. She was comfortable in the house for a few years but in late 1994 when she was 80, mother fell over and broke her hip. It was replaced but she never regained her confidence and for the rest of her days could only shuffle slowly around. A move was necessary as the house had steep steps to the front door and they became an increasing problem. It was time to consider the next stage down the slippery slope of old age,

My mother eventually agreed to move, the house in Charles Street was sold and the proceeds were put to one side in case they were needed at a later date to fund the cost of care for mother. She moved into a small ground floor flat in Bingley. This worked well for a number of years but she went into a gradual decline, she had always liked walking but now after the hip problem she had a bad limp and didn't even want to go outside the house. She appeared to have lost her spirit and started to complain about noisy neighbours stopping her sleeping. She was needing more care and attention than Connie could give and though she called and spent time with her every day she also had her own family problems and Freda and me were too far away do be any help So, in 2001 we decided that she needed to move into a care home. When it was first mentioned mother had not raised any objection to the idea but she soon let us know what she thought when we took her to see the various places in the locality. She didn't like any of them! It is awful to push your old mother into a home against her will but there was nothing else we could do. We persuaded her to move to a care home just outside Bingley in a nice country area, but it was not long before she complained. She did not like the staff or the other people in the place. We had to try and make her life as comfortable as possible so another place was found, this time not far from where she had lived in Bingley, and quite close to Connie's house. But again, it was not long before she decided she didn't like this place either. In fact, we all agreed. It was heartbreaking to see our old mother sitting there with a lot of other old folk in what was nothing more than a waiting room, close to the end of life's journey. So another home was found – The Beeches was between Bradford and Bingley, and she seemed immediately happier there.

I usually went to visit during the afternoon when the meal was over and most of the residents sat in the lounge. The care home was in a lovely, stone-built detached house in large grounds, it had once been the residence of a wealthy wool merchant and was surrounded by the tall trees it took it's name from. But as we entered the new millennium there were no wealthy wool merchants left in Bradford, just legions of old folk needing care. The lounge for those now living in the house had been the old drawing room, with the centre left for those in wheelchairs to move in and out. Armchairs were placed around the outside facing inwards and mother was usually to be found sitting in one, nattering to a friend or nodding off. On the way in I would pick up a spare plastic chair from a stack near the door take it and sit close to her. If she had been asleep, she would open her eyes, blink and smile often asking what day is it? As if it made any difference, every day must be the same in this place unless someone died or a new person came in. We would chat for a while then she would lean back in her chair and close her eyes again, leaving me with my thoughts. She never had much to say and I found it difficult to keep her attention. I think also by this time my mother was being sedated to keep her calm and sleepy. On one occasion she was asleep when I arrived, I sat down quietly close to her. A few minutes later she woke with a start and asked "What day is it, is it Thursday?" "No mother, it is Wednesday"... "Oh" she said and drifted off again.

While many of the others had visitors, some did not and would join in our conversation. One poor woman never had anyone to see her and always tried to find a seat next to my mum to have a chat. I liked to talk to her and make her feel comfortable. Towards the end, there was little feedback from my mother, and though I had much to tell her I seemed to run out of things to say. I could not go on about exciting things that would make her feel worse being shut up in this place. On one occasion I was thinking what to say next. I held out my left hand and made a motioning movement with my right, as if sliding a ring onto my third finger at the same time saying, "Mother, Beryl and I are thinking of getting married." Suddenly she was wide awake. "You are all right as you are," she said in a very clear voice. I thought that it was sad that she often didn't know what day it was, but still knew what was best for her boy!

The day my mother died

My mother faded and lost weight – always a bad sign, and we knew that the end was close. Now when I visited she would be in bed in her room. We'd talk for a while but she would slip in and out of sleep. I think she had prepared herself for the journey to join my dad. One evening Connie rang to say that mother had taken a turn for the worse and feared she had all but given up.

It was with the knowledge that she was now very close to death that I drove down into Bingley on 5th April 2004. I parked the car and in the grounds of The Beeches. When I entered her room she was sleeping peacefully but her breathing was very shallow. It was clear that any conversation we had today would be one-sided. I hoped that somehow she would hear and take comfort from my words as I did have something important to say, something I should have said many times before. I drew my chair as close to her as I could and looked at her face, faded, bony and wrinkled as it was. That was where I had come from. She had given me life. I was part of her. But what I saw now was not as I will remember my mother. I will always recall her as she was in happier times when she was younger, in particular at the start of WWII when my father went away to join the RAF, Howard was not yet born and mother and I were on our own. That had been a special time when I was four and five, and it had made us close, though I was never tied to her apron strings. Mother made a great impression on me, taught me to be polite and always to say please and thank you. It was from her I learned the difference between right and wrong, and it was her who had taken me to church. What I learned from her has stayed with me to this day. When I grew up and started travelling abroad I always first learned to say please and thank you in the native tongue, and at one time could say those words in eight different languages.

She was lying on her side facing me her eyes were closed her breathing was only faint I leaned close and kissed her cheek then whispered, "I love you mother." I do not remember saying those words to her ever before in my whole life, so I hope she heard me. When I was young I don't remember many hugs or kisses. There was never much show of affection in our family that was not our way. Maybe it was considered a sign of weakness. Mother lay still and did not react to me being there her breathing hardly perceptible while I sat quietly talking to her about my latest news. Now it was time to leave. I opened the door, then turned and looked back at my mother lying so quiet and still. I sensed this might be the last time I would see her and stood there for some time. Then I left, closing the door carefully as if I might have wakened her. Connie rang the next morning to say that our mother had died during the night. I do hope she heard me.

Throughout my life my mother had never held me back though I have done some dangerous things that no doubt gave her worries. Things like climbing around the battlements of the church in Masham when I was very young, riding my motor bike on lonely tracks in the Dales, motor racing and paragliding as I grew older and should have known better. But she never said, "Don't do it." Instead, her words to me as I went out the door were always, "Be careful." I'm sure she was proud of my achievements. When I was racing motor cars in the early 1970s mother worked part-time in a news agency close to where she lived in Bingley. "It pays for my cigarettes," she would say. Every Thursday when the motor racing magazines came in she would scan through them to see the latest race results, looking for my name to see if I had won. If I warranted a mention she would show the page to other members of the staff and regular customers. Years later when she had to move into sheltered accommodation I helped clear her house and found cardboard boxes containing every single copy of the weekly *Motoring News* Magazine covering the years when I was motor racing. She had saved every one.

It was a long journey for mother's funeral cortège to go from Bingley to Kirby road Cemetery Ripon but a place had been reserved there for her years before. Though my father had been waiting for 32 years they were finally reunited close to my father's parents who had lived so close to us in Masham when I was a boy. Together again.

CHAPTER TWELVE

CARAVAN UPGRADE

In 2009 with my savings and a small loan I bought a new mobile home. I had previously spoken to Toni Ashton who ran the site at Village Farm. I explained to him that I had limited funds and would not be able afford anything very luxurious. What is your top line he asked I told him my limit. I had talked to Toni many times over the years about upgrading so I was pleasantly surprised when three days later he called to say that he had found just the right van for me and within my budget. I was taken aback but now on the spot, it was time to bite the bullet. The next day I collected Beryl as I wanted her to see what she thought of it. He gave me the address of the Caravan Company and name of the person to contact. We rushed off up the A1 remembering to keep looking straight ahead as we passed Ornhams Grange, as I still can't bear to look at our old house.

We were given the keys and left to look round on our own. It was at the end of a long row clearly marked, I unlocked the door and pushed Beryl in first then followed could not believe my eyes it was superb fully fitted out complete with furniture, carpets, curtains cooker and central heating. We looked at each other and smiled. My immediate reaction was how wonderful and Beryl's face showed her approval and it was such a bargain, brand new but last year's model that they wanted to clear. While I looked round the outside Beryl went to look at other more expensive models. When she came back she asked if I wanted to look at some of the others, I said "No" it will only unsettle me as this is all I can afford. Just come and have a quick look she insisted. Well am I pleased I did as it made me even happier with the one I came to see. Some of the more expensive ones had lots of fancy mirrors and glass, the flashy type that gypsies like. We took another look round the one we like and came away very happy Toni had made a good choice at the right price. The next day I spoke to him and we closed the deal. He knew that my son Jonathan is a builder and to save expense for me he also agreed that we could demolish the old one and prepare the site concrete foundations and drainage ourselves subject of course to his approval and supervision.

There was the matter of disposing of this old caravan, Not an easy task as it had been extended many years before when a timber kitchen had been added and the remainder had been patched so many times on the roof and floor it would take some tearing apart but with the help of my two sons Jonathan and Tim, and the local farmer Charlie Kendal, it was dismantled, removed

to Charlie's neighbouring field and burnt. As his part of the deal he took the metal for scrap. When the outer aluminium panels were removed we saw that such timber as there was had all turned black with damp and much of it was rotten, no wonder my clothes were mouldy and I think it explains my morning sneezing fits.

Jonathan then laid the new concrete base and Charlie skilfully manoeuvred it into position with his huge tractor and coupled up the drainage system. We then connected the electricity, phone and plumbing.

My first night in the new centrally-heated, double glazed home was a truly wonderful experience. You may ask why I had put up with the old place for so long, well, the truth is it was not a priority, when I lost home and garage all I needed was a base as my plan was to see a bit more of the big wide world while I had the strength and the legs to carry me. I would be spending as little time as possible in the old van and as much as possible, 'some place else' Now in 2009 and well into my 70s my feet were not quite as itchy (and not quite as easy to keep warm in winter)! I was also a little bit more settled.

Outside the old caravan with my mother

CHAPTER THIRTEEN

NOSTALGIA

One night in 2008 Beryl and I were sitting in her house when she mentioned that her daughter, Shirley, had said how much she missed her father, Eric, who had passed away in 1993. "Couldn't mother write down the story of how they met and fell in love at school and college in Lancashire?" Wouldn't it be nice for Shirley to be able to share those years?

It started me thinking. I no longer had paragliding to distract me and charity trips to Romania were a thing of the past. Okay I was now 73, an age when perhaps I ought to have started slowing down but I had always been busy. I didn't feel like stopping now. Wouldn't it be an idea if I too put down the story of my life – I knew of nothing else to write about? The next morning as Beryl started making notes for her daughter I mentioned it, "Just write it all down in long hand don't worry about the spelling I will be able to understand and I will type it out for you then you can put it onto your computer." That was all the encouragement I needed and I pulled a blank piece of paper out of my notebook and thought, "now how do I get going? … I know, I'll start at the beginning with my earliest memory."

My life ran along fairly smoothly, I was now spending a lot of time working on the book, I was also selling the cutters on eBay that I bought from China and to market traders, garden centres and wherever else I could. My relationship with Beryl was sound, we met during the week once or twice to go shopping, or a trip up the Dales and weekends together at Wetherby – where number one priority during 'the season' would be football … especially if Beryl's team, Manchester United, were playing as she was crazy about them; jumping up and down, swearing and going berzerk if they were losing. I would try to calm her saying, "Beryl, it is only a game," – this would infuriate her. My interest in Motor racing rubbed off and she loved watching NASCAR, American big saloons racing usually round an oval with plenty of incidents. Fortunately we liked many of the same TV programmes and would also go out for walks when the weather allowed.

My book was eventually finished and published. The big publishers were not interested so I went down the self-publish route, unfortunately this also meant I had to handle printing, sales, and distribution but I was able to get an endorsement from a wonderful man Alan Titchmarsh and that was a great help getting my book into more shops and Garden centres.

Return To Croft

In August 2012 I received an email from Darlington and District Motor Club. They have been trying to contact me as they are running a special Nostalgia event at one of the race meetings this year and would like to see some of the old drivers and ex-champions from the past at the event, would I contact them? I spoke to Terry Wright the club secretary on the phone and said that I would be very pleased to attend as I had not been to the circuit since the early 1970s when I quit racing. A few days later a letter arrived with complimentary tickets for the two day event. I took my friend Roy with me, he had been around the motor racing scene at the same time as me we had remained friends and more recently been on a trip to Arizona together. It was good to have the VIP tickets and the special treatment that goes with them.

The circuit had changed quite a lot in the 40 years that had passed. The start line had moved from where I used to sit, (usually on the front row) revving my little Mini – my heart revving too watching for the flag to drop then try and be the first away and into tower bend. There were quite a number of drivers from my era, though so many years had past I did not recognise one or two of them – but one who I did remember did not want to remember me. Andy gave me the cold shoulder, obviously he has never forgiven me for showing him the way round Croft in my quick little Mini. Until I came on the scene he won most of the saloon car races in his Mini but I changed all that. The organisers asked some of us if we would like to present the awards to the day's race winners and we agreed. When it was my turn I took the trophy and presented it to Jon Waggitt, shook his hand and congratulated him then added "It is a long time since I stood where you are standing receiving my trophy, we exchanged a few words and he asked what car I had raced, I told him that the last car that I raced at Croft before retiring was a Brabham BT 30, "That is what I race, what is your name?" I told him and when he replied I could not believe what he was saying, "I have part of the bodywork from that car with your name on, I bought it many years ago with some more spares from a garage in Manchester. I live at Borobridge – come through if you want it I will give it to you". I could not believe what I was hearing, after more than 40 years, and a further coincidence that I happened to present the award on that particular race to him. I thanked him for the offer and said I would give him a call in Borobridge. We set off home after a most enjoyable and nostalgic day, though much had changed and the excitement of taking part and winning races was long gone it was good to be there and meet others from the same era. As I drove towards the A1 I noticed something that was very familiar and had not changed – the sign post pointing to East Cowton where at the time the Beeswing village pub belonged to my old school friend Wilf Jackson. We always called there to celebrate after a win, and occasionally to commiserate if things had gone wrong. Today we would give it a miss and head for home.

The following week I went to Borobridge. Jon made me welcome and true to his word he gave me the panel – still in good condition, bright blue with my name in white. I gave him a signed copy of my book and we enjoyed a talk about motor racing over a cup of coffee in his wife's café.

CHAPTER FOURTEEN

PUSSYCATS & TIGERS

I had almost finished writing the second part of my life story and was wondering how it should end. The first book had ended at a low point in my life so I thought it would be a much better idea to end it on a high note. Whilst I was pondering, the decision was made for me – suddenly I hit the buffers. During my 70+ years I have been fortunate to enjoy good health; with one exception, all my visits to hospitals have been to see others less fortunate. The crises in my life have been financial, serious enough at the time ... though not life threatening. Then along comes something really serious and it is life threatening. Often I have driven down Wetherby road in Harrogate on a sunny day and glanced across at the hospital thinking about some poor soul in there suffering, laid on their back gazing at a white ceiling – while I am out here able to gaze at the blue sky ... and on the good days be up there flying. Well now it is my turn to gaze at the white ceiling surrounded by other sick people, I have certainly hit the buffers! Now I am the patient not the visitor.

Last night when they dimmed the lights I lay in my bed listening to the noises around me. I closed my eyes and drifted back in time more than twenty five years to a hospital in Pordenone Italy. Then I was the visitor though on duty sat on a chair at the end of the bed keeping an eye on my friend Julia's father, ready to get him a drink of water or a bottle if he needed a pee, and as now listening to the sounds coming from old men trying to sleep, now I am one of them.

I lay on my back a tube connected to my arm, another from my waterworks leading to a container hung over the side of the bed. I had to remember that I could ease over a little towards it but not the other way as it could pull on the pipe that ran up into my bladder. I am not likely to forget as one night at home I lost my balance getting into my pyjamas dislodged the pipe and had to wait for an hour and a half in agony for the nurse to come and fix it. Eventually I slip into dreamy muddled sleep.

In the morning I looked across at the bed opposite, it is empty, late last night there was an old man in it. I remember watching for him to move as he lay there motionless for a long time with his mouth wide open gazing up at the ceiling, I wondered where he had gone as they don't send you home in the middle of the night!

I was sat up in bed observing the activity in the ward when the nurse and her assistant appeared on the daily round. When she got to the next bed I noticed from her identity badge that she was from Romania. Her name was Mona Lisa. I remembered a few words of the language from the time I spent there doing charity work. She arrived at the foot of my bed picked up my chart at the same time looking across the bed at me, I caught her eye and said in my best Romanian "Buna Diminatsa" she was so surprised she almost dropped the chart, "he speaks my language," she cried, as a huge smile spread across her face. We exchanged a few more words but I soon ran out of Romanian and she moved on to the next bed still smiling.

I continued to watch the staff rushing round with their different tasks. I could tell there was quite a difference between them and their attitude to the job it was obvious that a few were there just for the money whereas some of the others were more patient, caring and did the job with feeling. On one occasion when I had to have an awful uncomfortable biopsy the nurse held me so close almost in an embrace while we talked our way through the operation. She came from the same place as the pied piper, Hamelin a town that I had visited during my National service days in Germany so we had plenty to talk about. She was wonderful and such a comfort. I realise that it is an extremely difficult job dealing with people that are both old and ill made worse by having to listen to them when others are waiting for attention.

The next day the doctor came round accompanied by his entourage – he read my notes and asked how I was, then he told me to turn over onto my side and pull up my knees. I knew what was coming as this was about the third time it had happened, he thrust his finger up my back passage making my eyes water – then told me that in addition to my waterworks problem I had an enlarged prostrate. Earlier in the day I had talked to another patient who had just had an operation for the same thing, "well can I have the operation doctor?" I asked. He looked back at my notes then said, "we cannot operate until six months after a stroke and yours was only a few weeks ago". End of conversation and he moved on to the next bed.

A few weeks later I was back at the hospital, for an appointment with the outpatients department to hear the results of my latest tests. It was a long wait – they were running late and it gave me plenty of time to think and worry about what they might say. Eventually my name was called and I was ushered into a small room. It was not long before two nurses came in and sat down opposite, I glanced at their name badges. Alison did the talking and gave me the bad news – when she got to the word 'Cancer' an alarm bell rang in my head ... that dreaded word that we hate to hear. "But Mr Walker, there are different degrees of cancer, from the pussycat at one end of the scale to a tiger at the other end – I can tell you that yours is a pussycat." I listened in a daze as she ran through some of the options, chatted for a while, then gave me a prescription for more medication. As I left I looked across to the waiting area at anxious faces and wondered which ones would have the good news and who would be unlucky. As I walked along the passage towards the exit it was of little comfort that I could walk much easier without the dammed catheter strapped to my leg – I now had a much bigger problem to think about. It was a cold, grey December day. I paid the parking fee for the hospital car park ... in my hand carrying a little booklet they'd given me entitled *Treating Prostrate Cancer* and drove away thinking "what next? how long have I got?".

When I got home I put the booklet without opening it on the top of the bookcase then reached and turned it over face down I didn't want to see 'that word' every time I looked in its direction ... and that is how it stayed for a while until I had the courage to open and read it. I also demoted another book to a shelf where it could not be seen – I am a great fan of Aleksandr Solzhenitsyn and read all his books during the 1970s, I had only recently re-read, wait for this, *Cancer Ward*. I remember him talking about the Radiation machine and how it overheated with constant use, he describes it so well that as I read I could almost smell it.

The next time I went to the Hospital I had an appointment with a Consultant who explained to me the various courses of action. Radio Therapy was one of them. "You will have to go to Leeds every day for seven weeks for the treatment, but maybe it is a little early to consider that – in any case you could not have that treatment while you have haemorrhoid problems. You will have to get them seen to and in the meantime carry on with the medication, we will keep an eye on your PSA reading and just watch and wait."

I made my way home feeling rather disillusioned – no operation, no radio therapy ... just watch and wait. The weather was dreadful, cold with snow and ice. I turned up the heating in my caravan and put on an extra woolly ... but it was not easy to keep warm, and when I looked outside at the snow it was very depressing. From my kitchen window in the distance I could just see the top of Greenhow Hill, where the snow would be much deeper. During the late 1970s I had lived there through two rather harsh winters but I was younger then and healthy so much of it was fun – and the cold did not frighten me as it does now. Looking out of my front window I see the snow is about a foot deep and see no tracks as no one had been round the caravan site for days. I had tried to get my car out the previous day but it just sat motionless in the snow as its wheel's spinned so I had to give up the idea. I felt cut-off and isolated as all the other holiday caravans were empty and I was on my own. If I needed a doctor or nurse in an emergency it would be hard luck as they would not get to me unless on a tractor. I felt trapped and decided that I would have to move to where there were other people and medical help if needed as I now felt insecure.

My sister, Freda, lived nearby but we did not have much contact, when my first book was published friends and relations were enthusiastic but Freda chose to ignore its very existence and to date has never even mentioned it once. This hurt me and made me feel cool towards her, but one bit of good fortune was another relation lived not far away – Fiona, my niece, and she came regularly to visit me and gave me her phone number for emergencies. "Don't worry uncle Ken you can ring me anytime day or night and I will come round" that was good to hear and made me feel a bit easier.

I went to visit the housing department and asked about Sheltered accommodation. They were most helpful, put me on the waiting list and gave me the address of one place where I could go and have a look, talk to the warden and get an idea what such places are like. I did ... but didn't like it – it was full of old people and my thoughts were, 'I am not ready for this kind of place yet' and went home, turned up the heating switched on the TV and tried to settle down.

And now we moved into 2013, a new year but nothing good to look forward to and I slipped into a terrible depression. All my life I have been the one to try and look on the bright side – but there was no bright side. I had gone steadily downhill ... urinary infection with a catheter strapped to my leg for over two months, a mild stroke, haemorrhoids and now Cancer – *all at the same time.* Throughout my life good health had been my strength, on the occasions when I had lost everything I had checked myself and said, "No you haven't Kenneth you still have your health" and that thought had given me courage to try again ... but now there is nowhere to turn. I certainly felt low, in fact I had to see the doctor as I felt suicidal. She rather reluctantly gave me some anti-depression pills. When I got home I looked at the packet and thought 'I will try to manage without them and only keep them on the shelf in reserve.' Over the years as I enjoyed good health I did not realise that not only does illness give you pain and discomfort it affects your mind ... and that is even worse! I could not hold myself together and felt as if I was cracking up weak and gutless with no fight left in me

Beryl Moves

But worse was to follow when my best friend of many years, Beryl, who had helped me through my problems decided to move house and go south to live with her only daughter until she could find a house close by – my illness had caused her to panic and think "What would happen if I were taken Ill ... who would look after me? I have neither friends or relations in the North". I was devastated and felt that we had the best of both worlds, part of the week together and our own space in-between, I spent my weekends with Beryl and used to joke that I had a holiday every week, It had worked well for more than 18 years. I didn't want it to change – but change it did. A few months later I arrived at Beryl's house one day to see the For Sale notice on a post in the garden – my heart sank, I knew this day was coming but now it had arrived. The sleepless nights returned. I went to see the doctor again, this time with pain in my chest – she told me that it was stress caused by worrying about my problems and gave me some 'feel-good' tablets. When I got home I put them on the shelf with the anti-depressant tablets and there they stayed ... both packets unopened.

At a time when I needed support and a little understanding I felt extra pressure from Beryl. I realised that to move house had been a hard decision for her to make. It was the place where she had lived for 35 years, full of memories – most of happy times when she came over from Lancashire with husband Eric and young daughter Shirley to teach at a local school. On more than one occasion Beryl would show me round the huge garden naming the flowers and shrubs, many that came from Warrington with them. Eric had loved the garden and when he died Beryl took it on and for many years loved it, more recently given a little assistance by myself – but now it was far too big to manage; the pleasure had gone and it became a burden – another reason to move. Whilst I understood the logic of it I couldn't help feeling a great sadness as if I was the only loser in the situation and when she came under pressure from estate agents, potential buyers and time-wasters she would telephone me and go through it all. I tried to give her a sympathetic ear and listen to her problems but found it extremely difficult to give support when I needed it and knew that my prop would soon be removed.

> My best friend lived in Wetherby
>
> It gave her such a fright
>
> When I had a stroke
>
> She took flight
>
> And now lives in Basingstoke.

"Don't worry" is advice we are often given and give to others. But it is something that you can say "I will" or "I won't do". – like making a cup of tea or going for a walk, the only way to create a diversion to shut them out. When I went to bed reading would sometimes work; but often, when I put down the book and turned out the light, my problems would return – so I devised a system. First I would recite a few poems ... then I'd mentally revisit the 23 motor racing circuits in the UK and Europe that I had raced round in the 1960/70s and do a few laps of each (skipping the times when I had an accident!). My next move, to keep out the worries, was to revisit many of the 60+ sites round the world where I have flown my Paraglider and take off and land a few times (avoiding the incidents where I had a close shave!). If I had not managed to nod off by then the next move was to revisit the Dales on my Motorbike planning the different routes and mileages that I would explore later in the year when I was feeling better. Usually by this time I had managed to fall asleep or it was morning and time to get up!

LIFE GOES ON
(Fortunately)

But life goes on and my health steadily improved – I was able to sleep better, I put on a little weight and felt strong enough to take more exercise. My regular check-up at the Hospital showed that my PSA reading was not going up, in fact it had remained low, which is a good sign. The watch and wait had paid off!

Though Beryl's departure had left a huge gap in my life it had been partly filled by the unexpected response to the publication of my first book. Many who had read it contacted me by email, letter, and telephone – one or two even came and knocked on the door, friends old and new and this improved my morale when they praised my writing. I bought another motor bike, I had drawn a line under that part of my life some time ago, but only in pencil so it was easy to rub out and start again. Off I went into my beloved Dales turning the clock back more than 60 years.

For the past eighteen years I had spent my weekends in Wetherby with Beryl – now I was free to do other things, also free if I was not careful to be bored.

I made contact with my old friend Dave Elliot who taught me to paraglide, he now spends his time when the weather permits sailing the West coast of Scotland." If you fancy a trip Ken you are welcome", " but I am not keen on the water Dave" he looked at me and smiled, "The Idea is to stay out of it". Having been frightened out of my wits on more than one occasion on his adventures I should have said, "Thank you but no thank you" instead said I would think about it when I felt a bit stronger.

I had a call from Chris Seals a friend I used to go flying with, we had not seen each other for a long time and the following week he came to see me. Chris is an outdoor, extreme sports enthusiast and has tried many exciting activities. I remembered him buying a Blow Cart, a little three wheel buggy with a sail that you can race along the sand with, and asked him what he had done with it. "It is in the shed at York, do you want it"? I won't bother to type my answer only to say that a few days later he arrived with it and we agreed a deal, Chris being a generous man it was not difficult. He also told me that he had recently been training as an instructor to fly a dual paraglider taking pupils and learners up for flights. "Will you come up with me"? Without hesitation I replied, "Later in the year when I feel stronger and the weather is good I certainly will".

Sailing off the west coast of Scotland

It was not long before I received a call from Dave Elliot. "In a couple of weeks I will be sailing my boat from Stranraer back up the west coast of Scotland to a summer base near Oban. Polly, (his wife) will be working so I will be on my own. If you fancy a trip I would welcome your company – It  won't cost much, only the train fare from Settle to Stranraer, cheaper if you get a railcard." "Thanks Dave, I'll give it some thought, check on my Hospital appointments and let you know."

Now this offer sounded interesting but any trip with Dave Elliot needed a great deal of thought! it would be a new adventure and his trips were never boring – but some of the most frightening moments in my life have been with him and I have always vowed, Never again, I think I'll go!.

Though I was slowly feeling stronger I was not totally confident about going with him – after the long cold winter the weather was still cool. On my travels with him I had slept in a sleeping bag in a tent in some wild parts of the world ... but now after my illness I needed a good night sleep in a comfortable bed.

Two days later a parcel arrived in the post, I wasn't expecting one, but when I opened it I was pleasantly surprised to see two books and a length of new rope from Dave Elliot with a short note, 'Have a look at these books Ken, you may enjoy reading the one about Round the World Sailors – but have a good look at *Sailing for Dummies*. I have enclosed a length of rope for you to practice the knots and I will ask you a few questions when we meet'. I have learned a lot from Dave over the years ... maybe now he thought he would make a sailor of me too.

The trip did not clash with my hospital appointments so I packed a few items – including most important of all my pills and bought a Railcard. When I'd asked Dave what to take with me he said, "Wellingtons, water-proofs, and plenty of warm clothes" I was a bit taken aback expecting deck shoes and T- shirts – but did as he suggested as the weather was still not very warm.

On the agreed day I made an early start and got to Dave's house just outside Settle at 7am. We took the early train from Settle to Carlisle, a journey over the wild moors that I always enjoy (having read about the problems encountered and overcome by the railway engineers in 1870s). Also catching glimpses through the low cloud of some of the hills I had flown from with Dave. Next stop Glasgow where we changed trains, and on to Stranraer over more wild country – until we dropped down nearer the coast, passing numerous golf courses on the last leg of the journey. It was quite a long walk from the station to the marina at the side of what was the huge ferry port now moved further along the coast. Dave striding out at his usual brisk pace I had to remind him that I was not yet back on song.

The little 25ft sailing boat was just as he had left it securely moored, after a quick look over we put our bags inside and went into town to get a few supplies and have a meal then back for an early night sleeping on the boat.

The next morning we woke early to a grey day the tide was right but only a very light wind coming from the wrong direction I could tell that he was a little undecided – but I also knew that Dave would not ere on the side of caution and sit around waiting for perfect conditions. We set off, the little diesel engine chugging along at 5 knots, with no help from the wind, a long way to go at a very slow speed ... next stop Arran.

I stayed in the cockpit with Dave and he gave me the tiller – pointed out where we were on the GPS, and told me to follow the line on the chart. It was the course that he had taken on the previous trip. I kept turning it the wrong way, instead of left to go right and vice-versa but eventually got the hang of it. About an hour later we were out in the open sea I studied the gauges and felt a little uneasy when one read 48 fathoms – almost 300 ft of water below where I was stood! The boat began to rock, after a turn at the tiller I went down below and made tea then settled down and tried to stay calm as the little boat started to roll. I looked up at Dave stood holding the tiller calmly staring ahead. Behind us Stranraer disappeared in the distance, ahead nothing but the sea ... not a single boat in sight. This was another new experience for me and a bit unnerving in a tiny boat bobbing about in the great ocean miles from land (and in my eyes security) as conditions gradually got worse. But your options are strictly limited when you are well out at sea you just have to keep going – not like travelling on the motorway where you can pull in to the services for a break, you are committed and can only press on ... and when it is rough hope to sail through it!

Now out in the open sea the waves were higher, hitting the side of the boat causing it to roll further over each time. I stayed below in the main cabin looking out of the window. One minute nothing but grey sky – then as we tilt the other way nothing but the dark grey sea. I was scared. When I agreed to come on the trip I felt I was getting stronger and ready for a new adventure ... but not ready for this now ... or ever. I was scared and asked myself the question, "What am I doing here?" and just by a strange coincidence again with Dave Elliot! Some frighteners are over in just second or at worst a few minutes but this one went on and on for hours. I looked out of the boat towards the front where the deck was touching the water as it pitched over then back the other, the spray blowing over the font of the deck. I could not avoid thinking, how much further over will this little boat lean and still come back?

In the distance Ailsa Craig poking up out of the ocean like a giant mole hill. It remained in the distance for so long in fact that at one time I thought we must be going backwards. I had grown Ailsa Craig tomatoes and onions on my allotment at Masham during WWII but that thought did not divert me for long. I didn't feel sea sick, just sick and scared! "What am I doing here?" Kept ringing in my ears ... in the past year I had gone through many uncomfortable moments with my illness, now I was enduring another – but this one I volunteered for! I tried to read, Dave had given me a book called *A voyage for mad men!* I felt as if I could add a chapter to it rather than read it!

About an hour later we were getting close to Ailsa Craig when Dave called me up on deck. He pointed to an area on the island "It is now uninhabited but that is where they quarry the granite to make curling stones." Then he added "the wind has swung round just a little and I am going to put on some sail Ken, it could speed things up a bit and I need your help as I will have to climb along the boat to loosen the sail ... now take the rudder and listen to me, if I fall overboard this is what you must do – first, throw out the Danbuoy life ring and marker in front of me if you can – then cut the engine speed and come round to pick me up". Now I don't know if it was for my benefit to give me confidence or his normal way of doing things but he sprang up onto the deck, grabbed a shroud and proceeded along the edge of the boat with neither life jacket or safety line as the boat continued to sway. He casually loosened the sail then came back and jumped down beside me. "We may catch a little wind now and speed up a bit". He said as he unfurled the sail which billowed out when the wind caught it and I felt the pull on the boat as the speed increased a little from five knots to 7/8. Shortly after he cut the engine but not for long as the wind had picked up and swung round to the north. We had to take down the sail – more stress, "Ken I want you to take control of the boat while I go along the deck to the sail, put on full rudder and go round in a circle to get the wind off the sail then I can release it and don't forget what I told you to do in an emergency".

This is not what I came for, it was the first time I had been sailing – I had pictured a little boat gliding along on a calm sea, very little wind and a blue sky! I took hold of the rudder and froze. "I can't do it Dave" – "Of course you can, there is plenty of room you won't run into anything". I just had to do it – he was stood up on the deck by the main mast looking down at me and waiting. I took a deep breath and swung the rudder round to my left as far as it would go and we started to turn, he fiddled with the ropes at the bottom of the sail as we continued round in a circle then I panicked a bit as I could not tell when we had done a circle and when to turn back onto our course. But it did not matter, as by now he had fixed it and jumped down beside me laughing. I almost collapsed as the tension released when he took the rudder from me and turned us back on course. I felt a bit of a wimp – this is not how I have been on the many adventures with him but realised that I was a long way from my normal self. I went down below and made more tea. Like me he can drink tea any time. Before I had finished it he called me. "Come up and look at this Ken" I went up and saw something I had never seen before – as I looked out to the port side in the distance I could see a big wave like a mini tsunami rolling along towards us. Strange as it may seem I felt a little excitement rather than fear as I watched it creeping along towards us, "That Ken is the tide on the turn". I gazed in wonder, it is incidents like that that make up for the fear and I was learning a little about the sea.

After almost seven hours we arrived at Lamlash, Arran and moored for the night. I might have felt happier if I could have felt solid ground under my feet for short while but that was not possible there was no marina. Only moorings out in the bay – permanently anchored buoys that you hooked up to on a long rope. Drifting to and fro and bobbing up and down with the wind and tide all night I did not sleep well though ... quite warm and cosy in my sleeping bag after one of Dave's very good meals.

The next day was much calmer as we made our way up The Outer Firth of Clyde and on to the Crinan canal. Normally there is a fee for assistance negotiating the 14 locks but when they saw an 'old timer' with the grey beard they waved the charge and kindly gave us a little pennant to run up the mast. We received help through every lock – often the helper would jump on his bike and pedal along the lock side to meet us at the next one. They were all pleasant and helpful. This was my kind of sailing on the lock, smooth and leisurely ... I enjoyed it very much after the ordeal the previous

day. We only had one small incident when we got a plastic bag tangled in the propeller. I didn't worry to much as Dave was an experienced diver and he managed to remove it with a long pole with a hook on the end. A thick heavy duty plastic bag now shredded but still tied at the top and we wondered what it could have contained!

We moored on the lock for the night and took a walk into Lochgilphead for a meal and a little exercise. In the morning we made an early start and arrived at the final lock Number 14 about mid-day. It was a rather strange feeling in the last lock, perched up high – looking down over the great expanse of sea in front and below before the water level dropped as it was drained lowering us down to sea level.

It was quite a pleasant day as we sailed out into the sound of Jura turning to the north – the loch was quite smooth and for a time we glided along under sail. I was reminded of my paragliding days floating along, without any mechanical noises, the only sound the wind humming through the lines onto our faces as we headed for Ardfern and I was allowed to pilot. Dave always likes to show and teach new things ... and he knows that I like to learn – so now it was sailing. "Be careful not to get too near the Lobster Pots and keep an eye on the depth gauge as we sail round the coast to Ardfern".

I was by now feeling more comfortable with the tiller and realised that it was not as sensitive as I had imagined only changing direction slowly. He made me do a few circles and practice changing direction – most of the time I was even moving it the right way!

Ardfern ... Marooned.

The following day was wet and windy – no chance of sailing, so during the best part of the day we took a walk inland looking for the 'Cup and ring marks' a form of prehistoric art only recently discovered in the hills nearby and believed to be around 5000 years old. They had been revealed in 2008 after a storm and heavy rain, but we could not find them and the weather was getting worse so we decided to go back to the boat yard; have a shower, call at the book shop and settle down. I bought a book that Dave recommended about this part of the world – though quite a bit farther north on the Island of Raasay, *Calum's road*, an incredible story of very determined character.

The original arrangement had been that Dave's wife Polly would come up in the Camper van to stay and I would take the train back to Settle – but when she arrived they decided that as the weather prospects were so bad we would all go home. I was somewhat relieved, though I felt, as Polly put it, I'd had a baptism of fire – and it hadn't been the smooth enjoyable sailing trip that I'd hoped for. On the way back we talked of the trip but avoided talking about the next one ... only saying that I would like to go sailing again sometime!

Facing the Future

During the remainder of 2013 my health continued to improve and my hospital visits became less frequent ... unfortunately some of this is cancelled by the aging process – but maybe I am one of the lucky ones as my cancer is easier to treat than it is in many other parts of the body.

My many friends have helped fill the space left by Beryl but I take the train from time to time and go down to visit her in her new home in Basingstoke where she always makes me welcome.

As winter approaches my thoughts go back to last year's ordeal, had I done the right thing to stay? but so far, though we have had endless rain, it has not been as cold. I have again been offered sheltered accommodation had another look and decided again, that I'm not quite ready for that kind of place. But my mind is made up – I will defiantly stay for now and perhaps move before next winter. (or the one after!)

That was the second part of my life story ... but I haven't told you everything!

Nothing Easy

Available at: Amazon UK | Waterstones | Direct from Author

Nothing Easy
My Young Life, 1935 to 1977
by Ken Walker

For those interested in an autobiography that spans the 1930s to the 1970s, Nothing Easy will strike a special chord, portraying a boy growing up to manhood in his time and place before going off to National Service. It conjures up insight into the world of the Yorkshire Dales just before better roads opened them to the outsider. Motor racing enthusiasts will be able to follow the description of the sport-and some of the shenanigans that existed in the margins. Readers will feel compassion too, for the struggles and heartache,the yearnings and the lighter moments that make 'Nothing Easy'an influential picture of its times.

An absolutely fantastic book. Most insightful to a diverse and colourful life. Once started I could not put the book down. An easy read, the story of his life captures you from the very start. Thank you for letting us share it.

Nothing Easy

My Young Life
1935 - 1977
Ken Walker

ISBN: 978-0-9569839-0-9
250 pages
B&W photographs throughout